T0365107

# MOUNTAIN ROAD

# MOUNTAIN ROAD

## Not Dwelling on Yesterday or Tomorrow

HOOVER LIDDELL

iUniverse

**Mountain Road**
**Not Dwelling on Yesterday or Tomorrow**

*iUniverse books may be ordered through booksellers or by contacting:*

*iUniverse*
*1663 Liberty Drive*
*Bloomington, IN 47403*
*www.iuniverse.com*
*844-349-9409*

*Because of the dynamic nature of the Internet, any web addresses or links contained in this book may have changed since publication and may no longer be valid. The views expressed in this work are solely those of the author and do not necessarily reflect the views of the publisher, and the publisher hereby disclaims any responsibility for them.*

*Any people depicted in stock imagery provided by Thinkstock are models, and such images are being used for illustrative purposes only.*
*Certain stock imagery © Thinkstock.*

*ISBN: 978-1-4620-5860-0 (sc)*
*ISBN: 978-1-4620-5861-7 (e)*

*Print information available on the last page.*

*iUniverse rev. date: 10/23/2020*

# CONTENTS

# ACKNOWLEDGEMENTS

I wish to express appreciation to Lorin Oberweger for her work and contribution to the manuscript. Her clear insight, genuine spirit of support, focus, and attention to understanding the work was unusual and invaluable.

I am grateful to my family, the students, teachers, parents, friends, colleagues, and others with whom I have worked in the United States and abroad. I am fortunate to have a rich contribution from such persons through travel, reading, dialogue, and exploration as their energy, work and vision make this book possible.

# ON THE ROAD

# 1

# INTRODUCTION

There are many roads traveling the earth, and my journey begins on one in Africa.

On encountering and traveling upon the African road, I discover a life that deepens my wonder and a way of observing a world that I could not expect. I appreciate all that is alive and all that no longer exists: A world of people, land, and a spirit that shows how grand our universe actually is as we begin to journey into it and wander across it.

From my first day in Africa I am filled with excitement and wonder. I find that everything is fascinating and new. I am not distracted with the next moment. Let it happen!

As a youth in Toledo, Ohio, I tell my mother that I am going to run away from home and live a new adventure. It never seems to bother her. She knows how difficult it is to survive if I run away, and that I have no other place to go. So I never leave, and I socialize with the other youths and go to school just as they do, but I like to read, think about the world, and do things on my own.

One day, I am on a mountain road in the Great Rift Valley. I do not realize what a spectacular journey it is through the Serengeti plains and the planet's largest concentration of wildlife. The presence of Mount Kilimanjaro is spectacular and immense and dominates the earth.

I have no idea about climbing such a mountain but I know others have done it and that it can be done in five days. I will not tackle my first mountain until years later in California. When I do climb, it is with a team of five and a great event for us all to summit Bear Creek Spire (13,500 ft) in the Sierras. I learn more about human existence in fourteen days in the wilderness than I had in eighteen years as a San Francisco educator.

Over the years I find that learning from a mountain road adventure empowers the downtrodden as well as the affluent. Ascending the road to the summit I see our human capability deepen. The following year, after the climb, I run the New York City Marathon for the first time as I still live with the energy of the mountain world.

In the wilderness we learn the universe is timeless. There is only the living present. There is no past. It does not exist. The things that may have existed are no longer alive. The future is an image we paint, not an actuality. The present contains all there is. We understand the universe by being in the moment.

When I return to Nigeria from the Rift Valley in Kenya and Tanzania, I am again with students who are so enthusiastic about learning. I travel a short distance down the dirt African road to the school and find students who are filled with hunger, drive, and an excitement to learn. Nothing stops them from participating in as serious an education as is possible from a village without running water or electricity. It is inspiring to see them so determined to excel.

I teach mathematics and chemistry. In the first year, I work hard and struggle to master a British and West African system of education. Initially it is an obstacle getting familiar with this way of education and being able to deal with and move beyond working in a system of colonial origin and derivation. I find that the British system has a fundamental impact on student learning. The following year I teach the subjects in depth and find that we can all do things and understand the world in more profound ways. It is a great time in my life, living and working with the Nigerians, staying in a small village in the rainforest, and facing life and its adventures.

The Nigerian students are not interested in new practices or educational reform. It is the understanding of the subject that challenges them now is what matters. They are not influenced by any innovation, breakthroughs or past information that take them away from their mission of excelling on the West African or Cambridge School Certificate Examinations. For the students the examinations are a way to recognize the mastery of their work. They are all driven, focused, and serious.

Some of the Americans who come and live here are just as moved to contribute to African life as the Nigerian students are in their studies. It is through their independence, unyielding determination and unconditioned minds that they are able to live exuberant and youthful lives in a harsh land. They are able to immerse themselves into the African way of life and not be bound by American ways. Their image of being an American or a foreigner ceases to be significant. They seem to possess no fear. They come as rebels to discover another world. Some master African languages and write books; others question government authority and environmental destruction; and a few construct boats to sail up rivers for the first time. It is clear to me some people contribute more to life on earth than others.

To those who come and contribute I am moved to express the spirit and energy of their lives.

## Nigeria

It is as though life here should never end.
We do sing and dance and celebrate.
We take on struggles we never fear we shall lose.
We are young and determined to have our way in this world.

# 2

# TRAVELING NORTH

The school and the students make Nigeria an interesting place, but through life in Nigeria, and elsewhere, my deepest adventure and most serious encounters are often outside the school. They are sometimes on the road, in distant places, or in the wilderness.

The days and then the year quietly pass, though sometimes I am very tired in my first days in Ijero, Nigeria, a small village in the rainforest where I live. I seldom leave the village in the beginning. Instead, I accept the life that comes and goes. I am determined to learn from whatever things I face in the rainforest. Events pass through us the first year but they are harder the second year. In my first days often it seems like the only things that exist are the sun, the forest, the rain, and the earth as all else is diminished and seemingly insignificant.

What is hard about life in Africa is similar to what I recall from the days I was a seaman and would exist during monotonous and rugged days on the sea. When I sail to Brazilian jungle towns I know that it is the same struggling poor people living in Africa as there, except I never lived in Brazil, and I am living in Africa. I am starting life here.

I get through the days I face in the village and along the road. I am dedicated to survival. To start a life in Nigeria usually requires help. One would hire a cook or a person to wash clothes, go to the market and keep the house clean and in order. So generally you needed someone to work for you, but I never hire anyone. Often this means that I never eat regularly, that my house is in disarray from time to time, and I walk to the town and bargain for myself in the shops and market. It is not very long that I am in the village that I have a small motorcycle that makes my journey into Nigerian life and neighboring towns more alive. I am able to make the two-mile journey to town more frequently.

Soon after my arrival in the country a Nigerian civil war begins. It is a conflict caused when the southeastern provinces proclaim their own republic of Biafra. Of the many ethnic groups making up Nigeria, the three largest are the Hausas in the north, the Yorubas in the southwest, where I live, and the Ibos in the southeast. Presently there are 36 Nigerian states. The war mainly involves the Hausas and the Ibos, but the Yorubas are part of the national forces with the Hausas and other groups who oppose the breakaway republic of the Ibos. In our village we hardly notice the war. It is most evident that it is occurring when we leave our village and travel to other places. Most of the fighting is to the east and away from us.

The first year I pass a somewhat quiet existence, seldom varying my routines. I have occasional visitors and make local journeys but I do not frequently leave Ijero. The next year though I travel across the African continent through Central and East Africa. After returning to Nigeria I am hospitalized at University College Hospital (UCH) in Ibadan for sixty days. Fortunately I survive a hard and serious illness, and then I make a journey through several West African nations. And on the last school holiday before I leave the country, I am determined to journey deeper into Nigeria. It is a journey north. In my mind it is to be a road journey closer to home than the previous expeditions out of the country and I am excited about seeing Nigerian towns and people that I have never seen in the two years of living in the vibrant southwest region of the country.

I have always wanted to travel north. It is the way to the Sahara desert. I leave from Ibadan on the train. Train travel is cheap. I pay the one pound sixteen shillings to get to Kaduna. I travel second class and find the trip harder than I expected. I hear that third class is impossible so I did not consider it.

It is the Muslim New Year and the train is already filled when it reaches Ibadan. I look for a quiet train ride and do not realize the venture I am entering. The unbelievably large crowd anxiously awaits its appearance. When it does arrive, which is at one o'clock in the morning, I wonder as I look at those already aboard the train if it could always have been this overcrowded when it began the journey. All persons waiting on the platform now converge at the train doors. The huge mass of people is restless and wild. They pull, push, fight, and get beyond the black steel doors that never open. At first I wonder why the doors are not opening. It does not take us long to discover that we have no reason to expect them to open. People begin to climb up over the window rails and throw baggage into the train. The crowd crawls into every space there is. It is as though we are driven as a relentless herd to transfer ourselves into this standing, waiting metal vehicle. People crush, madly pull, and desperately fight to get onto the train. Everybody else but me seems to accept of all of this. I am beaten and worn down and feel fortunate to somehow be on board and still standing. I am in the middle of everything and hardly breathing and I am treated like everybody else. Who am I? I am certainly no better than anybody else. Though I curse and shout nobody hears or even notices me, but somehow I do manage to struggle my way on to the train. Somehow I am inside. The train is exploding with bodies. How is it possible for us all to be here on one train? All the seats are filled from long ago, before the train reaches Ibadan, which means that we are standing everywhere. Walking is impossible as we are a static, restless and impenetrable collection of people. It is ones rigidly defined space that locks one in and makes the ride so unbearable.

It takes almost fifty miles before I get a seat. It is around Oshogbo, which is a city on the Oshu River, a place where gods and spirits dwell. I have been to the city and I have met the Oba, or king. Could he imagine my riding through his town on this crowded train? At whatever time in the morning it is, the journey is hard and tiring and barely seems real. As I sit and see the passing land on a slow train moving north, daylight breaks and I appreciate this new place that we are encountering. I observe desert sand and flowers and there are tall red hills where termites dwell.

In this countryside the termites are not seen as pests as they are in the urban places of America and elsewhere where they are said to damage billions of dollars of human structures each year. This damage is said to exceed that of fires, storms, and earthquakes combined. Here the termites are beneficial insects in nature as they break down dead wood and return nutrients to the soil. They don't really destroy things out here. They productively eat the dead wood as they have for fifty million years and contribute to the natural balance of life. The termite is an individual as well as part of a community of thousands that has capabilities of self-organizing to solve problems such as finding food, building elaborate nests, and responding to external challenges of sometimes the highest magnitude. In the lives of insects, such as ants and termites, one sees societies transcending the individual, moving in and through the universe with the energy and productivity to make their worlds extraordinary places.

The journey is becoming so long and weary that I am beginning to realize the true size of Nigeria. Africa sometimes seems like an endless continent. After almost twenty-five hours we arrive in Kaduna. I get off the train in Kaduna and on my way to a cheap hotel and a guy who seems to have been drinking comes and asks me if I am an Ibo. I tell him that it is not his business who I am. A conflict is manifesting itself except he has a friend. The friend also wonders who I am and where I am from. I tell him that I am a black American. He is not impressed, but he is able to settle the situation. I go on to the hotel, spend but a night there, and the next day I go to a friend's place. My Nigerian teaching colleague, Sam Otuyelu, writes him that I am coming, so he is expecting me. He is an engineer who is from Ijero and he welcomes me.

After several days I go to Kano, which was like no place I have been to before in the south. It is a desert town and sand is everywhere one goes. It is the harmattan season and I am not prepared for it. It is a season of dry skin and intense cold in the early morning and night. There are only two seasons in Nigeria: the rainy season and the harmattan season. The rainy season is from April to October. In the south of Nigeria it can rain for many days non-stop. The harmattan is from November to March and is much more intense in Nigeria the closer I am to the desert in the north. It is a north wind that is cool and dry that comes from the Sahara desert and blows across West Africa. I should have brought warmer clothes for this quiet windstorm season. I pay the price with dry and ashen skin and at night I find Kano to be a freezing and cold land. I just cannot believe how cold it gets and I have no warm clothes with me. In the nights I suffer and struggle, but before I leave I go to the market and buy things to take to my family.

Early one morning I leave Kano and I can never forget the trip back. The day is cool. I walk to the motor park to get a bus. I am finished with the train. I hear that it is a good road to Kaduna so I pay my sixteen shillings and I get on. It is a modern and comfortable bus. All the seats are filled and three soldiers are among the passengers. The soldiers do not have to pay. I dislike the thought of them, as I am so far from home. The civil war and the question of my being Ibo bothers me and the possible encounter I may have with them. I am so accustomed to their questions and their asking for identification, but they have not bothered me. The bus starts and we leave Kano. All along the road there is sand and an occasional settlement of mud huts, a sameness of scenery that I think may stretch from Morocco to the Sudan.

When I first come to Nigeria I find that everything has a peanut taste. In Dahomey, now called Benin, and Togo that were bordering nations, everything tastes like coconuts as the food is cooked in coconut oil. The Nigerian food is cooked in groundnut oil, peanut oil in America, and I never really get accustomed to it. As I now look to the countryside I see farm grains and groundnuts. There are sacks of groundnuts stacked in huge pyramids that are a distinctive symbol of this world.

We cannot be very many miles outside of town when there is a loud noise. It seemingly comes from nowhere. It is a good bus moving fast on a good road. No one seems to pay much attention to the noise. I have no idea that it has any significance and I do not even bother myself enough to look out the window to determine or consider the source of the sound. I do not look up and I do not think that anyone else does.

All at once the bus is filled with panic. People are in disbelief. There is a definite pause and then transformation of life as the bus reaches a runaway state of confusion. I feel that that we are going to be in a disaster that may destroy us. **The loud noise came from the left from a tire. There had been a blowout.** The one thing everybody knows is that the bus is going to turn over because no longer is there any control, anywhere. Everything, everything is out of control. No one seems to have been in this situation before. Nobody knows what we should do, but the driver is doing all he can to ease the inevitable crash that awaits us. No one wants the bus to be over-turned, because if it turns over that seems like death. What else can the mind think but death and see the bus as a mass grave. Everybody on the bus could be killed or injured. Here I am inside the bus and everything around me is so strange and alien.

I cannot understand Hausa and all the things they are saying, shouting, and crying. I cannot even speak to anyone. I am now very far from anyone and any place I know. I seem to be nowhere at all. I am out here on a desert road where I have never been before in my life, but the accident has already begun and where the bus goes is where we all must go also. There is no thinking ahead that matters.

There are a thousand different things that may happen. If death strikes, here, now, it will just be too unbelievable. My mother will never get over it. I was just taking a casual trip to the north, nothing more than that. What about the things I have left undone in coming here? But we must all die sometime and somewhere and people do die in the desert. They do.

Then the bus turns over, touches ground. Everything is chaotic and in disarray. There is no peace. My mind and body no longer seem to connect as I feel separated into pieces as the bus slides and tosses and is filled with confusion. There is a feeling of madness in a world of collapse and destruction. It seems as though everybody on the bus is falling on me. It makes me angry to have all of these bodies and people lying on me as they cry in their pain and madness. What will happen to us? All parts of me are ready to break, as the frame of my body and its parts seems particularly brittle. The passengers and the bus seem to be scraped along the road. There are all of these people, constant noise and confusion and nowhere to go. The bus comes to a rest.

We are through the accident. The bus is lying on its side, shattered and broken. People are breaking glass and trying to escape. Nobody is calm. Everybody fights madly to get outside. People are climbing all over me and I am swearing and calling them names but nobody hears, and nobody cares. When everybody is out, I walk out through the front window, which has long been broken. I have scratches on my arms and legs and an exhausted mind. It now seems that everything happened so quickly and some of us have been hurt. A bus comes to collect the sick and wounded to go back to Kano and the others wait for another bus to Kaduna. I go on to Kaduna, where I leave and make the long journey in the friend's car back to Ijero and leave the road behind me and give my attention to the school term we face.

I leave Nigeria and return to the United States. I travel to California and I work in San Francisco as a teacher. I get married there. My wife and I have a daughter. With our one-year-old daughter we move to Kenya, where I work for a year as a teacher for the Kenyan government. We have family travels throughout Kenya and into Tanzania and we are among abundant wildlife as we travel the East African world and the plains of Kilimanjaro before returning to San Francisco. When my daughter graduates from college we return to visit East Africa and to be amongst the wildlife and I climb Kilimanjaro. We return to San Francisco and my wife and I continue our lives as teachers, parents, and grandparents.

# 3

# YOUTH

A relentless revolution begins in our youth. Life awakens it. It is unusual for its presence to remain throughout one's life. The school is often a place where such freedom vanishes. Schools should not deter or dishearten this energy of youth that is in us all. The energy that is in us when we are young gives expression to our creativity, curiosity, wonder, joy, and human freedom.

Our grandson, Kyras, enters our lives bringing immeasurable energy. Youth are at the beginning of life and learning. As we observe them we see freedom and tragedy and learn that there is no certainty. At an early age they are spirited with immense energy to play, climb, run, learn new words, and become familiar with other children. They are able to engage themselves in independent activity and to give attention to playing games, finding a fascination with books, listening to stories as well as exploring and discovering objects and observing images from surrounding objects of reflected light.

Children learn to make this world their own. They love the world and being a part of it. They are not outside of life as they live through its moments.

Though they are born to explore the depths of the universe as well as their own mind, sometimes the world suddenly changes for them.

We are shocked when we learn that a doctor finds an excess quantity of copper in our grandson's liver cells. Blood tests are taken, and then there is a biopsy. The jaundice eyes persist. Much attention is given to the possibility of hepatitis, but nothing indicates its presence. There is a chance that he may have acquired the disease from other youths whom he is around. There is endless uncertainty and unknowing. Serious attention is given to any presence of copper in the environment and its processing by the liver.

No one ever figures out the copper mystery and eventually he gets through it. What starts with stomach pain follows with medical tests and questioning the symptoms that are never explained as he moves on with his life. It is a moment and an event that he is able to survive.

When I write about a grandchild it refers to Kyras and events that happened before our other two grandchildren were born. They too would have early health concerns. The second grandchild, Kyle, has asthma but it does not affect his energy and exuberance. The third grandchild, Paige, has a rare pancreatic disorder. While she has surgery and other medical treatment the strength of her spirit is extraordinary and it is hoped that she will one day overcome the condition.

When Kyras is born it does not seem an unusual year to be born until the September 11, 2001 attack. The United States government is unprepared for the type of attack it faces or to improvise a defense against such an unprecedented assault. It is not a time that it has ever encountered. It awakens the nation and the world. America's challenge is to be a conscientious global citizen and not separate itself from poor and struggling nations and communities. It may take generations before we enrich the world and environment of our children. We must cease being a nation furthering its own self-interest. For us it is going from the needs of a single nation to the well being of the entire planet.

Schools are places that also perpetuate inequity by serving the few and maintain an inertia that sustains sameness. By not questioning tradition and society, those in school mechanically follow others. Whether we get an education or are uneducated, we do not revolt against school, organized religion, or culture but we fit into routines and customs in such conforming worlds. We do not deepen our human adventure.

In what environment are children free? It is one where the child finds out about himself. It is where parents, teachers, and others are truly concerned that young people discover who they are and know themselves.

Each child should be a revolutionary and question life and the world. He or she should be on a quest for the truth; such a person who seeks truth is living a religious life. Any ambition or self-interest whether spiritual or worldly does not bring about a mind that is intelligent, clear and free.

For many of us when the energy of youth leaves us, we do what everyone else is doing. We live second-hand lives. We are just one of the crowd. The energy and revolution in us as youths lasts but a moment for most, and never comes again. It disappears and vanishes. So the schools are places of vanished revolutions. The world of our relentless energy leaves, dies. Schools are not places of importance. No one stops us from learning. What matters is that an individual is thinking deeply about things, and learning about life, the world and him or herself, whoever he or she is.

When children are free and moving through life, they leave no trail or mark. They inquire into the questions of life with scientific observation and without self-importance. Schools can become insignificant in their lives in the absence of good teaching and deep inquiry. Before our grandson enters school it is evident that children want to learn new and unknown things on their own. They are motivated to make sense of the world and are driven to understand it. Children can understand what is invariant across language and mathematical worlds.

Invariance

I often share a story I hear about a five-year old youth who later becomes a mathematician. He counts five rocks and then he counts the same rocks backwards and he observes they are five also.

It astonishes him that there are five both ways. He learns there is invariance, or constancy, in the number of objects that does not change no matter what order or process is used to count them.

This is also true in other things such as the gravitational pull on a body by the earth is the same yesterday as today or from moment to moment.

Children observe things accurately and sharply and take in more in than one realizes and live with uncertainty as they probe deeper into the world, inquiring about such things as matter and energy. What are they? They question the truth in hearing of a yellow moon in a song and wonder how it is possible. Or they see an unusual word like Tao and wonder how it is pronounced. Or they question about rot and decomposition and the impermanence of things.

We separate ourselves from life through conformity, authority, and holding on to an obsolescent and empty world of culture and tradition. The known world of the past and the future, the projected past, are the thoughts that fill our lives and consciousness. What does our consciousness contain or consist of? The content of our consciousness is the past. Whatever we realize or are aware of has already happened. A free person lives in the present and it is where creativity, intelligence, and insight exist in our lives.

I regularly attend one of the poorest and most isolated schools in the city. It has a capable and dedicated principal. The school performs low in some areas but remarkable in others. The teachers and students are enthusiastic and energetic. They start each day with announcements on the playground.

When instructed the students shout out, "Ready to learn."

The adults respond, "Ready to teach."

It is with great energy that most days begin, but how many in the school internalize this morning energy? Some do.

Which students are ready to learn, who are at one in their surroundings, are regularly exposed to books, and can respect, communicate, and learn with other people?

Which teachers are there and ready for students to be well educated, to be capable of teaching themselves, and understanding what students are learning by expressing things in their own words?

One day a week I teach mathematics to a class of fifth grade students. They are capable students. Many do advanced mathematical work with great enthusiasm. One day Superintendent Carlos Garcia observes a mathematician in the class and the students solving problems such as:

$$\log_3 27 = ?$$

Many of the students understand the answer is 3, which impresses the superintendent. He learns how bright the students really are. They are mainly black, Samoan, and Latino students. He understands the racism, poverty, and isolation of the community that the students and their families exist in.

There have been six lockdowns this year from gunfire shot around the school. It is the poorest school in San Francisco, surrounded by public housing and intergenerational poverty. For forty years I have worked with this school. What amaze me are the occasional times when great talent and capability are evident in the classrooms in spite of the seemingly insurmountable barriers and setbacks. In their time at the school there are those who pursue academic excellence by motivating and engaging students to become independent learners. By using both new and untested approaches they learn in a spirit of innovation and transformation. They are working with others at different times to find productive ways of learning. The school at one time becomes a distinguished school in California, as does a nearby school.

The minds and thinking of young children excite and fascinate me. One day I am at a community meeting at another school in Hunters Point. A kindergarten teacher introduces me to a child in her class. She tells me how well he can read. He demonstrates this by reading things on the wall around the room. I am amazed at how his mind is unhindered as he performs with total attention to what he is doing. He is able to sound out and get through words that are difficult for some adults, sometimes with minimal assistance. His ability to read and process all he encounters inspires those who know him and his unusual attention and energy.

Reading

Why do we read? As youth why do we eat, play hard, and talk to others? They are all part of life. Some things we rebel against. However, if we are not reading, playing, getting angry, or being good and other such things then we are not truly alive.

Counting

Sometimes we learn of the enormous energy of youth through their learning process. I learn this on a visit to Lowell High School. I talk with two teachers. One is a teacher in the school district, and we talk about her son, a child I never meet. She shares a path her child takes. The other teacher is his physics teacher at Lowell High School. He tells me this youth is possibly the smartest student to ever come through the school. The physics teacher lets me look at the advanced placement examination in physics taken by the student. He uses it as a model to show other students, and seems deeply moved by the intelligence and understanding demonstrated by the student. He also remembers another student from the school that received the Nobel Prize in physics in 2001. This Nobel Prize winning student writes as a youth that he spends the majority of his childhood reading books. He seems obsessed with it.

The teacher says her son as a youth is fascinated with counting to a million. He would count each day and start the next day where he left off from the previous day. He reaches a million when he is four years old. The teacher believes the amount of attention he dedicated to this counting task or project is a significant part of his learning. I also think that the level of attention one gives to something shows us what we are capable of doing. The teacher's son finishes Lowell High School then Harvard and she says just recently he received a doctorate in particle physics from

Berkeley. The teacher herself spends much of her life working in the poorest communities in the hardest schools in the city. She is dedicated in her work.

In another part of the city at a school where public housing projects are across the street, kindergarteners are learning Chinese. Many of the students are Asian and white but not all. Four are black. Their teachers refuse to speak a word of English from the first day of class up until five months later. The teachers are thrilled at what the students are able to speak and hear. They find it exciting beyond belief and the students themselves are aware of what they are able to understand and express. All students should be able to perform in such programs when they are young, enthusiastic, and capable of absorbing what exists in the rich worlds they are immersed in.

On several occasions my daughter asks us to write about our grandson as my wife and I see him. We write about his probing energy and life in the world. Sometimes one's mind is limited to what a child is capable of processing. He clearly can see 200+300 is 500 just as 2+3 is 5. Our daughter reads the things we write and collects them. One day my daughter asks me to write a letter for our grandson that he will one day read by himself. I do. It is a brief note about a journey into the California wilderness.

For me the wilderness is a place that offers a rigorous life and where one understands self-discipline and human capability. It is also a place where one discovers the insignificance of self-importance. The wilderness is unlike school because it is not an artificial place. It does not give rewards but is a place of challenge, wonder, exploration, awe, discovery, mastery, and possibility. The wilderness communicates to us at the most serious level because it is a place of life and death.

The note I do write to my grandson is about an adventure I have on a wilderness road. It is an event I pass through and move on. Our ventures in life sustain our youthfulness and our energy.

# 4

# SAN FRANCISCO AND CHINA

"Are we in China?" My grandson asks, who is visiting from Maryland.

"No," I tell him.

We are in the Chinese consulate in San Francisco. It is a large building and I estimate more than a hundred people moving about and it seems everybody is speaking Chinese. I hear no English spoken except for the guard whom we ask for directions. He is a young white man and he informs us where to go. We wait in line to request visas to travel to China.

Several months ago I was in this consulate for a celebration of the Peoples Republic of China, which was founded on October 1, 1949. At the event is talk of the growing economic strength of the Chinese government. It is also stated that California is one of the leading economies in the world and that China wants to strengthen it ties with the United States, California, and San Francisco. The persons who are moving to San Francisco from China seem like they will be well educated and working in seemingly important jobs. They are like the American students who finish prestigious universities in the east and come here because they think that San Francisco is a world-class city. The poor and minorities who cannot live here by entering the city's exclusive society leave. Whites and a few from other groups dominate as the privileged of the population.

At the event I meet a lady from China who is a medical doctor and works at the University of California medical center. She has a young child and is very concerned about the school the child will attend. She clearly wants the child in the best school, getting the best education. Certainly many parents want such an education for their child, but they are not as determined of having it happen as this lady who seems driven and capable to transcend any impediment.

When we reach the window to request a visa, I tell the lady behind the window that I plan to visit several schools in China. I do not know that she understands me. She examines the passport but she never responds to me. I do not know if there is any additional approval needed for such a request. Even if she may acknowledge what I am saying she takes no further action. We leave the consulate, but before we walk down Geary Street to Laguna Street religious demonstrators draw our attention. They protest against their persecution by the Chinese government. Within China there are also clashes of ethnic and religious minorities who are seen as separatists by the Chinese government that does not permit mass demonstrations by such groups. There are a number of groups within and outside of China who struggle against Chinese oppression for their own self-determination.

# 5

# BEIJING

Beijing

The streets in the Chinese cities are very clean. People are constantly sweeping whether it is in a poor neighborhood or on the sidewalk surrounding a new high-rise. Traffic and pedestrians are everywhere. I read that there are 16 million people and 10 million bicycles in Beijing. It is a city of construction sites, wide roads, skyscrapers, numerous apartments, poverty, and great and growing wealth. There are also old buildings of earlier ages and ways of life, from times of emperors who ruled over the masses and peasants living among the alleyways connecting courtyard homes.

I do not experience the dirt in the air from the dust, pollution or weather conditions that I hear about before coming. The cool weather seems to maintain an acceptable air quality. Like India, the laborers move through the streets carrying impossible loads of materials on carts, bicycles, and their backs. There are no forklifts where human labor and toil are so cheap. Limited and scarce resources mean that everything seemingly gets recycled, even food and its scraps. One sees bicycles loaded with enormous pounds of cargo.

It is sometimes unclear and strange when one awakens and is aware that he or she is on another continent, in another country, in another city. It is an amazing realization to grasp that one is in Beijing, China, having reached a distant place on such a long journey. It is a unique and totally new situation that exists.

I think about San Francisco eighth grade school children who come to Beijing. They are from the Alice Fong Yu School visiting the Beijing Experimental School. Alice Fong Yu School is a public school in San Francisco. One student says it is an awesome trip coming here attending school and living with a family. Some say that the two weeks of being in China teaches them the most they have learned in their entire lives. One student finds his immersion into Chinese life to be like entering into a dream and leaving reality, and another says he is glad he did not die. A different student says there will never be a trip like this again because it is an exchange between two totally different worlds. One student says that one must be here to experience its life. It cannot be done while sitting in a classroom. Still others see China quite differently. When they arrive in China they feel as though they have not traveled far from home. In fact, some feel at home. They are comfortable in this foreign land with different customs.

Some of these students observe that people in Beijing walk a lot, bicycle a lot, and are seemingly in fairly good physical condition. Though there is a focus on fitness and a concern for health, many people smoke in public places and contradict this observation of health and fitness. It is a disturbing fact.

The teachers say that the children on this trip are amazing in taking care of themselves and each other. The trip is a great event for them because, most of all, they are all safe during the entire trip. The Great Wall and the Forbidden City are seen as incredibly majestic and inspiring to them.

There are students in the Beijing Experimental School who have visited the United States. One such student at the Beijing school says that there are challenges living in a one party political system. He says that he wants more of an American style education. He feels it allows for more emotion and social development. He appreciates seeing an American student playing soccer just for fun. He says that everything in China, whether playing basketball or the violin, is pursued very seriously.

I learn from our guide, Gilbert, that the Chinese are very patriotic. He talks about the communist party that rules the country, but he himself is not communist and he lives outside of their thinking. There are fifty-eight million party members (five percent of the population). For many Chinese their support for China does not mean loyalty to the communist party. In America there is much attention to freedom, but here discipline and order seem as essential. Gilbert talks about those dedicated to the party, but he is very clear in his view and where he stands. He has lived in the United States and has been a businessman in New York. He, therefore, does not philosophically believe in communism or socialism. He sees free enterprise as a more advanced system to the Chinese way of life. He makes it clear that he is his own person and does not comply with the government expectation to direct his way in the world.

Gilbert is our guide throughout China. He was born in Shanghai but now lives in Beijing. He is an excellent guide who is confident, well read and spoken, and very knowledgeable about China and the United States. He seems very qualified for the job he is doing. Gilbert sees himself as an individual who practices his free speech. This makes him stand out because among the Chinese your self-identity so often comes from the group.

One sees soldiers march around Tiananmen Square. For me it is a place of world drama. I learn about the youth and the sacrifices made to end the Qing imperial dynasty and to bring about a nationalist government in 1911. The contemporary movements in China are also driven by the youth. In the twentieth century student movements liberate China from foreign domination, as well as move China from an insular nation to a global and international place.

It is in 1989 in Tiananmen Square when one Chinese student dared to be run over and killed by blocking the movement of a tank, seemingly challenging and standing against the army. It is a moment when the Chinese youth movement impacts the world. In the end hundreds and possibly thousands of people are killed or imprisoned by government forces. It is interesting to learn that though this Tiananmen Square confrontation is seen throughout the world at the time that it is almost unknown in China. The government controls such information. Many Chinese are unaware that this standoff even took place.

It is evident that there is a silence regarding dissent throughout China. I see soldiers walking in formation through the multitude of persons passing through the Square. It is interesting that it is now almost twenty years after the event and it is as though it did not happen. It seems as though the lone student and his action would be seen and understood by many here as profound and revolutionary. It was a time when students protested and demanded government reform. The protests were violently put to an end by the Chinese Army, and there was a resurgence of conservatism in the country. This was followed by a push for economic reform that is now visibly changing the country. Its impact is opening China's economy and further connecting it to the outside world.

For some the China of today is changed dramatically. In 2008 foreigners and the youth see this new nation as a place where a productive effort is made to demonstrate crisis management, such as the disaster relief in response to the Sichuan earthquake. China produced a great 2008 Beijing Olympics, an example of its achievements and its participation in free trade and global markets.

The conflict at Tiananmen Square is seen as counterrevolutionary by the government and school textbooks barely mention it. Some fled China in 1989 because of the event. For them it was a time of fighting corruption and a protest for freedom and democracy. They see that China's economic transformation creates tough challenges for the nation, as inequality and social discontent still exist just as they did prior to the event in 1989.

Today government authority controls China. The student led movement that ended with deaths of hundreds when tanks came through the streets and opened fire is unknown to most of the youth today, but China is changing. For ten years that the Alice

Fong Yu school of San Francisco visited Tiananmen Square the students were never told anything about the Tiananmen Event, but in 2009 they were.

A prevailing Communist Party goal is to help the poor and to make things equal. This is why the visit to Tiananmen Square is so interesting to me. It is here that I buy the Little Red Book of quotations by Chairman Mao Zedong. I read the book years ago and I now reread it. The book states that without revolution it is impossible to lead working class people and broad masses towards transformation. It deals with combining theory and practice, working with the masses, and exercising self-criticism. It seems an awesome task moving hundreds of millions of people from an undeveloped country to one of power and prosperity. Mao Zedong states that the people must become competent. Revolution empowers those struggling with oppression and who stand against imperialism, exploitation, and the bureaucracy of domination. The book is fascinating to me. It inquires into the contribution of the poorest citizens in a time of revolution and change, and realizes one eliminates war when country, class, nations and borders are ended. After the theory and assumptions made in the book, life went in other directions. National reforms actually happened in China that lead to catastrophes where many citizens and counterrevolutionaries are killed and destroyed. Today innovation has transformed China from collective farms to a more free market economy.

My wife truly loves the history of places, visiting and seeing them first-hand. There are significant events and places in China that she has read about, discussed, and found fascinating. It is why it is so meaningful to her to be in Beijing and to visit the Forbidden City and the Summer Palace.

The Forbidden City is to the north of Tiananmen Square and was the imperial palace during the Ming and Qing dynasties. The construction took from 1406 to 1420 to complete and required more than a million workers. A deep moat and a high city wall surround it. It is now known as the Palace Museum and is the world's largest palace complex. The name Forbidden

City refers to the fact that no one could enter or leave the palace without the emperor's permission. During its history it was occupied, ransacked, plundered, and looted by European, American, Japanese, and Russian forces. Most of the buildings were rebuilt many times, although they maintained their original architectural style. In 1912 the last emperor of China abdicated. Under an agreement with the Chinese government he remained in the Inner Court, while the Outer Court was given over to public use. Traditionally the Outer Court was used for ceremonial purposes and the Inner Court was the residence of the emperor and his family. He remained in the Inner Court until he was evicted by a coup in 1924.

The last emperor ascended to the throne when he was almost three years old in 1908, following his uncle's death. He was treated like a god and unable to behave as a child. The adults in his life were strangers, remote, distant and not able to discipline him. He served as a ruling emperor from 1908-1911. He was a non-ruling emperor from 1911 to 1924. As a non-ruling emperor he and the imperial court were allowed to remain in the Inner Court of the Forbidden City as well as in the Summer Palace.

We visit the Summer Palace. Like the Forbidden City it is of extraordinary human dimension. It is a luxurious garden providing royal families rest and an imperial social life. In 1860 the British and the French ransacked its literary works and treasures, fought amongst themselves, and then set it afire. It took three days to burn it to the ground, but we see the ruins as we move through the park. Another attack to the palace was during a rebellion in 1900. The park was reconstructed after both attacks. The Summer Palace has a magnificent landscape and grand views. There are numerous buildings and halls, pavilions, corridors, and bridges. The natural elements are its gardens, trees, lakes, and winding roads. It is a great day for my wife to observe the Forbidden City and the Summer Palace.

# 6

# BEIJING VISITS

We stand on the Great Wall knowing it as an enduring symbol of China. My wife struggles to reach the highest tower as we ascend the wall. It is a vast place for my grandson to find his way. He tires and struggles to move along as our daughter follows along with him. We are among the hundreds of people, mainly Chinese, moving about and all are seemingly in awe of its existence. It is the world's longest human structure that stretched more than 4,000 miles across China and the largest man-made structure ever built. The forces of nature and human destruction have reduced the wall so that less than 30% remains in good condition. Many of the ancient sections of the wall have eroded over the centuries or have been destroyed or torn down.

It seems as though the Great Wall is hundreds or thousands of disconnected sections. How can they all ever be found? Over time some portions have collapsed and the bricks have been taken to build houses and roads. To us it is now a quiet and interesting place, but it once stood as a military fortification with watch-towers, and holes along the wall to allow archers to shoot arrows, and with a wide road built to allow horses to gallop along its length. Smoke signals and gunfire signaled the number of invading and opposing soldiers. This military fortification seemed endless. It is said that more than a million men once guarded some sections of the wall and that millions of persons died during the long centuries building the wall.

We are located forty miles from Beijing on the Badaling Great Wall. It is said to be the most well preserved section of the Great Wall and is situated at the outpost of the Juyongguan Pass. It was built more than 600 years ago to protect China's border from northern intrusion and invasion. It is visited by millions of people from China and elsewhere.

It now stands peaceful and awesome, but for centuries it protected dynasties as an effective defense structure with an organized military presence. When China's dynasties were unable to defend its northern border, twice invaders took power over them by getting beyond this wall. It no longer stood as a barrier and border that separated China from its invaders.

Though many of us on the wall today are aware of it as the separation and military barrier it once was, it has now become more. It was built to isolate China, but to the visitors who come here now the Great Wall is a bridge. It is not separating China from others but connects it to the rest of the world. As it presently stands it gives an awe-inspiring view of China that transcends its original purpose, and prior military history.

Hutongs

One day in Beijing my grandson and I take a taxi to the Hutongs. The Hutongs are passages and lanes around which communities have been formed. More of the Hutongs are destroyed as room for urban roads and skyscrapers is sought. We hire a pedicab to carry us around. I wonder to what extent we will stand out as two black persons moving through the area. It has not been an issue anywhere else in Beijing nor is it here. We seem almost unnoticed as we travel. We find ourselves part of a world that is unknown to us. We ride through narrow alleys looking into doorways and houses and pass a school. We visit a home and a lady shows us around. She is proud of the compound. The woman shows us the bedroom, and the common living room, kitchen, and the courtyard that are shared. Down the alley is the communal bathroom that is shared with other neighboring residents. We walk around on foot in the area and find people friendly and engaged in various games, conversations, and items for sell. We buy nothing. We have no camera and we take no pictures. There are small shops, eating areas, and women cooking. Older citizens sit together playing cards, mahjong, and Chinese chess.

"Hutong" is originally a Mongolian expression meaning "well". In the old days, people lived together around a well for water and the "passages" they made formed today's hutongs. The Mongolians came from the north invaded and conquered China in the 13th century. The main buildings in the Hutongs are almost all quadrangles formed by four houses around a courtyard, just as we visited. Some have survived and many have been torn down and replaced by modern buildings as dwellers have moved to new housing while the aging neighborhoods exist beside a new age and world that surrounds them.

The Hutongs are interesting places because they are where poor and ordinary people live. I learn that in the last fifty years the number of hutongs has decreased from seven thousand to thirteen hundred. I read a book by an American teacher who lived in a hutong and shared a courtyard home in Beijing for two years. The hutong neighborhoods have existed for eight hundred years and are now being destroyed for condominiums, high rise buildings, shopping centers, and wide streets for more motor driven vehicles that displace bicycles and pedestrians. The once past glory is becoming an obsolete way of life.

Foreigners once flourished in old Beijing. They are able to afford Mongolian ponies and endless picnics. It is a good life for them. Whatever the Chinese think about such a life is insignificant to the foreigners who celebrate their lives here.

Because of the low rent, the central location, and an atmosphere of a close community, the residents do not want to leave their dilapidated homes. As the city now welcomes commerce, business, and material advancement it allows thoughtless destruction of the hutongs. Those who do remain ask where are those who care, and when are they coming? Saving the hutongs seems hardly possible as even those who support them, and see them as significant places are not willing to live in them. The families move out, their homes become rubble, and the community vanishes. In a moment they are gone. As the hutongs are being destroyed, the city rebuilds itself.

I know a Chinese teacher in Beijing whom I met in San Francisco. Hidi told me to let her know when we are in China. When we arrive in Beijing I contact Hidi and we make arrangements to meet at her school. When my grandson and I return from the hutongs, we join my wife and daughter to take a taxi to the school. When we arrange for the taxi at the hotel I am asked if we have any authorization to go to the school. It is the same concern I had in the Chinese Consulate in San Francisco when I told the clerk that I would be visiting schools in China, and she gave no response. I never knew if my request to visit schools was understood or acknowledged. I intended to visit a school in Beijing, and another school in Shanghai that had 10,000 students. I was to meet a group of Chinese educators in Shanghai and we were to visit the school together.

At the hotel I tell them that I work with the San Francisco schools and I have made arrangements to visit the Beijing school. They are satisfied with the response. In the taxi to the school we again pass Tiananmen Square. The school is located very near the square. We get to the school and there is a gate that is guarded by soldiers. We let them know that we are to meet a teacher at the school. They are very cooperative and ask us to wait. After ten minutes the teacher Hidi comes and welcomes us to the campus.

We are on the campus of the Experimental School of Beijing Normal University. Hidi is a young and enthusiastic teacher who is happy to see us. She shows us around the school. She introduces us to teachers and students. The students seem glad we are there and to hear or discuss any questions or comments that we may have. I met Hidi when she brought a group of students from the Experimental School to San Francisco. They had stayed with families, and visited Alice Fong Yu School a San Francisco public school. The students who came amazed me in their fluency with the English language. They were creative, confident, and excited about their journey to San Francisco. Their deepest and sincerest expressions are for their host families. Their humbleness, kindness, honesty, and appreciation are clearly evident. It was a great evening hearing about their transformative life experiences in San Francisco.

We are now on the Beijing campus as I talk with a student who presents herself with the same awareness, seriousness, and capabilities as the students who came to San Francisco. She knows about American cities and universities and other things that shows her diligent interest of life in America. She speaks near perfect English with no accent and expresses herself in a way that shows she has mastered her education. While we are talking we go to the school playground. Many of the students are playing basketball. My grandson loves playing basketball. They seem fascinated helping him and with American basketball. He is six years old and seldom has the strength to get the ball up to the basket. They are happy to have him join them. My grandson loves shooting the basketball with them. All of their attention is on getting him the ball to shoot baskets. My grandson seems as at home as if he's in Maryland playing, and the students are elated with the unexpected experience of feeding him the basketball and watching him shoot.

Hidi and my family leave the school and walk through the streets past the hotel where the Alice Fong Yu students from San Francisco stayed while in Beijing. We then look for a restaurant where we can eat, but they are all closed. None seem to be open until Hidi finds a place that opens for us. While we are in the restaurant she telephones her husband, Andy, who joins us. He understands English better than he speaks it. We are happy to meet him and he seems very excited that we are here. He works for a company that produces electronic communications materials for teachers and others. He is very familiar with American movies, video games, and seemingly any electronic device. Andy is extremely enthusiastic about his work. He has a great deal to share about media and the jobs he has worked on. He is as full of life as anyone we meet in China. After lunch we all crowd into their car for a visit to their home.

They live about thirty minutes from central Beijing. They live in a housing complex of high-rise condominiums. It is a newly built development. It almost seems like being in Manhattan, New York as we take the elevator up to their unit. Inside, Andy's parents welcome us. They too live with them. They lived in the hutongs for thirty years prior to moving here. They are very friendly and welcoming and seem so glad to see us.

Andy loves to play billiards and a billiards table almost completely fills the living room space. He asks me if I play the game. I do not. It matters not. Other worlds are revealed as we move through the house seeing the electronic, photographic, video, playstations, and books. My grandson is excited with all of the gadgets and devices. The place is filled with the contemporary information age communication devices. We bring books from San Francisco and a mathematical puzzle that we give to them. They give us books on China.

The women are busy preparing food, when two young ladies who had been invited to the occasion, join us. They speak English well and are very interested in learning more about life in the United States. My grandson and Andy go outside to play basketball and other interesting games. When they return the food is served. It seems perfectly prepared with vegetables, noodles, fresh fruit and drinks. It is probably the best Chinese food ever in our minds. We have our photographs taken. Every one there is included. The evening is as true and as joyous a time as we have ever experienced. It was a special Chinese occasion.

Hidi and Andy had invited us to a wonderful Beijing family visit. Andy's mother and father had been very genuine and accepting of our visit. We were also pleased to meet the other family members. After I return to San Francisco, I write Hidi and tell her how grateful our family is for their kindness and untiring spirit. We appreciate their diligence and understanding in doing everything in their power to create such a remarkable evening.

# 7

# STORIES

On our fourth day in Beijing we visit Tian Tan, the Temple of Heaven, which is a large park filled by tourists and residents. From early morning and throughout the day and into evening it is a lively place with dancing, kite flying, singing, and different games from badminton to Chinese chess. I am astonished at the talent from Peking Opera selections to the Tai Chi experts. Most of the persons are older but are so impressive in their performance that makes it so vibrant and alive.

I learn the park first opened in 1912 to the public. The masses had previously been banned from even watching the emperor's procession from the palace to the temple where he would pray. Now anyone can visit the Temple of Heaven. I purchase a magnetic spinning top from a stand that is selling science toys. The top fascinates observers as it seemingly moves on the edge of space and reality. I am never able to study it as I cannot get it through immigration in leaving the country. They tell me that the magnets that it contains are not allowed items to carry on the plane.

As one learns about the five thousand years of life in China, the centuries sometimes appear almost mythological. I read and learn stories about the people who are here. The emperors, warlords, and dynasties are now gone. What of those here today? Rulers and emperors conquered other tribes to establish nations that are formed out of battles. Those who are benevolent as well as those who are cruel rule societies. In our travel through China we learn of archaeological finds that contribute to this ancestral existence. Excavations of written records, scripts, and numerous objects survived the ravages of time. The finding of these relics reveals previous levels of existence and human discovery found by accident and by chance.

In moving through the world some people are changed by a vision or sometimes by getting beyond the continued monotony of life and going beyond its containment. For me being in China is a breakthrough from images and thoughts of things that never were. China itself surrounds me and defines itself. I read and learn stories about the people who are here. The emperors, warlords, and dynasties are now gone. What of those here today?

Dedicated to school

I read about a student suffering from a congenital spinal disease. Since shortly after her birth, she has been unable to stand or sit. She has had several childhood surgeries that do not change her condition, but her intelligence is equal to other students her age. Her father, therefore, decides that she should attend school at age six, and every day he carries her back and forth on his back. His health deteriorates when she is in the fourth grade, and he is completely confined to bed. To prevent her granddaughter from becoming a dropout, her grandmother decides to dedicate her life to her granddaughter's study.

The school day is not easy for a seventy-eight year old retiree who is in poor health. She has undergone two surgeries and has had her spleen removed. She still takes a twenty-minute walk to the school every day and attends every class. Some subjects in the curriculum such as English, physics, chemistry, and geometry are too hard for her to follow. To keep up with the lessons she takes a lot of notes and frequently seeks assistance from other students. When she finds something wrong or missing in her notes, she immediately returns to school to consult the teacher, even late in the evening. She has short-sided vision and one day she falls down on her way home and loses her glasses. It takes her more than an hour to get back from school.

Her granddaughter is a hard working student and ranks among the best in her class and grades in her various examinations. She passes all of her classes in primary and middle school and passes a high school admissions examination for computer training. She is invited to Beijing to receive an Outstanding Student Award at Tiananmen Square. At the awards program she cannot help but think of her grandmother who is at the very moment still attending school for her.

In the many stories of the Chinese they all reveal new things and some of them are unusual. I also know of stories of Chinese students living in San Francisco. San Francisco is a first place of settlement for Chinese in the United States. From the lives of the millions of people in China there are many personal journeys for them there and as others reach America.

Learning English

While teaching in San Francisco I learn the stories of many Chinese students. I meet one student who comes to the US from a farming village in China. His family is poor. While living in China his father had an aneurism, and sometimes fell in unexpected places and was unable to move. At times the student has to move his father by himself, other times he is assisted by others. The family is able to migrate to the US. When I meet the student he is attending high school and he tells me he has a job as a bowl washer in Chinatown. He tells his co-workers that he is applying to attend UC Berkeley and they laugh in disbelief. He takes advanced placement classes. Initially they are a great struggle for him. He asks himself why he is taking classes with such difficult reading assignments when he has such a hard time understanding English. He then starts to read easier books and the language and ideas become clearer to him. He is able to change from being the poorest student in the class to the highest achieving. He becomes the best student in the school.

A Student World

One day I am walking down the hall of a San Francisco elementary school. It is one of the lowest performing schools in the city. It is populated with poor students from the public housing projects and poor Latino students from the Mission district. For many it is a place of poverty and disappointment. I read an article posted on the wall written by the only Chinese student in the school and how grateful he is in being there. It expresses a vision of learning and self-determination exists in the worst performing schools. This student sees a great school where others outside see it as hopeless. It shows that remarkable things do occur in the most troubled public schools:

> I am thankful to be a student at this school because I have plenty of great teachers to teach me, and this school is one of the few schools that has as many afterschool programs such as a math and science program, student council, and afterschool computers. I think I am one of the lucky ones because I have had an opportunity to join the best school in this San Francisco district.
>
> I am thankful to be a student here because I have lots of friends here. My best friends are at this school. Even though I have moved, I still come to this school because of these friends.
>
> Also, I have learned a lot of cool stuff like secrets and shortcuts to math. When I learn something new, I will remember it, even though I do not have a good memory. I've learned other things like science, art, geography, history, and many other subjects in school.
>
> One of the many reasons I like this school is because it is integrated. I like an integrated school because I get to meet a lot of other kids and make more friends.

I am thankful because our school has a lot of money to pay for field trips to Audubon Canyon Ranch. We also have a lot of school supplies. Like pencils, erasers, paintbrushes and paper.

I am thankful because we also have a lot of sports like baseball, dodge ball, tetherball, basketball, football, and kickball and plenty of balls to play with. We also have a computer lab which has a lot of programs which will help me with future jobs. Some of our science programs will help students become scientists or make good business strategies. I am also thankful to be a student here because I get to walk around the neighborhood selling our products. This will help me become a good businessman.

I'm going to make the school better by helping my classmates with their work when I am done with my work. When there is a student in need, I will be there. If there is a student in trouble, I will be there. I will also help with recycling. I will clean whenever I get an opportunity to do Broom Brigade. I will sell a lot of tickets or candy when we have fundraising programs. I think that when I help, I am not only helping the school but the whole neighborhood.

I will make the whole district proud of us. I will try my best to help the school as long as I can. I want to make this school the best because it is the best to me. I think I am lucky to be in this school with such a good principal. This is the best school in the whole San Francisco School District.

San Francisco
Elementary School Student

# 8

# XIAN

China is emerging as a place of significance as is evidenced by bulldozers clearing the way for skyscrapers and modern cities. Ancient sites are dug up as this is happening. In the fast growing cities of China thousands of relics are discovered and some are thousands of years old. Some are destroyed in a rush for the country to modernize itself. There has probably always been digging going on in China long before this modern era. We arrive in Xian. It is thousands of years old and its residents say that it is China's first capital and that it was the capital under thirteen dynasties and was the capital for more than a thousand years. I am told that about eight million people live here. Though it is smaller than Beijing and moves at a slower pace it still stands as a significant place in China.

My daughter, Maleka, buys a book about the Terra Cotta warriors. She then waits in a long line to have it autographed. The man signing the book is a villager who among others was digging for a well in 1974. He struck a hard stone object and had other villagers help him remove it. No one expected the object to be a terracotta solider that was one of thousands of figures buried more than 2,000 years ago. Though the villagers were searching for water they made one of the great archaeological finds of the century. To avoid risk and damage to the discovered figures a giant hall was constructed over the excavation site to provide protection. We are now at the excavation site. My daughter is amazed that the farmer is there and she obtains his signature. He is there more than 35 years after the discovery.

The warriors, chariots, horses and other figures are part of the tomb of the Emperor Qin Shi Huang (First Emperor of Qin) who ruled 2,000 years ago. It is said that he unified the Chinese feudal states and standardized written script, weights, measures and currencies. He is also said to have ordered the burning of books and the deaths of scholars. The terracotta warriors were the underground army guarding his tomb.

It is said that the emperor had construction of the tomb begin shortly after he became king at the age of thirteen. The tomb took 39 years and 700,000 workers to complete. It had pearls in the ceiling to represent the stars and rivers and lakes were represented by liquid mercury. None of the soldiers look alike as they have distinctive, individual expressions. They are life-size figures about six feet high in military outfits.

The interesting thing is how the emperor had so hoped he was able to provide himself eternal protection after his death, but he really became insignificant and forgotten and his death is like that of any other individual. It is the terracotta warriors and the farmers digging for water that bring renewed life to his name. It shows the uncertainty of life and the illusion of privilege and power.

As emperor he was dedicated to bringing the past into an unknown world beyond himself. He commissioned 8,000 life-sized terracotta warriors to serve him in his afterlife. We now observe the impact he is unable to know.

# 9

# SHANGHAI

We reach Shanghai late Friday afternoon. I try to reach a friend from San Francisco. He is traveling with a group of other educators. It would be the only chance of visiting the Shanghai high school that I would have, but I am unable to reach him. I get a message from him on Saturday. We never meet or talk person to person, so I am unable to visit the high school. We do visit the Yu Garden and the Shanghai Museum. The Yu Garden is a 400-year-old classical garden built by a government official for his parents. Gilbert, our guide, is very thorough in his detail about the pavilions, halls, rocks, trees, and plants. I find the place very overwhelming and exhausting. I am never interested in such things.

Our hotel is not far from the Bund. There are old and new buildings that show that Shanghai has been influenced and exploited by nations such as the British, the Americans, Germans, Dutch, French, Russians, and Japanese. As I see the remnants of these occupying nations I am moved by twenty-first century Shanghai as a place of commerce and a global information center. One sees it as a continuously transforming city by observing life by the Bund or the waterfront area along the Hangpu River.

In the Shanghai Museum are galleries of bronze, ceramics, pottery, paintings, sculpture, furniture, jade, and other things. The gallery that interests me displays the clothes, textiles, artwork, creativity and metal wares of ethnic minorities of China.

The library is also a fascinating place. I purchase a map of China and a book on the five thousand year history of China. I read the entire book about China's emperors, religions, dynasties, inventions, and invasions. I find the Chinese Imperial Examination System interesting. It lasted for 1300 years from the seventh to the twentieth century. Before the system was used, appointments to imperial or high-ranking government positions were recommended by individuals of aristocratic rank. The Imperial Examination System meant that appointees to civil service positions were not to be selected through special or inherited privilege, but through an individual's own abilities.

Theoretically, any male adult in China, regardless of his wealth or social status, could become a high-ranking government official by passing the Imperial Examination. Commoners could now attain positions that were once restricted to aristocrats. For centuries, it is said, that emperors from humble origins replaced existing dynasties. Once in control these emperors realized the government required the administrative services of a multitude of bureaucratic workers and the civil service examination became a means of accomplishing this. France and Britain when needing public servants in their imperial outposts in the nineteenth century use this meritocratic strategy.

Under some Chinese dynasties the imperial examinations were abolished and government positions were simply sold, which increased corruption and reduced morale. Education in China was valued because of its possible pay-off in the examination system. The civil service system enabled the government to discover and utilize talent. The examinations are said to also be responsible for limiting China from advancing in science, as the examinations were restricted to such areas as literature, the arts, and Confucian classics. They excluded other areas and discouraged the development of new concepts.

As we leave the Shanghai Museum there is a worker washing the front of the museum. Workers everywhere are continuously cleaning the city in the places I see. The hotel we are in is as world class as any hotel I have been in. When I awake in the morning I reflect on the city. It is Sunday morning. I sit in the hotel room looking out. I see the city knowing that it is the largest city in the People's Republic of China, and is its commercial and communication center and one of the world's busiest seaports. What was once a fishing town is now a booming metropolis. When I am entering the city and leaving Pudong International Airport, I realize that I am in a different world where things are being rewritten constantly. I see the Transrapid Maglev train which goes from its subway station at the airport along a 30 kilometer route in 7 minutes and 21 seconds and reaches a maximum speed of 267 miles per hour. It is the SMT, the Shanghai Maglev Transportation Development Company. Coming from the airport one sees the numerous expressways already connecting the city, and those that are being built. There is also a ceaseless building fury evidenced in the skyscrapers that are going up among those that already define the Pudong skyline.

As I look out the hotel window there are cars, buses, bicycles and pedestrians that coexist in streets where city movement does not stop. The cabs in China seem in good condition and have reasonable and affordable fares. Twenty years ago bicycles were the most ubiquitous form of city transportation. In the pictures I saw of China bicyclists always crowded the street traffic. Shanghai now bans bicycles on many of the city's main roads to ease the congestion. One still sees many bicycles and there are still bicycle lanes. One also sees Traffic Assistants who help provide safe crossings. Many of drivers have been bicycle riders, as well as pedestrians, so they seem to be aware of the life on the streets. What keeps traffic flowing seems to be an awareness that the larger and faster vehicles do not wait for you in any open traffic situation. I do not notice air pollution from the vehicles as it is cool and there is not a haze that one may assume. With the growing Chinese economy there is a rapid increase in private car ownership in recent years.

Looking at the steady movement of life the impermanence of the city is very clear. The city moves on never stopping, never looking back. Through the transience of life and movement it is still clear that there is a wealth gap in the city. I am told that a million dollar wedding is nothing novel in Shanghai these days. Even as I look from the window I see old apartment buildings existing among the new high rises. They are of another age and are quietly being eliminated. I wonder if people live there, but clothes hanging on the clothesline show there is life within.

# 10

# THE WEALTH GAP

The government promises to narrow the widening gulf between the rich and poor, and reports that the number of billionaires in China is among the highest in the world. It states that the price of becoming one of the world's biggest economies is environmental devastation and social disunity, and that China's most pressing problem is corruption.

Government officials identify the wealth gap as the most critical factor leading to disharmony in society.

Some say that the lives of hundreds of millions of peasants have failed to improve in the last half century.

As everywhere those living in poverty know that even money intended for them is often appropriated by corrupt local officials, who pocket it or divert it to business investments. Most of the poor know that they have to concentrate on making a living and finding enough to eat. They have no time to wait for the government.

China has moved more people out of poverty than any other country in recent years. Some hope for better times and that China can ignite the western provinces with the fervor for reform and change as in the east, as well as eliminate the ethnic tensions and labor unrest.

Many of the Chinese who move to San Francisco excel in its schools. The students are determined to realize their educational goals. They are highly motivated and driven to work hard in maximizing their capabilities and they are seldom distracted by other concerns such as their racial and minority status.

China imprisons thousands of people for counter-revolutionary crimes or who are accused of belonging to hostile organizations. Dissidents of the government face detention, surveillance, and imprisonment. The government states that the welfare of the collective must be put ahead of the rights of the individual when there is a conflict arising between them. The government argues that other nations have a disturbing instability and social deterioration because of extreme and uncontrolled individual freedom. How long can China remain a government controlling one party nation? The United States incarcerates more individuals than any other country in the world. How long will the United States sustain a two-party nation?

A Beijing builder and designer distances himself from the work he produces. It is used for propaganda by the government, but he says there is joy in doing the work and not in its promotion. By not letting the facts speak, we attempt to make up things that mislead us. This leads to a life of entertainment and amusement. He says that walking in any direction in Beijing one cannot help but to question why one lives in such a place with such pollution and yet celebrate it with Olympic games. The air itself is as appalling as any social, economic or political condition.

A person transforms the world by his or her participation in or resistance to society. China is a place where some never leave the crowd: others find their own voices and live their own lives.

We transform our world by our own energy. We must understand a world that is not Asian, European, American, or African. We all create the destructive places we live in through our own selfish interests, prejudices, hatred, and nationalism.

All over Beijing are signs proclaiming One World, One Dream. To me it means one planet, one mission. Those who live such a life contribute to a profound planetary community. It is a way to change the slums and ghettos into intelligent places to live and to be a part of life's adventure. We can sustain a global mission where everyone has the energy to be literate and well educated where traveling the earth we pass through places sending expeditions into space exploring the universe; where we cooperate with others to understand how we deal with overpopulation, pollution of the earth, and the destruction of nature.

# 11

## TOLEDO

I have not lived in Toledo, Ohio for almost fifty years. Occasionally, I pass through town visiting family members; yet hardly encounter anyone else I know. In a recent visit, however, I see Robert Brundage. The Brundages are the only white family living in an all black neighborhood. For me the Brundages are original settlers in the Old West End as many blacks are. The father is a chemistry professor at the university. There are five sons. Though Robert moved to Boston to earn his doctorate in biophysics, he returned to Toledo to help his aging father. When I meet him in Toldeo, during this visit, his father has died.

Robert and I are the same age. I have known him since grammar school. We are always glad to see each other. I remember becoming close friends when we attended Robinson Junior High School together. We later attended Scott High School and the University of Toledo together. When he studied in the Boston area I visited with him before going to teach in Nigeria and later in Kenya.

In a recent visit to Toledo, my wife, Margaret, and I first find Robert Brundage while driving through the Old West End. He is on a porch talking with friends. How fortunate it is that we find each other again in Toledo after such improbable journeys for the two of us.

He tells me about his current work in the Toledo community. I later learn that the white residents moving back into the Old

West End encounter a life which one person describes as an island of middle class people surrounded by a different economic demographic. In San Francisco there is a similar dialogue about diminishing the predictive power of demographics. Poverty, education, race, and class contribute to such structures and systems. We perpetuate privileged groups of people and further their education as a society. In a twenty first century democracy every one must be well educated. How do we educate the world?

Robert has a deep interest in restoring old homes in the area. It is important to him to show Margaret and me the grandeur of these places that still exist. Margaret also has a keen interest in such places and finds them fascinating. She had met Robert before when we visited Boston some years ago, and is amazed at how unpretentious and idiosyncratically he lived. In Toledo he has noticeably aged. He has less teeth and lives outside of conventional society. I often have a difficult time finding him when I come to town as his lifestyle is one where he is seldom home and does not have to encounter bill collectors and others seeking him out.

I cannot show Margaret where I lived growing up in Toledo as the small world that our family lived in is now a schoolyard and the house is gone. The road and life once there have vanished. The city continues to change. I know that living there in those days comes from ones attention and awareness during those moments happening then. It is a universe where we only exist in the present. The past is no longer alive for us.

When Margaret and I visit Detroit, which is where she was born and lived her early life, we find a large field of thick vegetation where her house and other houses had stood. It is an interesting moment for me realizing the house she was born in, is no longer there. For her it is a profound moment to walk down forgotten streets and in her own way she re-lives a time of eight years of youth, wonder, and a life of curiosity and discovery.

Robert tells me about the work he is doing in Toledo in several neighborhoods and the society he struggles to transform. He shows Margaret and me a project of building houses in poor neighborhoods. We visit the Collingwood Arts Center where Margaret buys pottery and he discusses his work in saving Scott High School.

Some times when I pass through town I leave a note on his door letting him know that I am in town. On this visit, I learn before arriving that he is in Saint Vincent's Hospital, where my mother once worked. Robert is in intensive care struggling to recover from an assault and robbery by a youth. My brother, Vernon, sent me a newspaper article that described the incident. A fifteen-year-old black youth confesses to knocking Robert off his bike, hitting him on the side of the head, knocking his helmet off, and sending him to the ground. The youth fled with the bicycle and was arrested about a mile away from the scene and confessed to the crime.

When I arrive in Toledo, Robert is lying in the intensive care unit. Margaret and I look on. He has been lying unconscious for 12 days. I learn that a vigil has been held for him and that the mayor, environmentalists, artists, and other interested citizens have come to express great hope for his life. My father and brother also come. As I stand in the intensive care room every breath I hear seems so significant. I read cards in the room wishing him well with a deep anticipation for his recovery.

There are two cards that are particularly interesting to me. The first one is from someone who never knew Robert. It says that we don't know you but we feel you are such a great individual for society. It expresses an acknowledgement of what the life of one person can mean to our world. The second card is from a high school classmate wishing him well and is signed, "Scott 60." It expresses a spirit that is just as strong now as it was fifty years ago when we are curious and enthusiastic about the world and on our way to a life of adventure. No one wants Robert to die.

The next day at the hospital I see Robert's younger brother, Richard, who now lives in Columbus. We greet each other after fifty years, probably never thinking that we would see each other again in life. He says that it like a family reunion in seeing each other. He says that Robert's jaw was broken during the attack.

This caused massive bleeding to the brain from which he lapsed into the coma. Richard tells me that Robert's heart is strong, probably from the miles of bicycling he does daily, but there is much trauma and damage to his head. Robert has multiple areas of brain destruction and there is quite likely an issue of paralysis and other body damage and devastation. Initially there were positive signs that included specific motor responses from directed conversation to him, but those signs have not happened again. Richard says that it is just a matter of time. The next day Robert dies. I have to go back to California, but I do return for Robert's memorial service.

At the memorial service I meet Robert's two sons, two of his younger brothers, and family members from Massachusetts, Michigan and Virginia. As the cello solo is playing, the Unitarian minister speaks, the community members speak, and his brother David (who I later learn has performed at Carnegie Hall) gives the eulogy. I think of the earlier days of our walking to school together and appreciate Robert as a critical thinker.

He is reflective, thoughtful and a good listener. He sustains his youthful insight throughout his days. One person describes Robert's imposing intellect and even greater heart, and his ability to read between the lines of life, and take delight in the simpler things. He is naturally himself. He has no need to follow what others are doing, and is able to exist outside the routine of society. I know of his great love for music and remember the day we traveled to Oberlin University with his mother for a cello lesson. He gives attention to pursuing things that interest him like travelling from Boston to New York on a Saturday to buy bread from a bakery on 96th Street.

I have conversations with many people, and they all have good things to say about him. Several long conversations are with people I have not seen for decades, and some are with people I meet for the first time. It is great to see classmates. We are all older but there is such energy in the paths that we are crossing. The classmate I spend the most time with is Robert Frankel. He has been busy intersecting with the lives of many persons and we visit with a former classmate together. Robert Frankel talks about his family and a relative who he is dedicating himself to help. In our conversations we speak of many things. It is very important to him that he express that Robert Brundage would not have wanted the youth who attacked him and caused his death to be tried as an adult. He is very adamant in stating this fact.

During this trip, I also visit a newspaper office that had written a story on Robert's contribution to the city. The journalist talking with me says that Robert's struggle for the poor and the forgotten is what he lived for and that the youth who attacked him to take his bike has no realization that he is assaulting an individual who worked to change society and the system that the youth is imprisoned in.

My first teaching job in San Francisco is with incarcerated youth. I observe the lives of those of brilliant minds and those who lack an education. There is often sameness to lives that have faced concentrated poverty, racial discrimination, and a lack of personal responsibility without a determination to overcome adversity and to change ones life.

Robert had respect and understanding for all persons. He lived a nonviolent life. His death is tragic and senseless. I lived in Nigeria during the Biafran Civil War where there are numerous such pointless deaths. Our world is violent both locally and globally and it is up to us to change it. We must all be serious about living in a world where all individuals are well respected and well educated and none are oppressed or allowed to practice violence. It is what he worked for and died for. Though Robert has always lived a nonviolent life, we must realize that he is as anyone else when attacked without warning. He is like all of us.

# SAN FRANCISCO

# 12

## SAN FRANCISCO PROLOGUE

As I walk the road to school in Nigeria, I sometimes marvel at the interest and energy of some students. It is a village of dirt roads going past the school and beyond the village. The people living on the road are probably as poor as many other people throughout the world. Why do students who are bright and hard working want to leave this life and travel to the larger cities and beyond? They seek new adventure and to deepen their education.

I come to San Francisco from Africa. I reunite with a friend, Shyaam Shabaka, who I work with in Africa, where his name is Willie Ellis. I find a job as a teacher in the San Francisco schools.

There are no dirt roads in San Francisco as in Africa, but there is concentrated poverty in many areas of the city. I find there are endless reform measures in the United States but isolated and poor children continue to attend the worst schools and lead the least educated lives whereas the schooled, affluent, and upper class children sustain a self perpetuating existence that dominates society. The rich and the dominating class in the American system of education also maintain a mental testing culture that is a highly effective means of social control.

When children are tracked and separated by comparisons and rankings on tests it is unlikely that the mass of humankind will ever re-emerge into an unpredictable whole.

A meaningful education encourages the best qualities of youthfulness, curiosity, adventure, resilience, and insightful expression.

Many who are unschooled thrive in life.

They are unschooled but self-educated.

It is the questioning of schools and society that keeps them alive. Like all else they perish as they survive.

The slums, ghettos and villages of the poor must be transformed into intelligent places to live in. We need to eliminate poverty and subsistence existence and to create environments where students and citizens are in stimulating places to learn and live spirited, meaningful, and productive lives.

# 13

## WITHOUT PRIVILEGE

The failure of institutions of the highest learning, greatest wealth, and the most power to be open to everyone, means that they retain their privilege only for the successful, the esteemed, and the distinguished. It also undermines their legitimacy. The poor and minority are not absorbed by life in America. They are without privilege. They struggle hard in society and in schools for a second-class education. Those elite institutions remain as targets because of their exclusion, and they are continuously under attack.

In my years as a teacher in San Francisco, education for poor African American children has only rarely been one of noticeable opportunity. I was recently asked about the students now and how they have changed over the last forty years. It was thought that the old days were better and that students were more serious in those days. The truth is there has not been any real change amongst black students in San Francisco schools. They have changed as black society has changed which has usually been minimally. The youth have not lived any more productive lives than their parents. That expectation has seldom existed.

During my early years in San Francisco I was a high school mathematics teacher. I began teaching forty years ago and was teaching an advanced math class and almost all the students are Asian. I am surprised at the make up of the class. The names are new to me, but the students are eager, capable, and they are a great class. The Asian make up of the class is unexpected, but I do not see any issue. If the class had been all black females that would have been even more surprising, but I still would have accepted the class as it was. There is no indication that any interested or able student has been excluded from attending the class. It does bother me that there are such low societal and personal expectations of ourselves from those who are not here. The students in the school are almost all from poor families, but not as poor as the students in Nigeria. In Nigeria it is all black students, but in this class there are none. In Nigeria every student takes the same rigorous education. It is a challenging education no matter who you are. In the United States only the most serious students take the hardest courses.

In Nigeria learning is a great privilege. It is also the case with the Asian students. Some of them are immigrants, or their parents are. They come to America and suddenly everything seems possible. This is a place to start a revolution, a new life. There is great social unrest throughout the country, but in my years in San Francisco there is no sustained learning revolution from the black population.

In my first year at the school I am asked to teach an African Studies class. I am also the sponsor of the Black Student Union (BSU). The social studies department chairman who asks me to teach the African Studies class expresses how disappointed he is with the attitude of black students toward George Washington and the founding fathers and the little respect they show. It is an unexpected encounter. It is an unfortunate conversation about race, slavery, and the oppression that we are still living through.

I recall going to Washington's home at Mount Vernon with my wife and seeing the slave quarters there. On the day my wife and I go there, the woman showing us around tells us how kind George Washington is to his slaves, and how each day he writes them notes that they read on the tasks they are to perform. My wife remarks that she does not know how this is possible as the slaves were illiterate. The woman seems confused and unable to respond with any reasonable reply. She was living in an era that never was. My wife and I believe that no one who walks on the land of this plantation can be proud of the slave life and the oppressed laborers forced to work on the grounds overlooking the Potomac River.

To the social studies department chairman the founding fathers were brilliant and revered individuals. They had not started the system of slavery and many spoke against it. And though almost all of the founding presidents owned slaves, it was argued that many were sincere in ending it. But was it not the case that their lives and careers were enhanced by the enslavement and exploitation of others? There were also other individuals who lived at the same time facing the same human and social reality who did not depend on a downtrodden class of persons to further their lives.

This teacher is asking the students not to discredit the founding fathers for their flaws, but to only acknowledge their courage, hopes, and aspirations for the country they created. He saw history and the past in this light and the students did not. For him, that these students to ignore these men meant accepting a pretense that they live in a country that came from nowhere. He wanted the students to have no prejudice toward them.

I understand his passion for the founding fathers, his acceptance of their importance, and his belief in them. I question their past greatness. He is pursuing a past that never was. We romanticize things that never were as we invent history and the past. Years later I work with his sister at another school. She is a humble person and sees learning in a different light. She is more open-minded about students and their thinking and understands that people do seek fuller lives.

What runs deep in us is the courage of those such as that of Rosa Parks, who comes to a San Francisco school. She stands against the slavery perpetuated by the founding fathers. It is a way of life that continues and becomes a part of Jim Crow laws of race separation that further dehumanize black people. As a town citizen on a city bus, she courageously opposes the practices and laws of segregation that were used to control, terrorize, and subjugate blacks until the 1960s. Her action changes life in America. It is important that such voices and lives give meaning to our world. Those who dominate American society sustain a second-class way of life that dictates others for hundreds of years.

There are some things I personally do learn about such matters. As a student in school, for me history classes, just as so many others, are perpetuated by an unenergetic system. No one ever challenged this world. It is outside of school that I engage with those who examine the reality of slavery, its cruelty, and the courage of its resisters. I learn about the speeches and writings of abolitionists, testimony of escaped slaves, and the witnesses to this brutal way of life. This is meaningful to me as I grow up in the south where black people are hung and killed because white people hate us so. My mother tells me that they do not even allow us to walk through their neighborhoods. There are other times I observe such intensity toward other persons like that of the attackers on September 11, 2001 and their hate for America, or the genocides in Europe and Africa.

America is a nation of racial and class divisions. In the American history textbook that we were subjected to in school slavery was treated as though racism did not exist. The textbook gave no attention to the lives of abolitionists or slave revolts. In its description of the discovery of America by Columbus, it tells of the 1492 landing in the Americas, but discounts previous journeys and other explorers who reached here from Europe and elsewhere in the world. It did not mention that there is evidence of journeys from places such as Indonesia, China, Japan, West Africa, and Europe before the celebrated 1492 discovery. In its account of the 1492 discovery it assumed that it was natural for one group to dominate another as the Europeans dominated the Native Americans. There are no counterexamples such as five-hundred years earlier of the contact with the Vikings and Native Americans. The brief Viking Settlement was not marked by domination or oppression.

It is likely that many others from the world had reached the Americas. There is even evidence that Native Americans journeyed from North America to Europe. This means that individuals have long explored the planet by questioning and challenging boundaries and seeking new worlds. There are those who break away from ordinary life and thinking to do things that have not been done. They are not bound by routine. They observe and bring about dramatic change in the world. Though their lives and the transformations vanish in time, their questioning of the state of the world deepens our existence in a profound universe.

Even today after hundreds of years there still exist chronic and persistent problems regarding human rights. In living and traveling in Africa I find there are Americans in countries that are selfless and dedicated to bringing human freedom. However, the United States government still provides assistance to places where dictators deny human rights as well as imprison and kill its citizens. These countries also support American interests. I often find that the US government seems to use the language of democracy at home but practices imperialism, dominance, and supports dictators in foreign countries and developing nations such as in Africa.

I teach the African Studies Class in the early seventies after I returned to the United States from Nigeria. I am so eager to share Nigerian and African life with black students, and any other students who are interested. I have read many books on Africa and I have traveled across the continent and have visited Zaire, Liberia, Ivory Coast, Kenya, Uganda, Ghana, and Tanzania. My life in Africa is a transforming experience. I am twenty-four years old when I teach there, and it is a profound time in my life. Before going to Africa I had also visited Brazil as a seaman, and had gone to Bahia that had been another place in the new world where many Africans were brought. At this time I am seriously interested in information about black people and the new things and stories one would hear. I am able to tell the class about such adventure and my first-hand encounters of living in Africa.

I saw Nigeria as a place of self-governance, black people governing themselves and their own nation. I had never seen a black nation that was as vibrant and spirited. The merchants, vendors, builders, and market women were busy, involved, and productive. The places are alive with business, conversation, buses, commerce, and automobiles. The large cities of Lagos and Ibadan have both African and Western styles of life. The African life dominates. There is not a European presence there as in some other large African cities. There are millions of inhabitants who fill the villages, cities, and other urban places. The presence of new language, food, dress, and clothes mystify and challenge the strangers who visit. It is a place filled with life and also a serious place as one observes ways of life that have existed for hundreds of years.

The Nigerian students are so eager to learn in the harshest of conditions. They study until deep into the night and into morning for their examinations using kerosene lamps, as there is no electricity or running water. In the dry season there is sometimes little or no water. Most of the students are poor, but learning is a privilege. It is the most important thing in their lives. The students are so eager to learn about America, and how the minority populations are segregated and discriminated against, and the great opulence and wealth of the nation.

I enthusiastically enter the class on my first day in Nigeria and there is total silence. There are forty students. I am new to them, but they have come to learn. I talk a little about myself but I talk most of the time about mathematics. When I first arrive in the country, and students learn that I teach math, they come to me for mathematical problems to study. I teach in Oshogbo and other places, and there are always those who are eager to learn.

It is sometimes assumed that Africa is a single rigid place of simple existence. It is rather a vast continent of various people, places, and experiences. Even within its societies is variation. It is much the same as American society which often goes in multiple directions. The American culture that produced slavery, white privilege, and segregation also produced revolution, black rebellion and resistance, and civil rights struggles. We are as bad a society as we are good; as rich as we are poor. So though I am in Nigeria at a time when I am immersed in great school and student learning, there are also African school experiences in which I struggle.

In my first year of teaching in Nigeria there were many things I am still learning. I am surrounded by a system of European education that I have not encountered before. I am limited in being able to find my own way. It is a textbook directed education and an examination driven system. I work all the problems and study the material intensely. I do not communicate it at a level that impacts mass learning. It is necessary to do so, because everyone in school has to take national examinations in mathematics, and so we all have a shared vision of doing our best. The second year there I become more effective as a teacher as I learn to master the European system of education. I worked with and learned from others who have been involved in this system in Nigeria, India, England, Ghana, South Africa, and Indonesia. We work laboriously with a common focus. In the end all of the students at the school pass the Cambridge University/ West African School Certificate examination in mathematics. It is a great adventure that holds and sustains our collective human effort and brings individual and school engagement. It is a great journey for us all.

Another interesting experience I have in the first year in San Francisco is an assembly during black History month. I am the school black Student Union sponsor and the president, Marvin Hall, is a militant, articulate, outspoken, and focused student. The two of us are the only ones who meet regularly, but no one is as serious as we are about the black struggle. No one can defy or disregard us in the mission we are on for the voice of the black and the poor. We go to the school administration about having a program for the entire school of two thousand students. We share our general plan and there are questions but total cooperation is given. It is hard because Marvin and I, along with the stage director and his crew who do the sound, the lights, and the curtains, have to prepare the program for the two thousand people who would fill the auditorium. It seems an arduous job to get serious thinking and participation. We fill the stage with large hanging photographs of African Americans. There are black students from the school who perform. I am so impressed with the talent of the girls who sing and the student who plays a piano solo. Music and sound pour and flow from within them. There is a black minister, Cecil Williams, who powerfully articulates the black experience. Many are moved.

Afterwards, however, several teachers come to me to tell of their concern about his street manner and the unconventional way he expresses himself. He has said that he worked all of his life to be different and he showed no need to be accepted by conventional society. Those who disagree with him do not discourage him. He says that he is at his best when things are against him.

Don't they know because he is a rebel that he does not do what others do?

Marvin Hall talks about us as blacks deepening our lives, and letting our power as black people become our self-definition. He says there should be rebellion by blacks against fitting into how others define for us what it is to be American. As a people we cannot live by what has been made up and invented by society and others.

I say that as blacks our past destruction cannot prevent our being here. We must change society and ourselves, and not be destroyed, or destroy others or ourselves. We must live in a world where no one is excluded or seen as insignificant. No privileged class should dominate us.

As black people who struggle to overcome conditions of poverty and race in San Francisco we know that our isolation as a people continues to destroy and marginalize entire communities of black children and families.

In these days it is a time of perpetual war among cultural and ethnic groups, which leads to systems of dysfunction. My situation as a new teacher having lived and worked in Africa is to express what I discover to be conditions fundamental to human existence. Such conditions come from a demand to change the greed, corruption, and prejudice of society by our individual action and responsibility. It is why the two of us, Marvin and I, have come together to organize ourselves. It must start with us as individuals and connecting with things bigger than we are. It is not just about individuals aware of who they are and what they can do but realizing a greater impact by connecting to a planet that must understand a greater adventure.

What is most significant to me that first year is working with Marvin Hall, the Black Student Union president. He is knowledgeable about human thought, self-organization, and power. He is able to learn on his own, at a serious level, and not depend on the school or a system for the truth. Marvin is as much a rebel as any student I ever know. He courageously stands up to those who rule by power and force, and he understands the meaninglessness and illusion of a group thinking it has power over others without diminishing themselves. He is the only revolutionary in the school. He leaves the school and I never see him again.

# 14

# DOWNTRODDEN

Schools of today, just like other organizations such as families, corporations, cities, or nations, suffer from the human impacts of a driving world of technology, information, urban devastation, global competition, and social transformation. Few schools of the past encountered such profound changes in which today urban schools struggle to survive. They cannot hold on to the illusion of past knowledge which is dissolving into pieces and being cut away from them.

The superintendent of schools, Waldemar Rojas, is from New York. He says to reverse the failing schools in San Francisco requires eliminating the existence of downtrodden classes of people. Schools that serve the poor and the disadvantaged are often ineffective. They are unable to impact the lives and minds of students so that they understand things deeply and perform them proficiently.

The question that should drive us all is what happens if everyone is educated to excellence not just children of the elite and those who live in affluent places. When students are not learning, schools are meaningless places. It is why schools themselves and others connected to them must continually review whether they are places that are productive, useful and significant in the lives of children.

In actuality, schools teach us nothing, but it is good being around other serious and motivated people in a learning community. As we teach ourselves there are ideas and people that help us learn by allowing us to see things as they are, and to see things that are true and profound for us.

To be a serious person in life we must become one with the world, immerse ourselves in our work, explore our beliefs and go beyond them, and we must detach ourselves from the familiar. The goal is human freedom from the prison of thoughts, such as race and class that makes us feel separated from the whole and no longer oneness with nature and all others.

Social inflexibility and disorganization bring limitation, and sustains failure for many children in schools in poor urban areas. Though blacks have changed the conditions of segregation and education in this country, in San Francisco few ever master the American system of schooling, or urban life. Some do.

A process often does not exist for teachers, parents, students, and the community to monitor and assess their own activities. To have corrective action and to effectively engage learning in rigorous ways, students must seriously understand the world, and that life is demanding. No one can save black people in San Francisco, but self-knowledge and self discipline can help us understand ourselves and our condition.

Poverty is a factor affecting all segments of the African American community. Both poverty and the conditions in which students live are considered obstacles to student achievement. San Francisco Unified School District data demonstrates that poverty is a powerful variable, but is not an insurmountable barrier to academic success. This is demonstrated in almost two decades of desegregation efforts where many students from low-income neighborhoods perform at or above the national average.

The population of black students in San Francisco schools is declining.

How do the students and the schools who serve them survive? Some of them set serious visions and goals and find ways to reach them.

There are more than ten city districts and neighborhoods where more than one hundred schools are located. There is ever changing movement in all corners of the city, and in some areas there is a broadening of experiences and an understanding of emerging worlds and new societies. Some places, though, change less as the people growing up in them, stay and maintain their neighborhood and world isolation.

Superintendent Rojas says that the urban crisis is a solvable problem. In some minds it can be dealt with, and is not a hopeless situation. He says it is a time when the nation is looking for ways to overhaul urban public education, and to increase expectations and performance of all students, particularly the lowest achieving groups of students.

Lives from poverty and failure rarely make it from one world to the next or any other world. Lives that are imprisoned by personal disaster seldom make the leap. It is a monolithic existence.

How do children counteract the special circumstances of growing up in America in its devastated urban areas? The inner-city slum is as unforgiving as any urban creation. The Bayview Hunters Point area of San Francisco remains one of the poorest and most isolated communities of the city. There are more than five thousand San Francisco students in public housing and a third of them live in the Bayview Hunters Point area. It has more than twice as many students residing in public housing as any other area of the city. The public housing impact is significant in their lives. The number of adults living there who dropped out of school is four times the city-wide rate with a functional illiteracy rate estimated at 50%. The welfare dependency rate is 89% and the unemployment rate is 19 times the city average.

Of the more than six thousand school children living in the Bayview Hunters Point area more than half are black; others include Latino, White, Chinese, Samoan, Filipinos, Indochinese, and other nonwhites. The demographics of the area, and the San Francisco school community, demonstrate noticeable change and transformation. The number of Chinese, Southeast Asians, and Latino children is growing at a greater rate than the black population.

During his first year, I accompany Superintendent Rojas to a meeting with residents of public housing, and discuss collaboration with them and the school district. They all spoke of how bad the schools and teachers were, and that they had been disrespected and diminished as people in their public school experiences. Their unconditional request was for jobs for the youth. All other issues were not as significant. There was a commitment to get jobs for the youth. There was an immediate response to this need. The jobs program expanded every year that the superintendent worked in the San Francisco schools. It had an impact on the community as those involved learned, and participated in a conventional way of life. This is a breakthrough experience for some.

Another important outcome occurred with the Superintendent's meeting with the residents in a community meeting with Sunnydale and Geneva Tower residents. This meeting was well attended. Many questions were asked, and answered, and opinions were discussed. The most significant thing about this event was that many public housing residents had an opportunity to meet the superintendent, and see him in their neighborhood. They appreciated the respect he gave to the community. They were grateful and looked forward to working with him. The superintendent had grown up in a poor neighborhood in the South Bronx, and was able to clearly communicate and to understand the world of those who are poor and the least successful. As a result of the community meeting collaborative activities were started and continued. Next to the youth job program in its impact, was the establishment of technology and computer centers in poor neighborhoods.

A question that was asked by a member of the community is this: Should the students from public housing and poor neighborhoods be treated any different from other students?

It is an interesting question, to me, that can easily be dealt with from a view as to how things should be, but not how things actually are. In theory everyone should have the highest quality and most challenging education that is available. It is important that there is one high standard for all, including minority and poor students, because they live with double standards throughout their lives. It is not what is supposed to be, but we do not respect the lives of all others. There is nothing that we love with our total being. This is why we have a society that has produced circumstances of immensely rich people who have everything and others who have nothing. How do we change this society? It is when I, as an individual, revolt and breakaway from society's corruption and greed.

There are schools of poverty that completely change their way of education and create exciting places of learning. There is a sense of urgency and transformation in their action.

There are also the communities and schools which struggle. In a section of the Bayview Hunters Point area called Double Rock there are about three hundred students who live in public housing. More than half are black and the other groups are mainly Southeast Asian, Samoan, and Latino. Of the three hundred students living there only five are in the 12th grade. They drop out and do not make it through the system. Why is their education journey as it? There are various reasons why such situations exist. Some reasons are told by community members in a Delinquency Prevention Commission report.

The teachers do not communicate with students how to do the work and the kids get bored and want to cut their class.

There are problems being in the system. The students often feel they are caught up in a bureaucracy and have the sense of being screwed up before they get started.

Some parents don't realize their students are not in school. The students seem unconnected to the system.

Some parents don't get involved even though the absences appear on their child's report card. There are some parents and students who are not interested. Find ways to engage them.

The downtrodden are the oppressed, the overwhelmed, the exploited, the underprivileged, and the powerless.

Unexpected Encounter

What are some of the situations of students and the world of school that I live, observe, and learn about? One day I meet a former student, Tommy, in a poor neighborhood of San Francisco. It is such a great occasion to see him again. He was a student during my first teaching job in San Francisco. It was a school about fifty miles south in La Honda, California for San Francisco delinquent youth. Tommy is a popular student who gets along with others but does not care much about school. Place value and the binary system are mathematical worlds that are momentarily engaging to him, as they are to most of the students who venture an interest into their existence. When Tommy leaves the ranch he finds himself in and out of schools as do many of his classmates. It is unusual that any of them are ever serious students. They are more aligned with lives on the edge of society. Schools have no real effect on them and most continue a life in and out of the criminal justice system. This is the life that he too has lived. Though he never pursued school life he is still the energetic person who had passed through the school system without bitterness, or even looking back. Tommy recognizes me immediately on the street and I am able to remember him and his name. After working with many students for many years it varies as to how ready one is in the moment of encounter. We both are as familiar as the first day we met. His enthusiasm and personal nature still shine. I thought that I had seen him on the corner of Market and Van Ness several years ago. Tommy said that it could not have happened because he was serving time in the penitentiary. He had just finished serving four and a half years of a nine-year sentence. He was so happy to be out again. He said that he was not certain how his parole worked out, but a former counselor at the ranch school was interviewed for the jury. And though he was not selected for the jury he thinks that the counselor had something to do with his early release. He is uncertain, but grateful for the break he received. He told me he had been in San Quentin, Soledad, and other prisons over the years. He had been out and free for two years and that things are going well. I asked him what had changed his life. He says that at one time he thought that everything in the world belonged to him. He would just take things and it took much of his life to learn to respect other people's property. He learned that he had to change his behavior. I am reminded of when we lived in East Africa and the Masai lived in the Great Rift Valley. They believed that all cattle belonged to them and they would take them from ranches, farms, and other tribes as they see no harm in taking back what they thought belonged to them in the first place.

Tommy had asked me to give him a ride. As we ride along he wants me to let him out for a moment. While I wait, a guy approaches the car and asks me to let down the window. Tommy tells me to keep the door locked. I try to raise the window as the guy threatens to damage the car if I do not open the window, and listen to what he has to say. I refuse to talk to him. The next thing I know is that Tommy rushes back into the car. He gets into the backseat but another guy is forcing his way in also. I try to drive away, but the second guy is able to get into the car. He is attempting to rob or harm Tommy, it seems. He had hit him several times, but Tommy refused to give him anything. Tommy tells me to keep driving. We need to get out of the area. The assailant puts his hand inside his coat and tells me he has a gun and that he will shoot me if I do not stop the car.

I think to myself that it is too dangerous a place for me to stop. I keep driving. I do not know if he will shoot me or not. I do not feel any gun next to my head, but I know I am immersed in a circumstance that I have never imagined. Is this a life and death situation I wonder? Will this guy actually kill me? We don't know each other at all. If he does kill me it will devastate my wife.

He tells me to reverse the car while he continues to struggle with Tommy. As he does, I drive ahead slowly. He is desperate with his threat to drive him back. I stop at a service station and get out. He gets out with Tommy and goes back to where we had all encountered each other. I think of his having a gun and using it. It shows that life is sometimes valueless and does not matter. I know that my life is no more important than his or anyone else's. It seems so easy to be killed at times. Had I escaped death?

The Urban Poor

Those who live in the poorest and most violent neighborhoods in California are sometimes talked about and written about in newspapers. Though I observe both the sameness and the drama of street life, I also visit San Francisco libraries, and I sometimes read about the hard lives of others.

One student lives where drugs are common while stores, banks, and produce markets are nonexistent. It is the hard life of a youth, his struggle and conflicts. Unfortunately he lives in this violent urban world. After visiting with friends he goes outside on the street. A gunman jumps from a car and fires at close range more than a dozen shots into his body. He dies within the hour at the hospital. He is another homicide in the escalating murder rate that is as high as it has been in twenty-five years in the city. The youth had not dealt in drugs, but his life was severe and hard. Those who knew him say that he never had a fighting chance from his earliest days. He loved his parents who refused to raise him. His father, a heroin addict, died when the youth was fourteen years old. The father had children with four other women. His mother is addicted to crack cocaine. Loving and well-meaning relatives, whose lives were already overloaded with their own survival in the world, reared the youth. His childhood was one without the parents whom he loved. Soon after he was born he was sent to live with a cousin who had her own miseries and demons. She drank Irish beer, which she warmed up with a floor heater.

The youth had a younger brother who was born with drugs in his system. The Social Service System in investigating the matter of living arrangements discovered that the youth did not live with his parents, and ordered him legally removed from their care because of neglect. He was sent from his cousin to live with his seventy-five year old aunt. She gave him attention and the material things she could. In school he struggled to learn, beginning in the first grade. He repeated the first and third grades. A tutor was recommended, but he never saw one. His father was living in a homeless shelter and he seldom saw his mother. In the fourth grade he was assigned to special education. His aunt was eighty-five years old and weary. He was confused in middle school from being immersed in a world with different teachers and rooms and in finding his way around. He never mastered school routines and he never became engaged in the life of the school. It never happened.

In the eighth grade he was recorded absent 145 times, twenty of them were excused. He was examined and found moderately retarded. A teacher requested that the school district send him to a school for troubled youth, which had smaller class sizes. He was denied the placement because it was stated that his problem was truancy and not a learning disability. Even though he continued as a non-attending or no-show student in the eighth grade he was assigned to a high school that scored amongst the lowest in California in academic achievement. At sixteen he was eligible for a program that taught living skills. He was accepted and started showing up every day and learned how to get a job and how to use a computer. An advocate for the youth asked for a waiver for him to continue in school past eighteen years old in order to earn the missing credits he lacked. The effort to assist and support the youth turned out to be in vain. His fragile family situation was further diminished when his cousin died of cirrhosis of the liver and several months later his aunt died. After his cousin died, he is in a state of noticeable deterioration. He never finishes the ninth grade. His aunt's sister becomes his foster parent even though she is only ten years older than he is. He stops going to school.

His foster parent encourages him to get a job. She wants him to make something of his life as he was not a felon, and is not into drugs. He holds one job for a week. He then attempts to get a job at a hospital but is frustrated by the bureaucracy. An error on his birth certificate has his age wrong, which prevents him from getting a California identification card for tax purposes. He needs his mother's signature to correct the mistake, but she never signs it. He said that his mother asks for twenty dollars to sign it and he did not have it, so she doesn't sign it. He then spends his days running errands on his bicycle and hanging out on street corners, and getting into trouble. Several days before he is shot, he is attacked, beaten, and taken to the hospital with a head injury. He never reports the attack to the police. On the night of the murder the police find his body lying on the ground outside his childhood home. Forty or fifty people stand around as his body is shattered with holes. The paramedics come. They wonder about the life of the victim and his bullet filled body that still shows signs of electrical activity. To them the questions are fleeting and the answers do not matter to them, because they are just there to save his life.

On the way to the hospital the paramedics try to save him by pumping air into his lungs, compressing his chest, administering intravenous fluids, and plugging the holes in his body. Before the ambulance can reach the hospital he is dead, or close to it. A team of twelve doctors, nurses, and technicians take over cardiovascular pulmonary resuscitation, and search in vain for signs of life. Within five minutes an ultra-sound confirms the heart has stopped.

A doctor calls his foster parent to report the news of the death. She does not seem surprised. Seven days after the death is the funeral. Relatives say they are tired of coming to the funeral home. It is where they came for the service of the youth's father, cousin, aunt, and older sister who died from a drug overdose.

Now men who were once from the community are coming back, walking the streets, and bringing hope, because they say stopping the killing is too important a job to be left to the police and other outsiders. One person says he does not know if he can bring the resources and presence that is needed, but the fact of the matter is that they are doing something. They are not just sitting back saying how bad it is. They come to change hearts and minds, to promote economic self-sufficiency and education. Some who come are veterans of past anti-violence campaigns, and feel that daytime meetings and rallies in churches and parks only preach to the converted. They want to go where the killings are occurring, and talk directly to possible killers and victims. They come without connection to the police or newspapers so they have no association to outside authority and no motive to enhance their own image.

These men came up through these same hard streets as the killers and victims. They show it is possible to move through this life in a positive direction. Our societal mission is to have the best possible education for each child. All children can acquire a love of learning and become engaged in its adventure.

There is a lack of concern for persons living at the bottom of society, and their state of uncertainty. It is amongst such persons that a deep human spirit dwells. As long as there is a downtrodden group of people there is no human freedom on the planet.

Black students in their battle and struggle as an underclass learn to stand against bureaucracies such as schools, the police, and the court. For some youth, life in San Francisco is imprisoning.

I recently read an article that states the dropout rate for black students nationally is greater than 50%. It states that more than 70% of the dropouts are either unemployed, incarcerated, or not looking for work. San Francisco records show that of the number of black students who entered the ninth grade four years ago only 38% of them are still enrolled four years later. There are various dimensions to this situation. In San Francisco many such students live with high levels of crime and violence, substandard housing, inconsistent school rules and expectations, drug abuse, dysfunctional families, inadequate health care, failing schools, and persistent poverty. These factors can lead ones thoughts to situations of hopelessness and helplessness. Such thoughts are impediments to one's education. In actuality no one can stop us from learning, regardless of the thoughts that exist in the world.

Though many black students in San Francisco are more concentrated in high poverty schools, in many ways they are like all other students in the city. Some are poor and are unchallenged by school, and some are energetic and capable. Recently there is a story about students from an elementary school in Hunters

Point. While attending high school, these students were all killed. One youth was shot in the chest. His elementary school teacher describes him as outrageously brilliant and articulate. He would sometimes come to school to visit her on his motorcycle. Other teachers at the school describe him as handsome, incredibly smart, and with a sense of righteousness and dignity beyond his years. Some residents say that they want to move out of Hunters Point to where calm people live. Those who live here, like us all, cannot be saved from the way the world is. How do we change the world and ourselves?

Hurricane Katrina

Hurricane Katrina comes to the Gulf Coast in 2005. When it hits New Orleans it shows the poverty and how racially divided the city is. Most of the white people leave town before the storm arrives. The poor, mostly black, are left behind. They seem to have existed in the poorest possible conditions. At first, no boats or buses are sent to rescue or evacuate them. Telling them to go to the Superdome further destroys them as people. Some are left on their own to die. We can never assume that others will save us.

I read about an elderly white gentleman from New Orleans, whose family had lived there before the Civil War. He wanted to remain in the city until the water began to surge around his French Quarter house. He decides to join a convoy of other affluent residents from other areas. He carries his dog and a gun with him. In driving out of the city the travelers display their weapons through the window. Many of the black residents are poor, and very few have cars.

One sees pictures of dead people floating through the city face down among the sewage, and other pictures of those sitting in wheelchairs where they died. I think about America and the democracy that it proclaims to be, but this is an illusion. In a democracy every citizen is to be a participant in the society. Why are there still second-class citizens who have not been a part of the country for hundreds of years? The situation is further complicated despite the courage and determination of the rescuers who do come. They are dedicated to saving life and helping others. A friend I know who flies in tells me about how their helicopter is shot at from the ground in their rescue effort.

Many struggle against odds and the unknown in their effort to survive. I learn about a family of twenty. To save the family, three of them jump from a three-story window into eight-foot deep water of the flooded city. Though none of them are strong swimmers they are able to make it several blocks to reach an abandoned boat. They spend nine hours ferrying family members to higher ground, and help others when they can. They are from a public housing project where residents had screamed for the attention of passing helicopters. Some set off firecrackers. No one came. The water is rising so they make a move. They say that there are too many members of the extended family that have to be gotten out. The odds seem against them as the family includes a newborn baby, a great-grandmother, and a pregnant twenty-two year old. When they fight their way out of the flooded housing project, they wait around for days on dry land. They say they take a harrowing bus ride to Houston. One of them is threatened by gunpoint by a rival public housing gang.

They all reach Houston after sixteen hours of travel. They are told that they may not be able to stay, but then a woman steps forward and invites all twenty of them to stay at her house. In the most trying situations the presence of the human spirit is profound. The woman is asked why she is taking in total strangers. She tells them that it is the human thing to do. The woman says that being human matters to her. She says they can stay as long as they want.

It is said that the children of the homeless, the incarcerated, the abused, the addicted, and other poor must meet the same standard as any other child. They have to reach the high levels as others if they are to be meaningful contributors to society. Some of them do, and show the greatness of the human spirit.

I come across another study when I am visiting the public library in Hunters Point. I read every old newspaper there, and learn about life in that section of the city and the black San Francisco experience. I come across an article that had been reprinted from the San Francisco Examiner (2/17/66). I looked up the Examiner article that was about slum youth success. The title of the article: "Harvard Gamble Pays Off."

The boys who learned their first lesson in the slums when they probably never dreamed of college made their mark at Harvard.

Harvard's deans said today the college has won its gamble on more than 200 youths it has admitted since 1957 who never would have qualified if judged on their College Board test grades.

The 200, chosen partly for their courageous response to a poverty-stricken upbringing, are no ordinary scholarship holders.

Most were raised in city slums. Many attended unaccredited high schools. More than 50 percent are Negroes. A few are the sons of maids and migrant workers.

The results of one of the first college recruiting efforts of its kind were termed "amazing" by Dean of Admissions Fred L. Gimp.

Eighty-five percent of those selected have graduated, a number with honors and one with a Rhodes scholarship.

The students have kept pace academically with their more fortunate associates from the nation's best preparatory schools and its academically strong public high schools.

And they've done it, Dean Glimp says, "without over-compensating, without burning all the bridges of their past behind them."

They are individuals overcoming great odds to discount the ideas and thoughts of others who assumed they were incapable of profoundly moving through a society that looked down on them as second class.

One evening my wife and I attend a community meeting to honor a prominent teacher. Also present at this event is the superintendent of schools, Ramon Cortines. My wife and he talk about issues and problems at the school where she teaches. This is on a Friday night. On the following Monday the superintendent saw to it that all the major issues they discussed were dealt with. He later left San Francisco and became Chancellor of Schools in New York City. My wife and I would one day visit him in his Brooklyn office in New York. Later he becomes head of schools in Los Angeles. These were the two largest school districts in the country.

My wife and I also talk with the teacher who is being recognized. When the two of us talk to him after the presentation he is quiet and composed, though he has received national attention for his work. It is an interesting and worthwhile encounter that we pass through. The teacher is Jaime Escalante. He is at the time working in Sacramento. That is where he went after teaching in Los Angeles. A movie, *Stand and Deliver*, was made of his work at Garfield High School in Los Angeles. It was a poor urban school of predominantly Latino students. I once visited the place, and met the principal who worked to have a serious academic school. Jaime Escalante's students surprised the nation in 1982 when 18 of them passed the Advanced Placement calculus examination. The testing service found the scores suspect and asked 14 of the passing students to retake the test. Twelve agreed to do so and all 12 did well enough to have their scores reinstated. In the years that followed there was a phenomenal growth in his calculus program at the school. In 1983 both the enrollment of students and the number passing the Advanced Placement calculus examination more than doubled with 33 taking the exam and 30 passing it. In 1987, 73 passed the exam.

Initially he was discouraged by the students' poor preparation but some were willing to take more demanding math courses which heartened him. He did not try to teach calculus until his fifth year at the school. There had to be classes in geometry, advanced algebra, math analysis, trigonometry, and calculus available to students. These courses were open to all students who wanted to study them. He worked with feeder junior high schools, summer programs, college classes and tutoring classes for students to complete the course work for calculus.

When the Garfield principal was asked if the students could catch up with the students at affluent Beverly Hills High School, he responded, "No," but that they could get close. The children of well-educated and wealthy parents have advantages in school. Escalante attempted to reduce those advantages. He did not use academic tracking for special students. If students wanted to take his classes, they were allowed. Students who never would have had the chance to be selected for gifted or honors classes enrolled in the courses and succeeded. By 1987 Garfield was one of the top schools in the country in the number of students taking Advanced Placement calculus examinations. They surpassed Beverly Hills High School.

One wonders why we tolerate a society where it is alarming that poor Latino students can perform at the same level, and beyond, as wealthy white students and others. Some children are labeled as second-class students. We are fixed and close-minded on race, and class in our image of others and of ourselves. In 1991, Escalante moved to a high school in Sacramento as a math teacher. It is when he was teaching in Sacramento when we talked with him.

He, and the students with whom he worked, demonstrate that assumptions and prejudice through separate systems of education is artificial and meaningless. Jaime Escalante died in 2010.

# 15

## SEPARATE SOCIETIES

To be worthwhile places schools need to be where one learns about life for oneself and where the isolation of social class ends. We make schools of separate classes and accept them as routine. When San Francisco began as a city more than 150 years ago there are schools of single races. There are white schools, Chinese schools, and black schools. The schools that whites attend are for the privileged community. And then, as now, the whites were assumed to be the most able students and scholars. There is little reference to those white students who know less than the blacks or Chinese, or to those who are dropouts and uninterested in school. The schools for the Chinese and blacks are established for the poor and the downtrodden. From the very beginning there is a system of advantage and of discrimination. The practice of authority is still maintained where one group dominates others. Today some of the schools attended by the poor may be worse off than when the city first began. Nowadays poverty, race, housing segregation, joblessness, immigration, and other social realities complicate a San Francisco school's capability to have a meaningful education for everyone.

The schools I taught in never expressed a mission of serious learning for all students. Later when there is such a mission expressed there is never one with the ability to carry it out. The earliest San Francisco schools practiced separatism and racism. These elements and factors were not discussed, or exposed until such a school system was legally challenged in the courts. At a school district meeting in the 1950s when the question of massive segregation within San Francisco Schools was raised, the superintendent claimed to have no knowledge of it. He and the board failed to take any action to change the racial segregation of the school children. Of the numerous issues brought to the court, one held that a San Francisco dual system of education was maintained through attendance zones, hiring practices, and residential segregation. In another case the court found the school district used intelligence tests, which were racially and culturally biased, for the purpose of permanently placing black children in Special Education classes.

Other court findings showed that in the school district fifty-four elementary schools were racially identifiable and thirty-two were racially imbalanced. By state standards one hundred nine of the one hundred twenty two elementary schools were racially imbalanced. From 1964 to 1969, twenty-three of the elementary schools that were identifiably black become increasingly black. The district had knowledge of practices that prejudiced the educational achievement in predominantly black schools, but took no corrective action. The district did not follow a recommendation that the most qualified teachers be assigned to schools enrolling a large proportion of minority students.

In the 1983 settlement the plaintiffs were able to show that San Francisco had a history of racial discrimination. Eighty-six percent of elementary schools still were racially identifiable. The school district and the state of California were accused of using practices that perpetuate a dual school system. The case was the third in a series of actions. The first case was dismissed, and the second case resulted in finding segregation of black elementary school students, but is reversed by a higher court. In the pre-trial of the 1983 lawsuit, the plaintiffs assembled three thousand exhibits for trial. It traced the history of discrimination and segregation in San Francisco from the Colored and Chinese schools in the 1850's to the segregation of housing during the 1940's and 1950's. In trying to reach a court settlement there was no serious impediment except for certain schools in the Bayview Hunters Point area. A settlement team was formed and the parties drafted a proposed consent decree that the court found fair, reasonable and adequate. The decree identifies nineteen historically segregated schools for special desegregation treatment.

When I start teaching in San Francisco in 1970 the black population is at its greatest. The Bayview Hunters Point area has the largest black concentration. It is filled with life brought by the thousands of people from the south who started to come in the 1940s to work in the booming wartime shipyards.

The San Francisco Bay Area shipyards were concentrated in the urban areas and sprawled across hundreds of miles from San Francisco to Napa in the north, Sacramento and Stockton in the east, and San Jose in the south. In the decade before 1940 America's shipyards had produced 23 ships. In the five years after 1940 there were 4,600 ships produced. The San Francisco Bay Area shipbuilders built 1,400 ships during the 1,365 days of World War II. It averaged more than a ship a day.

One day I go to the San Francisco Public Library to learn more about the numbers of the San Francisco black population.

The San Francisco Public Library is often fascinating to me. My experiences with libraries since a young age are as places where learning is open to all. They are places of self-direction, questions, and quietness for the ordinary and the privileged to engage in exploration and human contribution to the world. One day I get to the library early before it opens. There are forty or fifty persons outside its doors, and many of them are seemingly eager to enter. As the door is about to open everyone crowds around the entrance. Someone asks why is everybody so damn excited about getting into the library? Learning, information, and books came as responses. There are people from various backgrounds it seems, but many are poor. They are persons with no computers of their own, but the library has hundreds. They themselves have little access to books and information. The library has a spectacular display of the collective genius of humankind. They have no place to clean up and to wash their face. The library has free public bathrooms that exclude no one. I read an article that says the black population in San Francisco increased by ten-fold from the 1940's to 1950's. I wonder how accurate the article is. I sit at a desk on the fifth floor and gather several documents with the assistance of the librarian. I am interested in the San Francisco population and I calculate these population numbers from census data.

| Year | Total San Francisco (SF) Population | Total black | Total Hunters Point black | Hunters Point Total |
|------|-------------------------------------|-------------|----------------------------|---------------------|
| 1940 | 634,536 | 4,846 | 7 | 14,405 |
| 1950 | 775,357 | 21,616 | 11,080 | 51,405 |
| 1960 | 740,316 | 74,383 | 17,541 | 37,486 |
| 1970 | 715,674 | 96,078 | 20,586 | 30,064 |
| 1980 | 678,974 | 86,414 | 15,769 | 21,638 |
| 1990 | 723,759 | 79,039 | 17,432 | 27,899 |
| 2000 | 776,733 | 60,515 | 16,144 | 33,484 |

The ten-fold increase for the black population from the forties to the fifties is not the reality I find in the census data that I collect. There is no expert person or organization that has information, or knowledge that is certain or lasting. Those who are said to be experts with certain and accurate data cannot be relied on. We have to question all claims of authority. Though I was not there in the forties or fifties at this time I do accept the census to be reflective or a possible approximation of the city and the Hunters Point area. It is amazing to me to see the blacks living in Hunters Point increase from 7 to 11,080 in the decade. Another interesting phenomenon is that in Hunters Point in 1990 there are 6,085 Asians and in 2000 there are 9,227 Asians. It shows the changing demographics of the area.

Bayview Hunters Point is the poorest community in San Francisco, and has the least educated children. It continues to have the highest rate of homicides in the city. The schools have been the least served for many years. One black person spoke of the schools in the 1940s and 1950s as having teachers who did not care about teaching them anything. They had the impression that blacks were not going to become anything or do anything in their lives. There are four elementary schools in Bayview Hunters Point when the Consent Decree begins in 1983. There is one of these schools I have interest in since I came to San Francisco in 1970. My wife is a teacher there. It was originally named Sir Francis Drake.

Some of the community members say they learned that Drake had participated in the slave trade, and the community renamed the school Malcolm X. Though it has the poorest students in the city, some of the teachers I know there provoke and stimulate learning. They relentlessly work to contribute to the students and the school. One teacher had worked in Ivory Coast, West Africa and taught physics and science to the fifth graders. He introduces West African art projects for the students to explore, and learn about another world. There is an East Indian teacher who had taught in Kenya, and brought energy and resolve for a serious education.

One weekend several of the teachers were working at the school. As they were leaving they were robbed at gun point. The assailants wear ski masks, and put the guns to their heads. After the teachers are robbed, one of the assailants shoots his gun into the air to show that it is loaded. It seems a way to demonstrate that they are authentic robbers and criminals.

Why is this violence so deeply present in the community? Humans once had a natural resistance to killing other humans, just as other species have. In recent years we have increased this capacity to kill through wars, gangs and the military. Soldiers have been trained and traumatized for a violent world. This process has now reached the children through television, film, games, computers, technology and other such entertainment, as well as through war. It produces a new breed of criminal who has been conditioned to kill from an early age. Children are influenced through the media and television and other ways before they have learned to read. The more they are disconnected from the actual world and other people, the more violent they are capable of being.

One day my wife is covering the class for another teacher and asks for help to deal with several boys in the class. A minister from the community is in the school, and tells my wife that he would be glad to handle the situation, and show her how to deal with the students. He walks into the classroom, and immediately the students call him a fat black bastard and ask who does he think he is. The man is shocked and leaves the room in disbelief. He lets my wife carry on with the class. He thought he understood those in the community. His questionable knowledge and expertise are meaningless and irrelevant. The students need ways to test their toughness and recklessness. They lack people in their lives to pay attention to them and their ideas. They need to prove they are hard and are not afraid. They need to prove this to themselves and to others.

The Decree set forth a special plan for schools in the Bayview Hunters Point area. Though the school district and the state argued against the existence of two systems of education, in San Francisco there had been an Educational Redesign Plan enacted by the superintendent of schools. This was done prior to the Decree being settled and approved by the court. This plan is significant because it goes beyond black and white students. It has the goal that every school's enrollment would have no ethnic or racial group constitute a majority of the students. In many ways race became a non-issue.

The district defined nine major racial and ethnic groups at the time. These were American Indian, black, Chinese, Filipino, Japanese, Korean, Latino, Other Non White, Other White (Caucasian). No regular school could have over 45% of any ethnic group and no alternative schools could have more 40% of any ethnic group. There had been controversy over these numbers as being considered too large by some members of the board of education, but they were approved. Over a short time they became acceptable and part of the district's thinking and practice. They were not challenged until 1994. One day Superintendent Alioto interviewed me in his office to become principal of a school in the Bayview Hunters Point area. I was a math teacher and had not considered being head of a high school. I was assigned to the school, and in a year I became the principal. I worked with Superintendent Alioto on several projects and was able to observe his firm human nature.

Though several plans had failed in San Francisco, in 1983 a settlement was reached through the court for the desegregation of its schools. The plaintiffs who were the San Francisco Branch of the National Association for the Advancement of Colored People (NAACP) filed the case. They represented individual black parents who were proceeding on behalf of their own children. They charged the defendants, both the school district and the state of California, with maintaining a segregated school system.

I understand that the 1978 lawsuit that led to the 1983 settlement was greatly influenced and largely determined by the school district. The 1983 settlement, known as the Consent Decree, was driven by the school district and was reluctantly accepted by the NAACP attorneys. The judge had advised the NAACP lawyers not to go to trial as he does not see how they can win as they would not be able to prove that the school district intentionally promoted or sustained segregated schools.

All parties agreed on a solution to transform schools would be reconstitution. The reconstitution process resulted in vacating the entire school staff and hiring new persons who are committed to holding high standards for low performing students as for all other students. It began with four of the lowest performing schools in the district and two newly created schools.

Three elementary schools were in the Bayview Hunters Point and one middle school in the Mission District, which was primarily Latino, are reconstituted. The schools and the students were the poorest, and lived in the most powerless communities in the district. Reconstitution is not used as a punitive measure but a possible first step in the academic accomplishment of a school. It is a time that the education of the nation's youth is described as mediocre and spiraling down.

The nation is a war zone with desegregation cases. The San Francisco strategy is different. To me the superintendent, Robert Alioto, makes it clear that this time desegregating the schools would work. Two lawsuits, a prior court order, and all other plans to desegregate schools over the prior decades had proved unequal to overcoming San Francisco's long history of racially segregated schools, housing, and neighborhoods. None of the earlier plans had been able to desegregate the schools in Bayview Hunters Point.

The superintendent is a tireless strategist who is aware of those around him who support him, who fight him, or who never even notice him. He exists at a level in which none of this matters and he is able to deal with it as he understands it. He does something no one else ever is able to do. He shows his capability of making a clear stand as he takes seriously the education of the poor and the powerless as well as that of all other students.

His unusual leadership is shown as he acts to reverse more than a century of racial discrimination in San Francisco, just as elsewhere in America. The school district and others work for a breakthrough in a city that has been racist throughout its history. The superintendent assigns the ablest persons and shows he realizes that the school system is capable of changing itself in how it educates minority students. The superintendent gets the consent decree started with attention to its creative process where he is able to make a commitment to its language, quality of participation, and its spirit of delivery as well as understanding the court directives. Leadership does matter as educational inequalities in poor communities seldom ever correct themselves because they have the fewest resources, organizational skills, and societal power.

Gary Orfield is the primary individual appointed as the court's expert. He was first a professor at the University of Chicago and later at Harvard. He seems at the forefront of desegregation scholars. He has worked with poor families in Chicago and knew that racial segregation concentrated poverty. I did not meet and work with him until the Consent Decree had been in effect for almost ten years.

I read several books which he wrote. I am deeply moved by his accounts of poor black people who reside in the Atlanta public housing projects, and the human condition which they struggle and survive. I also read about his account of how courts are dismantling desegregation cases that have been established by the case of Brown v. Board of Education. I have since worked with him on a number of projects with the San Francisco schools.

We visit district community technology and computer centers in the Tenderloin. Here Cambodian and Laotian students, and other community members work in celebration of learning and achievement with the least resources available to further their own performance. We also visit centers in Hunters Point and in the Geneva Towers housing projects—since demolished—to observe serious learning in places surrounded by poverty, violence and destruction.

We meet a Laotian student from Galileo High School, Sokly Ny, also called Don Bonus. His family had escaped the Khmer Rouge in Cambodia, and he had made a video diary of their resettlement in America, which was produced and directed by Spencer Nakasako, a Japanese American. Caring little about school it shows his struggles to graduate, the family tragedy, and harassment in living in the Sunnydale housing project, and other places, and a younger brother in youth prison. It is a story of triumph and survival. Gary Orfield states that it is a perfect antidote to simplistic "model minority" stereotypes about Asian students.

After the first phase of six schools (called Phase 1 schools) the sixteen schools in phases 2 through 4 operated in a much more traditional direction. There was more decentralization which allowed schools more opportunities to use added resources to change. In the end they are troubled schools with poor and minority students and no clear vision or goals. The first sign of a serious problem with the Consent Decree came in 1987 when the NAACP filed a contempt of court motion, because of a sudden reassignment of students from Consent Decree schools without approval of the court. Gary Orfield represented the court in working to resolve the conflict with the parties of the NAACP, the school district, and the state of California. Other conflicts that occurred were also resolved and an agreement was reached to maintain ongoing communication and oversight.

In 1990 the court ordered a full review of the Consent Decree by a committee of experts from all of the parties. The report was completed in 1992 and concluded that Phase 1 schools had produced significant gains but that the other sixteen schools had produced no such significant gains as a result of the large expenditures allowed. The report also found that Latino students suffered very similar issues of educational and social inequity without effective programs.

The federal court takes the case seriously. In the several times I am able to be in a meeting with Judge Orrick, I understand his deep interest in the case. I realize the struggles of sustaining the consent decree for poor students in their powerless communities. The judge does go to a Consent Decree school, and it is a significant visit for those who meet him. He works very closely with Gary Orfield, and the Consent Decree advisory committee. The group meets with him at different times to discuss its perspective toward achieving the goals of the consent decree. It is the court that allows students from poor and isolated communities to benefit even against sometimes overwhelming odds.

Here are some of the performances of Phase I schools which include two Bayview Hunters Point elementary schools (Carver and Malcolm X) and one Mission District middle school (Horace Mann).

One of the early measures of academic performance was demonstrated in the scores on the former California Assessment Program (CAP) which was administered to all California students at Grades 3,6,8,and 12. Scores from one year before and one year after Consent Decree implementation are shown in the following table for Carver, Malcolm X, and Horace Mann.

| California Assessment Program (CAP)—Phase 1 Percentile Rankings | | | |
|---|---|---|---|
| | 1982-83 | 1984-85 | Gain |
| **Carver—Grade 3** | | | |
| Reading | 31 | 92 | 61 |
| Written Expression | 26 | 96 | 70 |
| Mathematics | 37 | 99 | 62 |
| **Malcolm X—Grade 3** | | | |
| Reading | 4 | 83 | 79 |
| Written Expression | 20 | 68 | 48 |
| Mathematics | 25 | 86 | 61 |
| **Horace Mann—Grade 6** | | | |
| Reading | 2 | 74 | 72 |
| Written Expression | 3 | 44 | 41 |
| Mathematics | 1 | 49 | 48 |

Malcolm X and Carver were recognized by the State of California as California Distinguished Schools in 1987 and 1989 respectively.

In 1987 Horace Mann was recognized by the Department of Education as one of the outstanding secondary schools in the nation.

There was also tremendous success at the other three schools initially and over time.

In a court-appointed committee with Gary Orfield and other experts it was stated in 1992: "The Consent Decree has made possible one of the most extensive educational efforts that has been carried out in the last generation in an urban school district."

What are some of the factors that are in play at these schools? In many ways they are changed from abandoned factories to places that are ahead of their time. I do not feel that it is productive to attempt to replicate what went on in the six Phase 1 schools. What happened in them may never happen again. The superintendent, the judge, the parties, the plaintiffs, and the court expert are now gone. The students have all moved on. One of the ways they were ahead of their time is that their first elementary school classes were limited to twenty students ten years before the reductions of class size of kindergarten through third grade classes in other schools. The schools offered cutting edge technology by those who were capable and talented in using the computer as an empowering tool.

Reconstitution was used as a way of dealing with a legacy of failure in a school in which both those inside and those outside the school held the lowest and worst possible image of the school. Those within gave up battling for its reputation. Reconstitution in those schools did bring a sustained renewal. Principals at some of these Phase 1 schools served for terms lasting for eight years, thirteen years, sixteen years, and even twenty years. A vigorous campaign was used to recruit the best teachers available and who were interested in the challenge of these schools. The teachers all served for at least five years.

As a guide to rebuilding the school, a set of philosophical tenets was agreed to. The tenets were a way for a school to internalize its self-worth and to demonstrate a capability in a wider world.

The Consent Decree desegregated San Francisco schools and impacted the academic achievement of some schools. The district's racial admissions policy of no group exceeding 45% in a regular school or 40% in a alternative school meant that some Chinese students were excluded from attending certain high performing academic schools such as Lowell, Lawton, and Jefferson. In 1994 a group of Chinese American families sued the district. In 1999 the court ordered the district to stop using race and ethnicity in admissions decisions. The district had the burden of proving that vestiges still existed of the discriminatory practices that justified the Consent Decree in 1983, and that the race-based student assignment plan was still necessary to address the problems caused by the vestiges of the earlier segregation.

There were minimal expert reports that were able to link existing problems in the district to acts of discrimination by the government prior to 1983. In the end this meant that the dissolution of the Consent Decree was sought. It was terminated in 2005. The district adopted a race neutral "diversity index" which was intended to desegregate the schools based on socioeconomic factors, but the schools became more segregated and on December 31, 2005, when the Consent Decree ended, 50 schools were re-segregated. More than half of the re-segregated schools had 70% or more of one race/ethnicity, and 11 schools showed 80% or more of one race/ethnicity at one or more grade levels.

Another person I worked closely with for nine years is Stuart Biegel, the State Monitor for the Consent Decree. He issues an annual report as well as supplemental reports on his findings in visiting district schools and programs, as they comply with the Consent Decree. He, law students, and other educators working with his department made hundreds of visits over the years. Some schools wondered why they were visited as they are not Consent Decree schools and received no assistance from the desegregation plan. He made it clear that his team visited every school in San Francisco, because the entire school district is under a desegregation court order. He was a professor at the University of California at Los Angeles (UCLA) who traveled to San Francisco in his work to serve the court and the citizens of California. He became so dedicated to his job that he bought a house and stayed in both San Francisco and in Los Angeles. He was as diligent, focused, and organized as any individual who has come through the school system. This is reflected in the quality of his reports and communication with the parties of the Consent Decree, the federal court, and the schools. His job ends in 2005 with the Consent Decree.

Before the Consent Decree ended Judge William Orrick died. Judge William Alsup replaces him. He continued in the spirit of Judge Orrick. Judge Alsup had a profound presence in the courtroom as he is hard on all parties whose interests lie in sustaining inequality, and a second-class education for any student. These issues clearly matter deeply to him.

The court has been a final authority in cases involving poor and minority admissions to schools in California and elsewhere. In 1872 the California Supreme Court denied admissions to a black girl to a local public school in San Francisco because of her race. Separate but equal schools were upheld by the court. The separate education for the races mandated segregated schools. In 1924 the court specified segregated schools for Native Americans, Chinese, and Japanese students. Not until 1946 when Mexican Americans in California won a lawsuit in Orange County was segregation in the state eliminated. In 1954, Brown vs. Board of Education declared segregated schools were unconstitutional and formally overturned the "separate but equal doctrine."

The court did not specify how the schools would be desegregated and the power of enforcement was left to the states, many schools remain segregated. In California schools were not segregated by law (de jure segregation), but from housing patterns or de facto (in fact) segregation. De facto segregation comes from limited opportunities, economic or social disadvantage, or effects of historic discrimination. School districts across the state had to find new ways to remedy segregated schools. It is a matter that is still unresolved in the United States.

For me the impact of the federal court on life in San Francisco schools is significant. The federal judges play important roles for us to engage ourselves. The court understands that a system needs to be in place to respond to failure. The judges give authority to use Phase 1 school success to impact the district to the greatest extent possible. The district never reaches desegregating the school and impacting the academic achievement at the classroom level for all its students, but the court allowed San Francisco schools to educate the poorest and least educated students in the city in a way that had never been done. I find that the court in these years has an important mission of making the world less discriminatory and more democratic, and one that is less dehumanizing and more just. I do think that cases filed by black parents in 1983 and Chinese American parents in 1994 contribute to a deeper investigation into our human drama with public schools to engage the students of extreme poverty as well as the most highly motivated. Our schools, society and planet must be places that the lives of all children matter deeply.

# 16

## FACES

Many known persons come to San Francisco. I work in a school where a number of celebrated persons from society sometimes came to visit and talk with us at the school. There were educators, professional athletes, politicians, judges, scientists, and business executives. They held important elected offices, ran marathons, headed global companies, worked in countries in Africa devastated by famine, and sometimes reached high positions from impoverished lives. They had all achieved these places in life against various odds. Some were familiar and famous faces. Their lives had been accepted by society as noteworthy and commendable, but fame and fortune are things outside of oneself. They do not indicate an inner richness or peace within us. Though they seemed to live well known, and talked about lives in the outside world, often inside there is emptiness and disappointment. If one is inwardly rich then one is able to stand alone, and it is unimportant if one is known or unknown.

When I work with public housing residents I meet troubled and serious individuals. They live in various housing developments but all live in impoverished situations as I encounter the quiet and reflective, restless, confused, and the articulate.

One resident says that it took her until she was thirty years old to have the personal strength not to fear the dominant society. She says that it was because of the bad schools, incompetent teachers, and corrupt leaders. Like others who say that the schools dehumanized them, she never talks about her own lack of personal responsibility or lack of energy to learn. Her motivation to learn comes later in life.

The resident and I attend many school and community meetings together in which teachers, school administrators, college professors, parents, community advocates, and business people come. Invariably she is as profound and as serious as any person there. She is aware of those settling for meaningless knowledge to secure a respectable position in a superficial society that is deteriorating. The first time I visit her house I learn about the possibility of teaching calculus to young children. I later connect with others who have carried the idea further and I am able to seriously engage elementary school students in this world. It all originates in her overcrowded public housing unit.

In the meetings we attend together, she makes clear the necessity of examining the assumptions and status quo of society in which schools become meaningless places to poor children. She knows that when the poor and the oppressed are learning the reality of their own world, it becomes hard for outsiders to define and solve their problems in isolation of them. This is very interesting, because when we are seriously learning things the more clear we become of our own ignorance. She is a genuine friend who makes a deep contribution to the life we are living and shows that profound persons live in all communities in San Francisco. I find that she is a fresh and new voice at these meetings, and in our conversations, and does not fear or depend on the world and expertise of others to define and shape her life.

She deeply understands her world and courageously expresses it, but the community of public housing residents is limited and sometimes one of disorder and chaos. Their lives are in disarray and they live in confusion. After several generations some families still remain there. The constant reality is that the schools and lives in these developments have scarce resources and exist in isolation. They live in a community filled with crime, fear, drugs, and violence. It is a community that depends on a dominant society to save and support it, but this seldom happens because the larger and prevailing society is filled with hate, envy, fear, and greed.

The lives of public housing residents are filled with negative images of themselves and society. Their faces and lives are unreal and unknown to the outsiders who celebrate a life of success.

What is the meaning of education and why do we have schools? This question is not often asked because the existence of a school is accepted without question. Whether it has meaning or not to those involved in it does not matter because its reason for being is not examined. Rather it is assumed that schools are necessary. This is so for the dominant society to sustain its greed and power over the poor and others. We invent and project an ideal education for students that never happens. Some of the poor realize that schools do not serve or welcome them, and they resist the compulsion to attend and accept a closed and a judgmental system to educate them.

Schools are sustained by the thoughts of dominant groups and they resist change. Society is too determined to continue the status quo and does not accept change. It lives with illusion that things can stay the same. The truth is we live in a changing world and everything is impermanent. The price we all pay for the illusion of staying the same is a diminished life. Schools become meaningless places because of our limited view of the human condition.

Why are those living in poverty so down on the schools? What are the things that so deeply disturb them about their school experiences? Why have they not learned and why have they hated what schools had done to their lives?

Among those who come to San Francisco one year is a writer whom I meet. He wrote a book about poor people and their crisis filled lives. He describes them as faces at the bottom of the well. For me they are the same images and faces who struggle in poverty in San Francisco. They are those who are disturbed by the acts that exclude, separate, isolate, and segregate them, which are ways to dehumanize them. Those from public housing often view a reality filled with crises, poverty, exploitation, battlefields, limitation, and stress. Who hears them? Who values their existence? Each person must become a light unto oneself.

# 17

# BEYOND DESTRUCTIONS

Many educators pass through San Francisco. I work with some who are articulate and dedicated. Since I have been in the district, I have worked with all persons who have served as superintendent of schools. I work with some more directly than others. All have been capable, with varying backgrounds, and genuine reasons for serving.

Some persons I encounter express a serious vision to transform schooling in San Francisco and elsewhere. One individual is a San Francisco superintendent from New York. He is Puerto Rican. He comes here new to the job of superintendent. He fights hard for seven years in San Francisco until the day he leaves for a job in Dallas. He makes a swift impact as an educator in San Francisco. Not long after he comes, he is considered as one of three finalists for Chancellor of the New York City schools. He is not selected. It is interesting reading about him in the New York Times newspaper and then later discussing the matter with him. In New York they marveled at how much he has learned about leadership and schools. They see he has the courage and vitality to be a fearless leader. He talks about his first job of teaching emotionally disturbed students in Bellevue Psychiatric Hospital. He gets along with them because they know they are with somebody different and who is not afraid of them.

His job as superintendent is a struggle from the day he arrives in San Francisco. Many members of the black community do not want him as superintendent, but want a black candidate they believed to be the deserving person. One member of the black community promises to shadow him wherever he goes. It never bothers him, he says, because the person does not threaten to kill or shoot him or injure his family. It seems a mild threat to him, as he is from New York where conflict is normal and where one expects jobs to be hard. Even before he arrives in San Francisco there is controversy about his drinking while driving when he was working for the New York schools. I am impressed with his ability to communicate that the charges would be non-issues by the time he arrived as he would clear his the record of the incidents. He does. Just before he leaves San Francisco I share with him a story my wife told me about Gandhi in India. A mother goes to him because she wants him to help her son to stop eating sweets. Gandhi tells her that he will try to help her if she comes back in fifteen days. She does, and he is able to help the son stop eating sweets. The mother tells him that she is grateful for what he is able to do for her son. Gandhi tells her that first he himself goes without sweets for fifteen days so he can explore and understand the depth of the problem. He is then able to communicate what he learns to the child. As superintendent he had given his fifteen days of attention to numerous problems in the district such as the budget, student testing, bilingual education, and the academic achievement of poor students. It gives him a penetrating focus on actually running the district.

In San Francisco he leads and survives many battles as a superintendent of an urban America school district and is considered by some as one of the top superintendents in the country. He brings both energy and controversy to the district. The academic performance of poor students and all others is deepened. When he leaves the district various people view him differently at the time. A newspaper reporter describes him as one who exudes compassion and egoism. Many teachers say that they cannot stand him. They have never accepted his style. The president of the teacher's union says he is, "a dynamic force and extremely articulate and energetic. But he is difficult to work with. His management style is very top down and it clashes with the union, which is interested in building collaborative relationships." A member of the board of education calls him, "the best there is."

He is a strong leader who is not a conformist and does not accept mediocrity. A San Francisco newspaper quotes him as saying that the superintendent's job in Dallas interests him because it represents a new challenge because his job in San Francisco has become routine and monotonous.

Beyond all newspaper articles, thoughts, and past events is our human situation. Regardless of one's birth, path, or history, life is lived in the present moment. Whatever one may or may not have studied, learned, or been taught, in actuality we are here to live our own life, run our own race, and find our own way. As superintendent he came to San Francisco determined to express himself in his own way. He brought the expectation that there be no downtrodden class of students. He perseveres with this vision. Rojas is viewed as being more concerned about solving the problem as he sees it rather than seeking approval and avoiding blame.

After he leaves for Dallas newspaper headlines continue on as they always do. I observe those who write about the superintendent while he works in San Francisco, and notice that the journalists seldom understand how we all are engaged as a society in education and the learning of children and our own learning. In the end headlines that questioned San Francisco's test scores while he was here, published this headline after he leaves, "Test scores rise again in city's public schools." They questioned whether the six consecutive years of rising test scores had actually happened. When the students clearly showed significant gains for the seventh year, the press is silent on its case of questionable district academic performance and the work of the superintendent. He comes to San Francisco with a vision of eliminating a society of haves and have-nots. He had seen urban poor students increase their academic achievement for more than ten consecutive years in Brooklyn and brings that same expectation and vision to San Francisco.

Even after he leaves San Francisco test scores continue to rise, year after year. San Francisco's overall test scores are higher than any other major urban district in California, the size of the achievement gap among ethnic groups is also larger than any comparable district in the state. The gap is partly driven by the relatively high scores of students of Asian backgrounds, who represent 4 of 10 students in the district. Recently I hear a national black leader who comes to San Francisco to speak. He says that what is so remarkable to him is how the Chinese came to this country and mastered the white man's system. A black San Francisco leader tells me that blacks have to demonstrate that the black community does value education and learning.

Disproportionate numbers of poor and uneducated blacks lived in segregated and inhumane conditions. A social breakthrough happened in the civil rights era of the twentieth century and some lives changed. A generation after the achievements there still exist alarming dropout rates, an unacceptable life of criminal behavior, distressing numbers of children born to single mothers, and a growing gap in academic and economic achievement. How are young minds and lives empowered to radically change themselves within a society of failing schools, violent neighborhoods, and a destructive drug culture? The civil rights revolution continues with the young, the old, and all of those with the energy to question authority, society, and past knowledge. If we do not seek the truth with our own energy then our world becomes destructive and society controls and imprisons us. We live outside of the relentless revolution of change when we do not inquire, explore and discover what is true. When we understand that we are capable of standing alone in the world then society cannot destroy us.

# 18

# SELF-ORGANIZING

The school seldom moves anyone beyond the poverty and social background of the student. For most poor students it is what happens in the school, such as the failure to learn, which can be far worse, and more severe than the conditions of poverty and family background. The personal cost of failure to black and minority students who come from socially disorganized communities in San Francisco is profound. Drugs, poverty, gangs, racism, and weapons are all connected to the violence, fear, and failure rates in the community and the society. The school's action in response to the community and family life of poor minority students can be significant and crucial. There are breakthrough cases in the worst possible conditions where students from the poorest communities demonstrate the energy to empower themselves.

Isolated Communities

The world we all live in has not awakened to the urgency of action needed for the lives faced by children of poverty and the education in their lives.

As a society we have not eliminated the barriers for the opportunities for all children to learn and discover their energy to empower themselves and to be contributors to the world.

The poorest schools in San Francisco remain as forgotten and marginalized as they still stand in desolate and struggling neighborhoods. The situation of the children's lives is not about them in comparison to others. It is a needed understanding that no child can be pushed to the sidelines and forgotten. Rather than building a wall around one's life each child must be motivated from within to reach as far as he or she is capable. One day I ask students in a fifth grade class I work with to write a short statement about life around them.

These are some of the comments:

I wish that people would not be mean and stop talking about people that are homeless.

Segregation laws should be broken all around the world.

I wish that people would stop killing people.

I see things that I don't even believe in.

In my city people get shot for no reason.

Colored people should be able to do what the Whites do.

I wish people will change into good ones.

I hope for no gunfire or fighting in my neighborhood. People are being beat up and shot in my community.

There's too much violence. I wish people would stop it.

I wish people were not so disrespectful.

Sometimes I wish that when I go to my mom's house that they would not kill people.

I hope I don't get jumped.

No killing.

Some of the students in mathematics class are inspiring to me. They are as enthusiastic and as capable as any other students. Others are not. One day the principal and I visit a home in the public housing projects. There is an absence of predictability in families I find in visiting various homes. Some parents have strict expectations, but others are in disarray. Siblings from the same family may have totally different lives. One student, who has been receiving violence counseling, is capable and bright. His conversation can be articulate and thoughtful. No one knows what to expect from him. One day he destroyed a classroom by throwing chairs and papers everywhere. Another student had upset him. The family has been homeless but his sister is a quiet and bright student. She has no behavior problems in school.

The school works as hard as it can with the student and reluctantly the mother has him enrolled in a self-contained special education class. It was why the principal and I had visited her for the approval. I visit the student in the new school where an adult is assigned to him at all times. The principal at the new school says that he is adjusting well. The principal had once been a special education teacher.

The struggling students express these views:

They say they are going to college but provide no evidence

They appreciate a teacher who does not bother them about homework or grades

They say it is too much work to take hard courses

Many think they are stupid and cannot learn. They once thought they were smart at something until they reached high school. They find there are no experiences to change or encourage them.

They find that the teachers seem to hate their jobs.

They have either given up or feel like giving up.

They blame themselves for lack of success and feel there is no one who can motivate them to do better.

Those who are teaching themselves new things express these views:

They feel it is important to redo work and to clear up mistakes.

They do not feel fear in taking hard courses.

They observe that struggling students give up.

Some of them discover going through adverse and challenging times can empower them.

I have worked with this community for more than forty years. Some families live in the same community of public houses for generations. There are plans to establish a new community by fundamentally transforming the housing units by a revitalization of new properties and changing the life-style of the low-income housing communities and services. What happens to the families when they are relocated? Many leave and never make it back.

The lives of persons residing in poor isolated communities are dependent on persons with more resources than they have. The rich want to stay rich, get richer. They are not moved to reduce or eliminate mass poverty.

Organized minorities control governments and societies. They have the power to manage resources to maintain their wealth and privileged condition. They give attention to their special interest and of educating their own children.

In the life and education of the poor and others, a person is not free if he does not exist in a society where he is not able to completely stand alone.

A critical issue is to eliminate negative effects of schools for minority and underprivileged students. Few poor students are challenged to a rigorous and demanding education. The remedial and limited education they receive is monitored, assessed, and perpetuated. Most never leave school as serious learners, but as failures with significant disability. How do we know that this is so for poor and black students in San Francisco schools? School visitations, grades, courses, suspensions, and special education placements reflect the negative education journey of these students. Some practices at the schools are not based on any serious learning. There is always the issue of what quality of attention is needed to reverse failure for poor children. What worked in San Francisco at the Phase 1 schools? What brings about the change?

Two of the schools were newly formed, and four were reconstituted. Reconstitution meant that the schools removed all the administrators, teachers, and other adult personnel. A new staff was then hired to guide the students and the school community in its new vision, sometimes this included persons who had been previously at the school. There were eleven philosophical tenets that the new staff believed and accepted. These tenets bring learning and social adventure. Two of the tenets were the following:

## Tenet 4

All individuals can learn.

This tenet is fundamental. It is something that must be understood by the school and the student. Many poor students come to school from an environment in which education is not emphasized, sometimes resisted, and often not pursued. Therefore there are students who come to school who are not prepared for the education they encounter. They come without the skills to do academic work or to socially interact with others. It is important that the school works with each child until the student understands that he or she is capable of learning. This is not a trivial matter for some students. Once they themselves know that they are capable of learning then they can master the skills and information needed through their own self-discipline. It is also important that the teacher and the school realize that each student can learn regardless of the family background or educational environment. And once the student knows this then he or she can deeply understand and perform in a serious way.

## Tenet 8

If individuals do not learn, then those assigned to be their teachers should accept responsibility for this failure and take action to ensure success.

The methods used by teachers sometimes seem to make learning harder. Often teachers prepare well for their lessons but the students are not learning. Teacher effectiveness and student learning can be monitored. Teachers must do their best for each student in the class.

Not all students learn at the same level.

Students also behave differently in school. They can vary from explosive to indifferent to self-disciplined.

Students discover their ability to learn when they are curious and when they seek and find meaning and truth in everything they do. We can help them make their own way and understand the richness of life. Schools and teachers should provide intellectual, artistic, creative, and physically demanding activities that all of its students can participate in.

In addition to reconstitution and the philosophical tenets some other practices were the following:

Each of the schools had technologically rich environments (such as computers and multimedia) that was used in instruction.

The computer was an empowering tool that impacted and accelerated student learning. It breaks down barriers to communication while it also connects us to a deeper discovery and understanding of the universe.

There was a favorable adult to student ratio. That is, there were small class sizes. In my mind when we are engaged in learning the exact numbers of participants often do not matter. In life it is sometimes not finding a correct answer as much as it is responding when stakes are high and doing what is appropriate for the situation.

There was appropriate staff development in the philosophical tenets, instruction, and the use of technology.

In my discussion with principals who worked at these Hunters Point phase 1 schools they were exciting places because they were advanced, ahead of their time, had an edge in technology, instruction, and class size and were therefore able to outperform many other schools in the San Francisco and their students were primarily black.

So the phase 1 approach is to monitor academic achievement and eliminate as much as possible the negative school effects on disadvantaged youth from impoverished conditions. It is more crucial that those at the school know that every child can learn and that the child is also aware of this. Once these things happen, the student's academic skill and competence level become evident. This is the beginning of learning for all students where they can understand and contribute to the deepest human and world discoveries.

Students become engaged in learning new things without being put down. It is important that students understand life as it is. They do not dominate it nor do they fear it but teach themselves new things and construct personal meaning in their lives. They work with other motivated individuals.

Why is learning something new significant? The world is impermanent, temporary, and changing. To observe things as new is to realize the true and actual state of the world as it is. Recently I read work written from students at Downtown Continuation High School in San Francisco. They write of the world as they live, see and experience it. It is a school of immigrants, urban poor, the rebellious, and the forgotten.

> I am from a poor family,
> who works hard to have a small meal
> and survive each day
>
> I am from dreams and goals
> which I strive for,
> they give me life
>
> I'm from the cold streets
> of San Francisco
> where there's killing and drug dealing
>
> I'm from the Ghetto, hatred, disrespect
> I'm from Terror
> I hear footsteps of a menace
>
> We are the underspoken, the timid, the oppressed
> who sit on the bottom rung in society
> One has to rise above it all

We are not less than others
We are trying to accomplish our goals
knocking at the door to make our dirty streets a
community

It takes energy to change states and conditions, to reach summits, to transform schools and society, and to change ourselves. To those in the schools who experience failure, and who feel defeated, it is easy to give up and to wonder why one continues a struggle to change the state of society, schools, and the world. It is a real issue.

If students could express their understanding, and what was stopping their mastery or ability to do more, we could do more. But when they are not speaking about their own learning we make assumptions about what they are not able to do. Coming from the circumstance and background of their lives, they are at risk of not getting a strong or effective learning environment or the best schooling. Students who live in rich families and environments have more resources and possibilities to express and master understanding school and the world. Their condition is not as acute as other students. In some neighborhoods one may not be in the best place to get an education. In some poor neighborhoods school A is able to observe and monitor your competence and curiosity as you discover your learning and your proficiency. School B does not observe or monitor your learning or mastery but gives you remediation that is useless and harmful to your existing in the world. This should not be. We should be mindful of the lives of all students.

The superintendent says that we spend a lot of time trying to reform bad schools at students' expense. This is why he says the district reconstitutes schools.

What is troubling are the cases where young black and other poor students who are failing are devastated by school unnecessarily. They can live productive lives but are being destroyed. I see how school has not had a positive effect on them and their lives. Their minds are not being respected. Schools instead demonstrate numerous variations in ways to fail.

A fundamental issue with schools and learning is that of compulsory education. The knowledge in schools is fragmented, and never liberates us. Learning is more important than knowledge whether it is in a classroom or independent of school.

Violence, illiteracy, drug addiction, greed, and corruption are measures of poverty in the education of an individual and of a society. A society is not free if there is not a questioning of everything; including ones own assumptions and knowledge. Compulsory education or any other theory or policy cannot determine or accurately define how children learn. Some governments and other control oriented groups use a strategy to educate children so that within a generation they will have a group of true believers that do not question authority. Sometimes, for generations, we are totally isolated from life. In America it is the quantity of schooling and the amount of money it costs that create value and worth. By assuming such knowledge and expertise in schooling or anywhere else in society we cut ourselves off from life as it is. Self-teaching leads to a more interesting life and makes our schools seem trivial places. As a people and a planet we must educate ourselves; also as a city, a country, and a planet we must care about the journey of all of our youth.

Traveling South

One day I travel south with colleagues to a school in Inglewood, California. It has almost three hundred students. All are black. We are assigned a student to show us around the school. The school presents an exciting and engaging education for its students. It is a place that provides a learning environment which validates the language and culture of each student. Attention is given to providing a place where students are aware of themselves, the community, and the world. The education is based on rigorous standards, and an intellectually stimulating curriculum, one that respects the thinking of all its students. We learn that each student is provided a computer, and that cutting edge learning is practiced.

I observe student writing displayed throughout the school. As we walk around we read the posted writing of students about the community they live in, and the questions they have about the town, the citizens, and how the residents survive. It is interesting to discover these insightful student expressions.

Handwritten school rules are on the wall. One rule states that when passing through the halls one should keep ones hands to oneself. Another statement says that if one sees paper or litter scattered about to pick it up, even if no one else does. Be the responsible one, it states.

At recess we observe students gathering themselves in both independent and interconnected streams of activities. They organize themselves without being directed by any external system of control. They exist freely without authority, oppression, or subjugation. They self-organize with their own configured arrangements that form and disappear. To me this reflects the life of the school.

The genius of humankind is everywhere. Revolutionaries are feared because society and schools have not acquired the knowledge of managing a population of self-educating persons. Let them manage themselves.

# 19

# THE HARRINGTONS

The Harringtons are a San Francisco family. Three of them have passed through public schools as teachers. The first member of the family I meet is Robert. We are both math teachers at Mission High School. Robert is also a bartender on the weekends at Harrington's Bar on Front Street. He works Saturdays and I sometimes visit and we talk about school and life.

Robert has an interesting family. His mother had been a kindergarten teacher in the San Francisco schools, and even after she had retired she remained very energetic. She lived above Harrington's bar on Front Street. His grandfather had started the bar in 1937, and left it to Robert's father. The grandfather had a fascinating existence and had made an interesting journey into life. Anytime that Robert wished to speak with him he had to make an appointment.

The grandfather was involved in the early days of the Irish Republican Army and the Irish War of Independence from English rule. In the midst of battle and rebellion, he transported weapons and liquor. He was daring and successful. He had a lucrative life and became a millionaire. Circumstances became too heated and intense for him to stay in Ireland. He left his wealth there and came to America. He settled in Montana. I learned that in the late nineteenth century and early twentieth century of families from all over the country went to work in the Montana mines. The Irish had come in large numbers and became the largest ethnic group working the copper mines in

114

Butte. Robert says that his grandfather had gone to France and then to Canada before getting to Butte. It was a route that many from Cork, Ireland took to get there.

In Montana Robert's grandfather was successful in the copper business, but he left that life him behind, and came to San Francisco. He opened three bars, one for each of his sons. He did well financially, in managing the bars. I visit Harrington's Bar on Front Street on Saturdays, where Robert is working as bartender. Sometimes his brothers, Joe and Mike, are also there working. Robert and I talked about the world of the schools. There is usually much about San Francisco schools for us to talk about. I also discussed problems with his brother, Leo, who is a mathematics professor at the University of California at Berkeley. He studied at the Massachusetts Institute of Technology (MIT), and I was told that he is a leader in conjectural mathematics.

A problem I discuss with him one Saturday at the bar is the number of regions space is divided by 10 planes. The planes are in a general position so that no two are parallel to each other.

One plane divides space into 2 regions.

Two planes divide space into 4 regions.

Three planes divide space into 8 regions. (2 intersecting vertical walls crossed by a horizontal floor.)

In the case of 10 planes dividing space it may be impossible to see or to visualize the regions.

Mathematically the problem is connected to points dividing a line and lines dividing a plane. One observes a pattern, or system that calculates 10 planes dividing space into 176 regions; 100 planes dividing space into 166,751 regions; 1,000 planes dividing space into 166,168,000 regions; and going on endlessly.

Mathematical reasoning produces a formula where the number of regions is technical knowledge. One can mathematically determine a million or a billion planes dividing regions of space.

Technical knowledge trivializes the world and reduces it to routine thought that exists in its limited realm.

I discuss many things with Leo Harrington, and appreciate our dialogues about life, thought, and reality. It is evident to some who are present in the bar that he is an enlightened mind moving effortlessly through the mathematical world at the deepest levels. Others hardly are aware that he is there.

He shares this insight with me: If you know what you are talking about, then it does not matter how you say it.

He also shares this with me about teaching: There are some students who know more than their professors in certain fields of mathematics.

Robert and I sometimes talk about the world of technology and the desegregation of San Francisco schools. After having been selected on the original desegregation team, he is the district expert in its philosophical and organizational direction. Robert is profoundly captivated with the power of the computer and our human capability. He tirelessly pursues mastery of the computer and its widespread use in learning and in the empowering of the human mind. He is able to see its use in running a school or district in managing their data and organization, as well as its impact in everyday life. We both are interested in computers from their beginning, and we are fascinated in programming them. They bring a new world to us in managing information, and a fresh way to learn. We both teach computers to educators through the university. Robert had been teaching there and had recommended me as an instructor. It makes us both more serious educators. The early use of the computer, as a programmable instrument that stores and processes information, is fascinating. It seems incredible to see an automated machine manipulate symbols to perform complex and repetitive procedures so quickly, precisely, and reliably. Robert served on the original desegregation or Consent Decree team as Superintendent Alioto sought individuals to work creating a plan that gave serious attention to the learning and education of the underprivileged and underserved students in the district.

In the 1980s San Francisco schools were leaders in the state for student information. It reported data and information aggregated by the various subgroups of its students and shared it with all who made inquiry. Robert was in charge of the department.

Some years after the Consent Decree, Robert's son, Kenneth, decided to become a teacher in San Francisco. I had known him since elementary school. He was an excellent student and a brilliant chess player. Robert was pleased that he would be teaching in a Consent Decree school.

After the Consent Decree had so significantly impacted the original six schools, it moved on to other groups of schools, already in existence. They did not perform as successful as the original six. The Consent Decree, however, did further expand opportunities in later years with the creation of three new schools in Bayview Hunters Point.

One of the schools was Thurgood Marshall Academic High School with a focus on math, science, and technology. The school had been in existence several years when Kenneth started as a teacher. The school started with the high hopes of a rigorous education for all students. However, a number of students were failing, or dropping classes which frustrated teachers, parents, and students. Some teachers say that the commitment to academic excellence drew them to the school. For others it was the various ethnic, social, and educational backgrounds of the students. From the beginning the school did not have a unified focus.

Kenneth's first day in the classroom is devastating. He was having a private conversation with several male students about the class, and a girl storms out of the room calling him a racist, probably meaning a sexist. It is an unexpected encounter that he does not understand. The girl is outspoken and the accusation is draining. He barely gets through the day. He struggles with the decision to come back the next day, or ever again. Reluctantly he returns. The event had a serious effect on him, but he is able to work through it. I visited his classes and had conversations with him, and the incident became a non-issue. Kenneth is able to get beyond the matter, and other classroom management concerns, and to seriously teach mathematics. His father tells him what he learned from his forty years of teaching are:

1) Teach them something new, something that they do not know.
2) Do it in a way that respects them and does not put them down.
3) Let them know that you care about their lives, and value them as individuals, that their intellectual and social journeys in life are important to you.

Kenneth comes to school every day and works tirelessly. He is driven to bring the power of mathematics to all the students he is assigned. No one remembers the first days of conflict and uncertain direction. He is open to everyone's comment about learning math, and he is available daily to discuss mathematics into the evening. Some call him at home. Many students appreciate his insight and diligence, and they express this in their written comments about the course. He appreciates engaged dialogue with students of all interest and backgrounds. He has always been a serious student of math, and in exploring life. He graduated from Lowell High School, and in his senior year he was the top golfer in the city. When he was studying math in the university, he received an A in 39 classes. The only course he did not get an A in, he got a B+, but that was the highest grade in the class. I have visited his classes to talk to and work with some of the students.

One day his uncle Leo and I visited Kenneth's class to talk and work with some of his students. With much excitement Kenneth presents to the class a world of space, planes, and vectors. He reviews material they have discussed before and shows how it is connected to new and deeper problems. He then sets them free to explore and to engage themselves in the problems they are assigned for their class work for the day. He tries to make everything he says have relevance to the work going on. The entire class worked cooperatively in groups that varied both in size and in their approaches to the class assignment.

Two students worked the entire period on problems of equations from a point to a plane; and on points and lines of intersection. Leo worked with them for the entire time. They had no idea that he was a mathematician from Berkeley but seemed pleased to have spent the time asking questions and working with him.

I observed Kenneth as he interacts with all the students in the class and how much it means to him that every student had performed well in their understanding of the problems and in the mastery of the work. It is a mathematically meaningful class for him and all the students.

Leo and I walked in front of Thurgood Marshall High School back and forth, back and forth for an hour. This was the first time I had seen Leo in a number of years. He said that the last time we met was in his office at Evans Hall at Berkeley. We talk about technical knowledge and the impermanence of existence. Nothing is hardly unusual to Leo it seems. He is both a mathematician and an expert chess player.

Once he came to Mission High School and played four teachers simultaneously, blindfolded, and won all four games. He says at the time he wondered if he could pull it off, and he did to the astonishment of the players and spectators. It was something he had never done before.

Leo once had a nervous breakdown. I visited him in the hospital. When he leaves the hospital, he visits my wife and me. We have an interesting conversation about living in the present moment and the mathematics of information.

There is a dimension to Ken's life that I find unusual for a city teacher. It is his adventures in the wilderness. We are not serious about learning when we lack an appreciation for the natural world. With a lack of such understanding life is empty and abstract. Nature gives us a revitalization of our inner-self and we find the technical, physical, and mental skills to go further and deeper than we ever have before. A few teachers go out and seek great adventure and learning, and find them from within. This deepens their lives.

When Robert and I were both teachers at Mission High School, he loved to sail in the San Francisco Bay. I sailed with him on several occasions and I always am struck at the wonder of the Golden Gate Bridge. One year Robert took a leave from school and he and his family sailed to Mexico. The boat broke down and they had to abandon it and fly back to San Francisco. Today he anchors his boat in Steamboat Slough near Sacramento for much of the time. Robert still sails, and he also rows. He has rowed from Steamboat Slough to Sacramento. He would often think of rowing the Sacramento River from Red Bluff to Steamboat Slough. One day Kenneth takes on the adventure his father has spoken of. He sets off in his dory, a small rowing vessel, from Red Bluff to row solo down to the San Francisco Bay. It is more daring than he realizes. He hears a roar, not realizing it is from white water rapids. He soon finds himself in treacherous waters and somehow manages to struggle through two rapids. After six hours a sheriff's boat rescues him and puts the dory on their boat at Woodson Bridge. They tell him it is amazing he got that far.

He goes back. The next time he goes with his friend Jeremy Light, and the two of them leave Red Bluff at 9:30 in the morning, and row through the precarious waters and gravel bars to reach Woodson Bridge at 1:00 in the afternoon. They row in 35-minute shifts unless there are winds or strong currents that call for double shifts. They row to Hamilton City, Ord Bend, and to Colusa. On day four they make it to his father's boat at Steamboat Slough and eventually on to the San Francisco Bay. It took 7.5 days to row from Red Bluff to San Francisco. They had completed the 315-mile journey. Since then they have done the trip six times.

Kenneth Harrington teaches for two years and then he leaves public education. He works as hard as he can but burns himself out. He frequently hears it stated that all children can learn, but finds it to be really just talk and words. Society does not change, nor does the individual. Each year the students remain just as illiterate in math as when they arrive in the classroom. It is as though neither the schools, nor the students care about their minds or their lives. He leaves as a high school teacher to be an instructor at the university. He later teaches at a private San Francisco high school.

# 20

# SCHOOL VISITS

Ten years after the Consent Decree and reconstitution are enacted, a study shows how the schools are performing. The first six, Phase 1, schools show that they perform better for poor students than other schools. The black and Latino students perform best at these schools. In these schools the persons in them are building something new. Even the poorest schools, with the highest public housing populations, and students from the toughest communities find a breakthrough in academic achievement. They have a new vision and a new start. Those in them no longer feel as if the school is being punished because of the communities they serve, or sense any social disregard for the students who attend the schools. It is building new schools that meaningfully involve them.

In order for the district to make even greater transformation, the court orders it to reconstitute three schools each year until the black and Latino student achievement reaches the level of the six Phase 1 schools. Schools each make presentations to the visiting district team. This instituted district program is called the Comprehensive School Improvement Program (CSIP). I shall refer to this program as the Review Program and its members as the Review Team. I join this Review Team with Superintendent Rojas, Robert Harrington, and Linda Davis, who later becomes the first black acting superintendent in San Francisco.

The first year we visit nine schools. After the second year we had made 17 school visits; 26 after the third year; 34 after the fourth year; and 36 after the fifth. Several school visits stand out in my mind. During the first year six of the nine schools are elementary schools.

We go to one elementary school and we arrive there early for the morning assembly. The whole school stands on the playground for the morning announcements. I have not been in such a gathering since I taught in Kenya more than twenty years ago. I do not remember much about those days except it was half a world away from here, and I did attend such assemblies. The Kenyan school stood on the edge of the Rift Valley where earliest human life is said to have begun. It made my days of living there serious and reflective. It is just as important that I am a serious observer in this San Francisco school.

At this San Francisco elementary school the assembly is a daily event. The principal speaks. It is clear that she is the school leader and her deep feeling for the school is evident. Then, a black student speaks. This is the main presentation. He is a fifth grade student.

I learn that students regularly participate in this activity. In visiting schools I try to observe the seriousness of student learning and the depth, talent, and spirit of the teaching. There is particular focus on the performance of African American and Latino students, and the quality of their participation in the learning community. The Consent Decree schools work with 11 philosophical tenets. They are often words that are not internalized.

The student speaks of a place where all students can learn and how all individuals are worthy of respect. His understanding of the world and the school itself as a true learning community seems profound as I listen. In his own way he describes the organizational assumptions and beliefs of the school, and clearly expresses the vision of the school just as the principal had. I am impressed with how they began the day and how they performed as a school. It is one of the schools that graduate from the Review Process. I shall refer to it as the First School and write more about it later.

During the second year we visit another elementary school that stands out. It is the fourteenth school visitation. I shall refer to it as School Fourteen. From the moment we enter the school there is a feeling this is a serious place. The principal greets us and makes it clear that the school is ready for our visit. The school awaits us. The classes I observe are orderly and well run. I am impressed with the computer lab and the expertise of the teacher. Several years before the computer lab teacher came to the school, I visited this school to work with the principal with new computer software. I had known her before but she came to this school, but when I left after the visit that day I knew that she competently managed people and the school. Undoubtedly she was the person in charge of the school. Her leadership is evident. It had been a worthwhile school visit.

This school is more than fifty years old, and most of the students are poor. Three hundred students attend the school. I observe a class where a retired teacher is volunteering. The students are playing chess and are seriously involved. I am fascinated with the game and its possible effect on the life of the participants. The principal knew of my profound interest in the game and its effect on learning. Indeed, at an earlier meeting the superintendent had told principals that they should demonstrate school activities that the visiting team had strong or unusual interests in. There is deep silence in the room as the students from various races, background, and grades work hard trying to find the best moves. The game can provide children with a compelling way to overcome self-doubt and isolation that are so much a part of the lives of inner city youth.

I have played chess with students in a Hunters Point elementary school who had been taught by a chess master. How inspiring and hard they had played. The chess master was a black man from the East Bay who worked passionately with them to change their level of play. No one wins every game so they learn from their losses, and are encouraged to pursue their game at a more serious level when they are victorious, or struggle to win. For some it is a slow and a hard game to learn, but in the end they can find it a good game to play and are excited when they do master it. The students discover that chess becomes an encounter that uses intelligence and thinking in new ways.

I walk into a classroom that is striking to me as no one is teaching the students anything. They are in groups educating and teaching themselves. How engaged they all are. I am there for some time when the teacher approaches me, and speaks about the class. It is an unexpected atmosphere in which I find myself immersed. The teacher, Ms. Blumenthal, tells me about the various areas in which the students are working. She also has students in the groups discuss with me the work they are doing. I tell her how impressed I am at the self-discipline, and involvement of the whole class. The students are able to articulate what they are performing, which deepens their learning. Ms. Blumenthal tells me more about the groups of the students who are cooperatively working together. I am fascinated at the attention given to each student and the quality of the different learning centers in the room.

At one location are activities using balances to compare quantities of materials and to observe properties of matter. There is an ordered display of student work all around the room. There are bright colored blocks that are ordered and reordered as students build, discuss, and test numbers and concepts. Abstract ideas and concrete patterns are explored as assumptions, and misassumptions are communicated to me in the processes they pursue. It is important to me that they are able to use objects to complete tasks and to test and verify ideas. It is refreshing to see them sometimes individually or collectively searching for an understanding to a problem and discussing why it works, rather than seeing them respond to a teacher asking them questions to which the teacher already knows and holds the answer. There is stillness and quietness in the room. It is evident that the class focuses on its work and activity in a place of seriousness and order.

There is a center where students have journals and write things. When they write to Ms. Blumenthal, she always responds to them by the next day. Always. Student writing fascinates me. It is a way of expressing what is going on in one's mind. Writing is a way of illuminating what may be locked inside. The students have goals, solve problems, help each other work on tasks and projects, often evaluate and monitor their own work, and benefit from a serious learning environment sustained by the teacher.

When I observe the students performing their mathematics work it is clear to me that the actual world or physical world is not really based on mathematics, except by invention. Mathematics can help us to understand this world. I see a similarity with students playing chess and those doing mathematics. Once you know the rules and the meaning of chess pieces, then you manipulate them in different ways, and even become creative in your own game. The more you learn about rules, definition, and social presence of others, the deeper you get into the game. The same is true of mathematics. The more the students are given the chance to benefit from the learning opportunities of knowing the fundamental truths and rules (and expressing them) the more mathematically empowered they become in this human made universe.

In leaving the classroom I see the principal in the hallway. I ask who the best teacher in the school is, and she indicates Ms. Blumenthal. I also learn that her mother had been a teacher, and learn how much attention she gives to her class, and how much she loves to teach.

Other strong impressions about the school come from the cleanliness of the bathrooms. They are all impeccably clean, and without blemish throughout the school. It communicates that this school is a place which is significantly and thoroughly cared for. My daughter attended schools in San Francisco. I remember that in her four years of high school she never used the school bathrooms. They had been such horrible places for her.

All schools make a presentation to the Review Team. The length of each presentation is supposed to be one hour. Almost always the schools exceed the time limit. School Fourteen's presentation runs for one hour exactly. It includes a student and teacher presentation for each grade level in the school, as well as presentations from the special education and Spanish Bilingual programs. Some of the activities are those we had observed in our classroom visits. I had observed the special education presentation in the classroom, but it certainly makes a greater impact before the audience to see the teacher and a student who is unable to hear or speak use technology to communicate with us using a computer keyboard. Special education and disability makes me realize that someone can always do something better than someone else and some of us have strengths and abilities that others do not have. We are all disabled in some areas as human beings as well as have our own capabilities. The bilingual presentation displays a peer-tutoring lesson in which students help other students learn English, while strengthening their Spanish. The school choir performs and the principal ends the program as every group works within the time of its presentation. Every group performs well which means that the school has done very well. At the end of the year, School Fourteen graduates from the Review Process.

In contrast to our visitation of School Fourteen during the second year of visits, is a visit to an elementary school during the third year. It is the twenty-first school visit. Like most of the schools the Review Team visits, there are many inner city children who are poor and attending the school. Many students are from the Potrero Hill public housing projects. In some schools involved in the Review Process it is clear which will be reconstituted and which will graduate. School Twenty-One is interesting because the staff feels it has done a good job preparing for the visitation, and in the presentation of the school performance. This is also evident from a demonstration by parents and teachers protest at a board of education meeting after the school is recommended for reconstitution. Most of the schools reviewed know that they are schools on the edge, and that there is the threat or possibility of reconstitution. It is not a mystery as to how they became identified as a Review Process or failing school. This is demonstrated by a lack of student academic achievement with all students as indicated by seventeen district indicators. Many of the schools have the lowest reading and math performances in the city, and continue to decline over a period of years.

Despite these indicators, many schools feel that they are not fairly judged. Public schools in urban inner city America have long been at a disadvantage from a middle-class society. These school communities often speak of the overwhelming obstacles, hopeless bureaucracy, impoverished students, deteriorating facilities, and the impact of drugs and crime on the life of the school. They see themselves as remainder schools as the schools in the more affluent communities do not have these problems, and are able to focus on academic excellence. The alternative and academically successful schools get the most serious students. The schools that remain are for those students and parents who are less sophisticated and informed and must accept what the system forces on them. They become the oppressed. This is why they see themselves as the remainder schools. The affluent schools have less special education programs, less children of poverty, less suspended and expelled students and more parent interest and productivity.

These things are true, but they are not new. They are the same reasons that there is a court order to have excellent schools in the poorest areas. This does happen in some Phase 1 San Francisco schools. We have seen results and we can ask why are not all schools places where students question life and the world and are curious about the truth? In schools of the poor, or the affluent, when we dwell on things that destroy or that reward us, we are imprisoned. Life is moving on. Education has to stay moving on the frontier of life in its journey.

There can be transformation when the most dedicated and capable educators work in the toughest schools. The teachers at School Twenty-One perceived themselves to be doing an appropriate job for the students they served. The students were poor and the community was poor.

I remember the first time I visited the school there had been a robbery. Someone had broken into the school and stole a computer over the weekend. It was chaotic and unsettled. The school was surrounded by the public housing projects so this was not an unusual situation to occur. It did impact the school and those who worked there.

The teachers at the school express to the Review Team that they think they are effective at the school. They feel as though some teachers are outstanding. Parents come and support the school, and the teachers. There is also a partnership with a business that works with the school, and it expresses its support also. This however is not unusual for the reconstituted schools. Many feel as though they are doing a good job. School Twenty-One did achieve in some areas, but there was not a high enough school performance to prevent their being reconstituted. There had been a strong plea by the parents to maintain the special education program at the school. In the end those teachers are allowed to remain.

The School Twenty-One visitation is interesting to me, because those who are in the school believe they are doing a good job. This is true in most of the schools we visit. However, our Review Team did not observe this to be the situation at the school. They do not see themselves as teaching down to the students, but they have been doing it for so long that it is their way of life. The Superintendent during the visitation asked me, "Is there anyone in this school who can teach?" He likened the visitation to walking through a plantation. There is a mentality of dominating the minds to respond to orders and rules. No one understands the students are getting a second-class education. And though some parents thought that reconstitution was unjustified, not everyone was impressed with the performance of School Twenty-One.

A community member who worked with parents from the school shared with me that she met on a number of occasions with the school staff. She tried to determine what to do to change the academic performance of the students from the public housing projects. No one responded to her. She said that reconstitution would make the school more accountable to those children. She stated that it was time for people who are responsible to say that inner-city schools don't have to be provided the worst education a child can get.

A Neighboring School nearby School Twenty-One was a Review Process school the previous year. It also had students from the Potrero Hill housing development. It also had students from the military base at Treasure Island, however, it demonstrated student achievement and a learning community with high performance. The Neighboring School graduated from the Review Process while School Twenty-One was reconstituted. The two schools are approximately a half-mile apart. It is easy to assume schools so close with similar poor students would both perform with predictable low results.

At the Neighboring School each member of the visiting team had a student to accompany him or her around the school. The students knew a lot about their school and were very conscientious. It was good for them to look at their school globally as they walked and talked with us. It was a new experience for us and for them. There were interesting things occurring in the classes. There were exciting hands on lessons in the math classes and the science classes. The computer resource teacher impresses me. She seems so competent and enthusiastic about her work and about the children she teaches. She says that she drives seventy miles a day for a job that she loves. The school is very organized and focused on academic achievement. The students and teachers present a school where effective learning is occurring. The visiting committee writes the following letter to the students who show us the school.

"We were grateful to have the opportunity to meet you and to learn about your school with you on Thursday. It was good for the Superintendent and his visitation team to observe and to explore the school from an informed student's point of view. We think that we covered all of the classrooms and met all of the teachers and saw all of the students. There were many interesting things going on in the school and it was good to see the enthusiasm and learning throughout the school.

"Again, thank you for accompanying us. Keep up your outstanding scholarship, leadership and service to the school and all the best wishes when you attend middle school next year."

There was such contrast in School Twenty-One and the Neighboring School. One had been reconstituted after one year and the other graduated from the Review Process. One was a failing school and the other an emerging school.

We judge others because of their race, their place of origin, or what we read about them, or what another says about them. It is meaningless to invent a world based on past knowledge. We assume this knowledge to be reality. Nigeria and Kenya were both former British colonies. Both had similar school systems. I had expected similar teaching experiences in the two countries. But when I went to Kenya and lived there I found it to be a situation different from I had ever imagined.

In Kenya the school was less serious and intense than Nigeria. The Kenyans were more tranquil and more deeply influenced by the colonial British past. Nigeria was a much harsher life for Europeans, and there were less remnants of a former European glory that never was. In Nigeria there are deep student goals. In Kenya the school is on a road that is traveled by Jomo Kenyatta, the president of the country, and the school is always dismissed and students are forced to stand along the road and observe the presidential motorcade travelling to or from his Rift Valley home. There is never serious sustained study at the school it seems. Though both Kenya and Nigeria have European school systems, the Kenyan school was very different from that of Nigeria. In Kenya it is a similar problem to what I find teaching mathematics to black students in California. There is a lack of pursuing a subject at any profound level. My wife taught in a nearby school in Limuru which has sustained itself since colonial days. It offers a different level of education and students perform at high standards. For me student learning is not a question of race, nation, wealth or poverty. Does the energy exist to sustain serious student learning?

What happened in the classrooms at the Neighboring School that was more profound than at School Twenty-One? What was absent in the classrooms at School Twenty-One was that some teachers wanted to maintain their power over knowledge. In places that work students assume responsibility for their own learning and can determine how well they are doing. When students are dependent on authoritative instruction, extrinsic measures, and the judgment by others in their learning they do not increase their ability to evaluate and to assess themselves. They are disempowered as learners and end seeking new and different ways to learn.

High Schools

At the Second High School we come in through the back entrance covered with graffiti. It was a spontaneous and momentary decision. They had expected us to make the entrance through the front of the school. How much was revealed from the quiet and unexpected entrance? Only two people and a group of students on the computer made the school presentation. It did not represent a high school of 1500 students. There were also technical problems with the presentation. The superintendent was shocked at the absence of preparation. They scored only four points out of a possible twenty-five for their presentation. At a Board meeting many alumni, staff, parents, and students of this high school came to speak in support of the continuation of the schools teachers and staff. One student asked why the school only received four points for its presentation. The superintendent responded that they were lucky to get four and they should have gotten one. He publicly stated that they were that bad.

In the Fourth High School, we discover the paint in the bathrooms is still wet. I am always interested in the attention given to the cleanliness of bathrooms and the school stairwells. My approach is, "no graffiti." Its presence shows no excitement or enthusiasm for learning.

A colleague and I visited a geometry class in the school and then visited a math class in one of the district's top elementary schools. My friend said that he was more impressed at the geometry lessons of quadrilaterals and parallelograms in the fourth grade class than the high school geometry class. The elementary students expressed mathematical language and comprehension more accurately than the older students had. The elementary students were more deeply challenged in their class. During the visitation, a student in a social studies class asks me if I think that I can adequately access a high school this size in an hour. First I thanked her for her question. Then I tell her, "Yes," that I am able to observe this school, and express what I see, and make recommendations from my findings. I have been to more than twenty classes in the school and have visited more than twenty other schools. That in itself may not mean anything about this visit, but it is a fact I have been to every high school in San Francisco and I look forward to sharing what I have seen here.

One person shadowed the superintendent throughout his visitation recording notes as she followed him. It seemed a miscalculation to carry out such an act with the superintendent. He is both physically and mentally tough and never backs down from any confrontation. He did his job as observer and when the process was over the school was reconstituted. One teacher filed a grievance against one of the team members for harassment. It was without substance and dismissed.

The presentation of the Fourth High School was well done. The students and the teachers participating presented the school enthusiastically and performed with noticeable determination. They showed the artistic and academic strengths of the school. They were well prepared in showing student work in areas such as dance, literature, physics, and technology. The press was present and it seemed as though there had been such a great effort to save the school from reconstitution. Some students and teachers wanted to show the school was worth saving and be given another opportunity. It was not clear to me the exact strategy of some staff members; they seemed to try to intimidate the visitation committee. What added to the confused state of many of the teachers was that they disliked the principal, and questioned his capability as a leader. They seemed to want to save the school, but replace the principal.

The school newspaper, the West Wing, had won a special award from Columbia University for its reporting on such articles as the school's administration and reconstitution. They had written about the replacement of the previous school leaders, and issues with the present principal in which they say he had pressured them to do more positive articles about the school.

Having been a teacher at this Fourth High School more than thirty-five years ago, I have always had an interest in the school. From my earliest days at the school I am aware of the students with the greatest needs, who are often the black, and Latino students, as well as those with the greatest interest who are often Asian.

The students with the greatest needs are sometimes discussed summarily because of their lack of interaction with the school. Information such as dropouts, transience in and out of school, cutting classes, school suspensions and expulsions, and lack of academic productivity express their absence of educational attainment. They are often hardly aware of the school material they never see, which they will probably never master. In actuality their problem is not attendance, race, or poverty but an absence of learning. From the very beginning years it is evident that there are students who come to learn. They are self-motivated and often transcend what the school has to offer. They are the students with the greatest interest in being there. All ethnic and racial groups do have such students with the deepest interest in learning. Some students, when they leave, have been able to attend some of the most elite and prestigious universities in America. This has always been the case since I have followed those who have studied at the school. There have always been some students who have achieved at the highest possible level at the school.

In the last years at this Fourth High School there have been several bright students who have been killed in their communities as a result of living in places of violence, drugs, joblessness, and hopelessness. In state examinations the school is reported as performing amongst the lowest in California. However, in national examinations some students perform among the top public schools in the country, something few other San Francisco schools achieve. It shows there is human genius present here as clearly as anywhere else in the country.

The Fourth High School is the last high school that the committee visits. The seriousness of the visitation committee, led by the superintendent, is driven by student academic achievement and a high level of performance of the school as a learning community. There is also a court order that is based on the academic achievement for all students, elimination of racial identifiably in school programs, and the desegregation of all schools that is declared by an uncompromising judge. I have met with the judge, William Orrick, on several occasions while serving on an advisory committee to the court. He is fair, thorough, and profoundly concerned about San Francisco students and schools. His judicial authority makes San Francisco an empowered district. This is carried out despite opposition from some teachers, communities and some school board members. They were powerless to have an impact on the Review Process because of the strength of the federal court order.

Superintendent Rojas had come to San Francisco with academic excellence and achievement on his mind. There are a number of ways to monitor how students are achieving. He discussed with me the district in Brooklyn in which the student test scores had improved for eleven consecutive years. It significantly challenged him and it also provided him a direction that he would pursue as an educator.

San Francisco is considered a world class city but whose social tradition and history have not valued and respected minority groups of color. The schools would never have gained their present level of performance without a court order. I sometimes wonder if the citizens of the city would ever have made the local sacrifices without the court order, even in a hundred years, if ever. For the first hundred years of the existence of California, San Francisco schools were as racist as the rest of California. The

South held beliefs that were unquestioned and cherished during the civil war and for nearly a century thereafter. California and San Francisco were not different.

The Teacher's Union president stated that, "There have been times when he (Rojas) has moved me to tears when he talked about the problems of kids who are disadvantaged. She also had said, "But in terms of running the organization, people who work in the school district see it quite top-down, quite authoritarian and quite hierarchical. They don't see him collaborating or making shared decisions."

The superintendent did not disagree. "People may complain that there isn't as much access," he says. "But the people who had no access now have access."

This is true as evident in his meetings with public housing residents, convicted felons doing community service with the school district, grass root political activists, distinguished academic leaders and scholars, as well as concerned parents and influential business and community organizations. He is not predictable in the issues and people he supports and listens to.

# 21

# POVERTY AND SCHOOLS

I wrote earlier about the First School. I now continue with issues that it faced and dealt with. It was in a middle class neighborhood and few of the children who lived near the school attended there. It did not have a good reputation among those who lived in its neighborhood. One barrier to the school's appeal to its own residents was the fact that children from the Geneva Towers public housing project were bused there.

The towers are far from downtown. Tourists do not reach there. The tourists ride cable cars, visit the wharf, live in fine hotels, shop in elegant stores, eat expensive meals, discover city hills, cross bridges and never know of this side of the city. On the south edge of San Francisco is a modest neighborhood of small unit houses. Two eighteen-story buildings called Geneva Towers, built in 1967, hang over the city. There is an imposing fence that surrounds them.

Outside the fence are the Visitacion Valley and Sunnydale neighborhoods. I was once a school principal for students who live there. Almost all are poor but they are also unique, and living a life of uncertainty. It is a drug and crime filled world. The youth who live there are both the perpetrators and the victims of crime. I worked for many years on a community board to resolve conflicts in the area. We never had the hard cases of homicide, robbery, or drugs. There were cases of arson in the schools by youth, theft from stores, graffiti and gang related incidents.

After I left the area I read one day about an incident in the neighborhood where two black youth, about ten or eleven years old, had ordered two other youth from a car. It was a male youth who had been driving a female youth home from a nearby church. The younger black youth was intent on stealing the car, a carjacking. It was reported that he had a gun and was disturbed with how long it was taking the other youth to get out of the car. He shot him in the head, killed him, and rode away in the car. I never heard anymore about the incident, but I learn how uncertain and tragic life is.

When I worked in the neighborhood high school one day a Filipino youth who had recently arrived in the country was driven to the school. He got out of the car and shot a Latino student in the head and drove away. The next day the Latino youth was dead. It had all been over a girl. It is a deep tragedy in life that some youth suddenly no longer exist in the world; their lives are destroyed in an instant.

What of those who live inside the gates of the two towers? Two out of three of the adults are unemployed and without jobs. There is crime and vandalism here. They are rampant. I read a report that says that the security and maintenance cost more than a half million dollars a month.

The students at Geneva Towers attend the First School. The principal knows about the crime, poverty, drugs, and personal misfortune of the students from the neighborhood. She knows that when a black student from Geneva Towers enters school and acts different from other students, and is not a normal student it does not mean that he should be isolated, expelled, tracked, suspended, or put into special education. She moved to counteract the special circumstances of growing up poor in urban America by hiring parents to ride the buses and to assist in the classrooms. They had a visible presence and were welcomed in the school. The principal held parent meetings and student conferences in the towers. Teachers from the school went and knocked on doors and met with the parents. By this action the school had refused to be a mindless and inert bureaucracy in the life of its children.

In contrast to the First School, a nearby Middle School is also a Review Process school that is in the neighborhood of Geneva Towers and Sunnydale and located very near to these public housing projects. Those who work at Geneva Towers feel that the principal of the nearby Middle School does not strongly value, and support the kids from Geneva Towers. The school lacks the vision, and the effort demonstrated by the First School. At the end of the school year the First School graduates from the Review Process, but the nearby Middle School is reconstituted.

The superintendent had wanted the district to establish cooperative programs with public housing residents. This resulted in the district establishing computer centers in the public housing projects from the Tenderloin center working with the Southeast Asian community, as well as areas such as Geneva Towers and Sunnydale housing projects. I work with Ray Porter from the district. There was enthusiasm and excitement. Ray worked with Vernon Long at Geneva Towers to establish a successful center. A magazine article called, "Towers of Power," described how the Geneva Towers residents dealt with overcoming obstacles of becoming a technological underclass. Students after school fill the chairs at the workstations, compose stories, work on tutorials, do homework, produce a newsletter, and send e-mail to Europe, Africa, and Asia. Students are involved in learning at a deeper level and are not involved in violent behavior. Of the forty users half of them are adults who write letters, resumes, and over a hundred and fifty pages of a book is written about living at Geneva Towers. The vision of getting technology to the residents was happening. It had happened quickly because of the focus and serious interest of the residents and the school district.

The principal of First School says that she finds that it is possible to impact the lives of the Geneva Tower residents, because the centralized arrangement of families makes them accessible to members of the school. They are able to go knock on a door, wake up the residents and have them come downstairs to meetings. It works. It shows they are serious, and it brings communication, dialogue and change. The principal worked with students from

Potrero Hill public housing for eight years and was therefore able to penetrate this world of poverty, neglect, isolation, violence, and non-achievement. She and her school worked hard for educational excellence for all children. The principal eventually leaves the First School to become the principal at a civil rights academy. She carries on in her profound contribution to all youth and to the district. At the new school one day the principal walks 109 miles in 5 days with a teacher and parents to the state capital in protest for more funds for school supplies for children.

The crowding of poor people into the high rise Geneva Towers make them unlivable. The government and the residents realize how greatly they are mismanaged. The magnitude of the crime of such concentrated poverty is finally recognized, along with the need to eliminate such inhumane conditions. On Saturday May 16, 1998, I witness the implosion of the 576 apartments that are destroyed in fifteen seconds. They were recognized as a national public policy failure.

In the Western Addition, another area of the city, the city demolition in the name of urban renewal did not consider the voices of the community. In demolishing the Geneva Towers, the residents of the community agreed on their destruction as a way of eliminating a cruel way of human existence. In one report four years later I read that over one hundred families were scheduled to return. In another account I read that the relocating agency has lost contact with all but fifty families. I do not know how many families ever returned or the success of the government effort to get them back. What is clear is that the effort that once seemed as responsive to those displaced became insignificant in its promise.

As in many San Francisco neighborhoods there are more Asians who have moved in and transformed the neighborhoods. An elementary school principal says the elimination of the Towers brings positive reform to the neighborhood and the school. He says that the school is performing stronger academically with a new spirit from the zest of the immigrants. The neighborhood itself was built in the 1940s for low-income residents that included shipyard builders from Hunters Point. In San Francisco the black population is declining as it struggles to survive in the schools and the city. For me it is our own self-discipline and sacrifice that transforms us. The schools and the students do not ask or understand what changes them and society.

# 22

# SCHOOL OF CHANGE

These days in San Francisco, private alternatives to the public school system are met with jarring opposition. School voucher programs, for example, are totally rejected as they are designed to undermine public schools. The teaching of democratic ideas is opposed to parochial, limited, self serving interests of the few which is seen as diminishing education. The affluent would distance themselves from the poor and the disadvantaged would become further isolated in ghettos and forgotten. Segregated developments are the envisioned outcome.

Urban public schools across the United States have the hardest job of educating students who are denied challenge and success and who live in hopelessness.

There is shock and outrage by some when Waldemar Rojas, the Superintendent of Schools, announces that an elementary school will become a public private partnership between a private organization and the San Francisco Unified School District. It is seen as giving up on the poor and abandoning them in privatizing the school that is the first step to eroding the public school system.

The superintendent is a unique leader in that he is unpredictable, and will do new things to challenge conventional thought and practice to further the education of poor and minority children by providing them ways out of the worst schools.

An elementary school partnership is an example of his challenging the thinking of serious minded individuals who opposed him, and questioned his direction and strategy in dealing with poor children. Some support him. The school, whose students were among the poorest and least academic in the district, shows dramatic transformation in one year.

There had been four principals at the school in a year's time. They all came after the school was reconstituted. I met and discussed the school with them all. The latest principal at the school is an experienced administrator with a vision of excellence. She brings new teachers to the school and also brings in a private organization with strategies to empower poor students.

One day I am visiting the school and I am invited into the classroom of a fourth grade teacher, Ms Yvette Fagan. She is African American and was selected as teacher of the year at her previous school. There are thirty four students in the class all working at computers. (I have been in their regular classroom and they are just as engaged in learning with books, paper, and pencil.) The students are of various ethnicities but many are black. They are all deeply involved in a writing project. There is total attention to the lesson. I am asked to observe and to read the projects that the students are immersed in.

They are all writing about Martin Luther King, Jr. It is fascinating work because the students have all given some attention to the work before they come to class. This adds to the energy and interest of what they are producing. They are all writing about an interview that they had with their parents and relatives about Martin Luther King, Jr. and what his life meant to them. For some there is discovery of human encounter of another time and place. It is an activity that engages them. The students are all writing about the information they have gathered and are constructing it in their own way. They ask questions as appropriate while they work. Everyone is working hard on a project that provokes and engages him or her. In one year this school has been transformed from a place of disaster, chaos, and hopelessness to one of light, emergence, and learning.

The students are writing about experiences they have gotten firsthand about human conditions that they share with me. They also import graphics into their work and are able to produce an original report from their own investigation and writing effort.

There have been many newspaper articles about the school as a public-private charter academy. One San Francisco Chronicle article spoke of how well the parents had assessed the school after its first semester of the partnership. The parents spoke of the reading advances of their children and the motivation of children to work hard. One parent speaks of a child who is inspired by her teacher's love of mathematics. Parents speak of quality teaching, a longer school day and longer school year, the reading program, special art, music, and language instruction and regular communication among the parents, teachers, and children. They speak of corporate money that brought new life to a rundown school. The school is still one of poor minority students with a reading coordinator who is working hard in her mission to make sure that every student can read by second grade.

In the article a parent spoke about the fourth grade teacher who loved to teach math and science. She is inspiring to the girls in the class. The teacher had been excited with the math program and told a parent that she could not wait to teach this new curriculum to the students. Such enthusiasm impressed parents. The teacher said that the school curriculum also gave her the freedom to develop the teaching of social studies.

"While we're learning each other's history, I'm trying to teach the skills they need to be part of society," she said. "I'm embedding it in the curriculum rather than turning it into some self-esteem class. They are learning to listen to each other's presentations, to ask questions and evaluate what they've heard, to gather material without plagiarizing it."

One day I met with the superintendent and a representative of the of the private foundation. The superintendent says that, he is stunned by the lack of focus on educational achievement for students in this debate over the public-private partnership. He is talking about educational opportunities for at-risk and predominately minority children who have been scoring at the lowest national percentile range for at least the last 8 years. Where were these critics for all these years that this school has been failing? There have been books written about this school, it wasn't as though nobody knew that it was a struggling school. This is evidenced by many of the critics of the school. There are many of the same people who either don't have kids in schools at all or have chosen to take their kids out of this school or enroll them in private schools. The superintendent says it is much easier to respond, "No," and oppose something than it is to look for solutions. Instead he says he listens to the parents of the children who say that they want us to create this partnership for their kids and for their school. If those voices come from wealthy families we rush to support them, he says.

In this partnership he looked to open new worlds and uncover new talents.

A member of the Board of Education tells me that he always tells others that a public school is better than any private school. It is because the public school serves any student who comes. There are no students with special privileges and no students who are turned away from an education.

The superintendent and the board member are both from New York. They are both articulate and live determined lives. The board member had gone to jail for refusing to serve in the military. He was opposed to war. The two of them, often inspiring in their own way, are not able to come to terms on what the public private school matter means to them in their own social realities. It is an issue that does not get resolved between the school board and the superintendent.

The State of California and not the San Francisco School Board eventually supervises the school.

External School Observer

Stanley Shainker worked with the district, and he wrote a confidential report on the elementary school before it was associated with the private foundation. He was an associate superintendent who once worked with Superintendent Alioto when the Consent Decree and the San Francisco desegregation plan were initiated, and made their significant impact on the district. The original six Phase 1 schools demonstrated that students from poor black and Latino communities, and San Francisco ghettos could learn, and achieve at a high level. Stanley Shainker and Robert Harrington provided as much as any other individuals in the leadership and mission for the district.

Stanley Shainker left the district but has returned to work on several projects with desegregation, and he was also asked to visit the elementary school. He wrote two reports on the school. The first report was written the year before the partnership with the private foundation. He made a number of visits to the school. He talked with 17 teachers, two principals, 24 parents, and most other adults who were associated with the school. He made observations throughout the school, conducted interviews as well as attended school meetings. He made the following observations:

> Most of the teachers seem to distrust the District Office and to blame its past decisions for all of the problems of the school. Teachers see themselves as "victims" with little or no responsibility for doing anything to improve the situation. Since all the problems are viewed as someone else's fault, solutions are someone else's responsibility! That helps to explain why additional personnel positions or new programs are expected to be paid by external "add-ons" and not through any process of internal reallocation!
>
> Many of the staff seems extremely stressed and overwhelmed by the disruptive behavior of some of the African-American students. (A handful of young African American males do seem to take an inordinate amount of time and energy of the adults in the school.) It is clear that most everyone in the school—and many of us from the outside—are at

a loss regarding how to best cope with the extreme types of disruptive behavior that have been displayed by a few of the students.

There is little evidence of any genuine staff affection or caring for the students— especially for the African-American students.

Many African-American students seem to feel that they are unwelcome in the school and that the school really is not theirs. Some feel that they are treated differently—and worse—than the Latino students. Others articulate that, "no one here likes me or cares about me."

There seems to be little follow-through within the school. Discussions are started but not finished. Staff decisions are made but not implemented. Teacher ultimatums are given but not enforced. (Is this simply a symptom of stress or is it something else?)

Staff members seem to focus on doing "their own thing" and rarely were seen working collaboratively with each other or accepting collective responsibility. (I observed teachers walking past colleagues in the hallway when it was clear that they were having difficulty controlling students and not offer to help.) I have no responsibility for those kids. I teach—" or "that's not my job; that's—'s". One teacher observed that, "they don't listen to me anyway so what can I do?"

Unlike every other reconstituted school in the district that I have ever visited, there is no evidence of the District's philosophical tenets posted anywhere in the school—let alone, operationalized. (I found that quite telling!) What are the prevailing values of this school and staff?

There is evidence that the staff has had difficulty in setting priorities in this situation or in determining that some things are more important than others at this point in time. (This is the main reason that I feel important decisions impacting the school must continue to be made by "outsiders"!)

The parents with whom I have met have indicated that they distrust the superintendent because he has failed to fulfill "promises" that he has made to them in the past, that they want more staff stability at the school, and that they want the staff to have high academic expectations for the students, to communicate regularly with parents and to listen to and address parental concerns, and to operate a safe, well-disciplined school.

Stanley Shainker, suggests that planning and professional activities be instituted at the school based on the following assumptions:

The staff needs to let go of the past and perceived "injustices" and to move on.

The staff needs to focus on the behavior and decisions that it can control; not on what others control.

The staff needs to accept its collective responsibility for all of its students; not just those assigned to their respective classrooms. In addition, it is essential that the teachers begin working more effectively as a collegial unit to accomplish the priority objectives of the school.

The staff needs to increase its sensitivity towards the feelings and concerns for all students—but particularly the African-American students.

The staff needs to assume collective responsibility for communicating with and involving all parents—but particularly African-American parents—in the life of the school.

This was his first report on the school. There was also a book, *A Principal's Story*, written by Ken Romines who was assigned principal to the school in 1993. He described it as the worst school in San Francisco. There were times when it may have been. He said that he was assigned there to end the anarchy, and turn around the school with the lowest test scores in the city. The accounts that he writes about are many of the same that Stanley Shainker described in his first report. Ken Romines was focused, talented, and energetic and at the school for two years before it was reconstituted.

One year later Stanley Shainker returned to the school to write a follow-up report, given the school's new status as a "charter academy" under the auspices of the private sector company. He reported the following:

> I observed two house meetings, a number of informal, small group conversations involving staff members in the teacher work room, all of the classes, and interactions between staff members and students, and student-student interactions in the hallways, on the playground, and in the cafeteria. I also met with 10 parents (4 Latinos, 3 African-Americans, and 3 whites) in a group setting in which I solicited their perceptions of the major strengths and weaknesses of the school, in general, and of the school's specific programs.
>
> My overall impression is that the school is a much healthier place for both students and staff than it was last year. In terms of culture and climate the school was a "1" last year (November 1997) on a scale of "1 to 10". (In fact, I characterized it as the most dysfunctional elementary school I had seen in my 35 years in education!) After this year's visit I would give it a "7" on that same scale in terms of those two dimensions.

Some students (especially African-American males) continue to act in a disruptive fashion that makes it difficult for them to take advantage of learning opportunities and requires an inordinate amount of staff attention. But the students appear to be much happier than last year and relate to each other as well as to the staff in much more positive ways. There is less separation—and more voluntary mixing—of Latino and African-American students in the classroom, the playground, and the cafeteria. The teachers are more positive about the students, and willingly share strategies with each other for dealing more effectively with learning and reading problems.

This year there is a greater emphasis on academics in the school and significantly less instructional time lost due to student behavioral problems. Teachers are organized and prepared. Instructional materials and supplies are not just available: they are easily accessed and used! The staff has a common philosophy enforces the same set of rules, utilizes similar classroom management techniques, and implements coordinated instructional strategies. The reading and math programs are highly structured and appear to be appropriate to the students' learning needs. In addition, these programs challenge a wide range of student ability and interest. Unlike last year's "where everyone does his or her own thing" faculty philosophy, the school staff's efforts this year are collegial and coordinated.

This was his second and follow-up report on the school. It is still a school of poorest children. It has shown limited change over its first years as a new school. Its academic rank in the state slowly is moving upward. The coexistence of poor blacks and Latinos in the school is interesting. The superintendent states that the fights and quarrels between them is based on a life that is never questioned whether the reason is race, the economy, culture or ethnicity. It is not unusual for those at the bottom to be their own obstacles in liberating themselves. They seldom change their state of existence. Their lives are predictable and they put up with a societal attitude of what conventional society defines for them. Their lives are controlled by institutional bias that separates them through testing, grades, and social behavior. They are institutionally separated for instruction and this is perpetuated throughout their educational lives.

The brightest and most capable students do well regardless of any group they are assigned. They are self-motivated.

Schools are places of cultural replication and duplication. Student differences are not considered as elements that contribute to a school's inefficient functioning. Schools are thought to be neutral places, not reflecting the interests of any one group of society, but they are unable and inadequate to meet the needs of the various students they encounter.

Our educational system turns lower class citizens into workers subordinate to external control and authority. As such citizens, though they are alienated from such institutions, they are still willing to conform and believe in the world of the dominant society. They value the culture of the dominant group and devalue their own. The tradition and practice of school maintains the inequities of the larger society.

# 23

# LOWELL HIGH SCHOOL

Lowell High School is probably the most known school in San Francisco. It is San Francisco's oldest high school. It was established in 1856. For some it is also one of the top academic schools in the United States. It was renamed and moved on a number of occasions in its early years, until it was renamed James Russell Lowell in 1894. Since schools in San Francisco tend to be segregated amongst the wealthy and the poor, Lowell stands out as a place of the rich and the privileged. Because it is a prestigious public school, the representation of the student body is always in question, black and Latino students are and have been historically under represented where Chinese and whites have been over represented. The affluent and the privileged are often subject to question by the underprivileged and other outsiders. To the insiders or those in the school it does not serve them well when looked at as a clichéd privileged kid school.

One year in the early 1980's I participated in a conference of the top twelve public schools in America; Lowell was the only school included west of the Mississippi River. The schools were selected based on academic standards and indicators such as advanced placement examinations. Lowell still remains one of the top schools in the country academically, and in the number of advanced placement examinations taken by its students. At the conference there were discussions on the replication of school excellence. One principal from a school in Great Neck,

New York, said that it was not a hard problem. His solution: Select the right student body. This is systematically done in San Francisco, New York, and Boston as they select students through an examination or other academic achievement measures. At the conference Lowell, Boston Latin, and Bronx High School of Science were all represented and they each selected students for admissions by examination. Students of all the other public schools selected were from suburban and wealthy locations. Most of the schools had predominantly white students, except for Shaker Heights near Cleveland with 40% black students at that time, and Lowell High School with 40% Chinese students. The traditional successful schools are almost always those with a selective enrollment of self-motivated students. The status of a school becomes directly related to its selection of students.

At Lowell many students transcend the school. Regardless of the teaching staff, the students have strong personal goals to deepen their education beyond Lowell and to go on to college. The school sends more students to the University of California at Berkeley than any other school. The students are driven to achieve. There are 2500 students in a building made for 1800 students. There are always students crowding the hallways, studying with each other, learning from each other and teaching each other. At the conference the Lowell principal said that it was in these student study groups where the significant education and learning of the students occurred.

There is a special admissions policy to get into Lowell based on an examination in the seventh grade and on academic grades in the seventh and eighth year in school. At one time the maximum number of points obtainable is 69. Some students receive perfect scores. When the district is under a court order to desegregate all schools, Lowell as an alternative school is not allowed to enroll more than forty percent of students from any ethnic group. There were nine ethnic groups defined when the Consent Decree was enacted. These include American Indian, black, Chinese, Filipino, Japanese, Korean, Latino, Other Nonwhite, and Other white (Caucasian). At one time, in order to be in compliance with the court order only the top 40% of Chinese students would be accepted. This meant that some high scoring Chinese students who scored higher than those in other ethnic groups would be excluded. A court case was filed by parents of Chinese students because of the exclusion of their children.

The admissions system was revised by the San Francisco Unified School District. It was changed to a system where the students with the top 70% or 80% of the scores from the examination and academic grades results qualify and are admitted regardless of their ethnic group. A cutoff score is determined for automatic admissions. The other 20% or 30% are admitted by considering such things as (1) evidence of the applicant's ability to overcome hardship (2) Extenuating circumstances, such as a personal or family crisis or (3) personal achievements such as athletics, community service, or school leadership.

The system was revised and the ethnic composition of the school did decrease for more disadvantaged groups and increased for others. The school is approximately 4% black, 8% Latino, 18% White, and 70% Asian. There are fewer complaints of Chinese exclusions with the new system. Though some still are not satisfied. It is still described as a race conscious and illegal system by some. The graduating classes of Lowell are more than 600 students. One recent year only two African males graduated, another year three graduated. A major cause of this figure is that there are so few black males entering the school. The applicant pool is extremely low despite various recruiting strategies over the years. It is not a school where blacks or Latinos seek to study. They look for friendlier environments. Many who come regret it.

Many Asian students and their parents dream and work to get here from early ages. The principal, Paul Cheng, is a friend and a capable and clear thinking individual. I have known him for most of my thirty-five years in San Francisco schools. After 16 years at Lowell he becomes head of another struggling school in an impoverished area of the city, where he is a dedicated and effective leader also. He then works in a district outside of San Francisco and is now retired. He is one of the persons whom I was to meet in Shanghai for a school visit. We talked but did not see each other in our China visit.

While at Lowell he states that the intrinsic nature of the school makes it a self-selecting place. Many families know of its reputation as a privileged school. Black, Latino, and other underrepresented groups are discouraged because of this hard and elite reputation. With this acquired status, many students from even privileged groups are dissuaded from applying. The majority of the students are Asian. The principal states that the Asian parents sometimes stereotype black and Latino students as less studious and as trouble-makers.

The number of black students who are eligible to attend Lowell diminishes even more as black students from the outstanding academic middle schools are offered scholarships to private and elite schools. They seldom attend Lowell. There are few others in San Francisco middle schools with the goal or the effort to get there. It is not an issue of how many Chinese or black students who attend Lowell, but rather who is not attending because of artificial barriers of merit, and because of a rigorous academic education received by some individuals and not others. Why should some groups receive a different quality of education regardless of their family background or where they live? Need and merit are issues that are not resolved in our society. The dominant group disregards the poor as meaningless and their talent and voices are excluded.

When Chang-Lin Tien was Chancellor of Berkeley, he started a partnership between UC Berkeley and the San Francisco Unified School District called the Incentive Awards Program. He had a vision for students of the poorest backgrounds to be given profound opportunities. The program is designed to motivate high achieving, economically disadvantaged high school students and provides resources and support to enable them to achieve their highest goals. Each year an outstanding student is selected from each of the district's high schools. The incentive is a scholarship award and other financial aid. Each student is enrolled at UC Berkeley with an individually tailored support program on campus. The Incentive Award Scholars are young people who have overcome financial hardship, language barriers, dysfunctional families, and violent neighborhoods. Some of them are heroes.

The goal is simple: it is that the enrollment of poor and minority students match or approximate their population in society, or their school district. The selection committee has a clear mission. The black population in the San Francisco Unified School District was 16% of the students when the program started. Of the San Francisco graduates attending UC Berkeley, 3%were African American. However, 16% of the 70 Incentive Award students at UC Berkeley are black, and are all on a path to graduation. Also the percentage Latino and Chinese students approximate their enrollment in the district.

Chancellor Tien was committed to the highest quality of education for all students regardless of their family background or where they came from. With a deep social vision, excellence is possible across barriers of race, ethnicity, and culture. There is excellence in all groups. How exclusive are the schools and societies that we contrive? How inclusive of others are our expectations?

When I was head of high schools we would have meetings in various communities for parents and students who were entering San Francisco high schools. The representatives for Lowell, when talking about the school, would always have to meet in the auditorium or the cafeteria, because sometimes five hundred people would be there to hear about the school. There was always so much curiosity and fascination about the place. Some children work hard for many years, and seek to be a part of an alumni that includes ambassadors, authors, Rhode Scholars, scientists, a US Supreme Court Justice, Nobel Prize Winners, college presidents, and others.

The atmosphere at Lowell has been described as being in a pressure cooker. Many students work so hard to get there, and then their goals of going on and doing well continues to drive many of them. There are more than 2500 students attending the school. The largest single group of students is Chinese females. They make up 24% of the student body. The second largest group is Chinese males who make up 18% of the students. The third largest group is White females who make up 9% of the students. The fact that there are only two African American males who graduate in some recent classes of more than 600 students is insignificant to the school, and the city of San Francisco. Another year, only 2 females and 9 males graduated. Nobody seems to respond.

It is not unlike those blacks that populate the prisons, and is similar to the blacks who are displaced from public housing in San Francisco. They are quietly forgotten and eliminated from the city, and life goes on. As dominant as the Chinese students are at Lowell and other San Francisco schools what is the resultant effect? A Chinese parent who is also a Lowell graduate told me that as successful as the Chinese are at the school they still have no impact on the life of the city. A White teacher at the school disagrees with him and he challenges her to name a prominent Chinese Lowell graduate in an influential position in San Francisco. The one person she names is her dentist, which he says proves his point. What he is referring to are Chinese in leadership positions. It has not yet happened he concludes.

Many students thrive at Lowell, but the intense competitive academic nature of the school makes it an unhealthy and stressful place for many other students. There is also opposition to Lowell and its elitism and special privilege in having the most academically successful students educated separate from others. However, there still remains the demand for more schools like Lowell. Why is there the perceived need for more schools like Lowell in the city?

I have a colleague who is black and who has been a teacher at Lowell for twenty years. He has seen the stress, horror, failure, and disaster in the lives of students of all races, cultures and background. He has observed and interacted with countless students, parents, and teachers. He has also seen the achievement and academic excellence. He is not married and he has no children. I ask him if he had children would he send them to Lowell. His answer is yes. He is very certain that he would. He says that it is because of the academic challenge and rigor that each student in the school must face. This to him makes the school a worthwhile journey for the students. It is unfortunate that all of the San Francisco schools do not deeply challenge all of its students.

My first years of teaching in Nigeria showed me much about life and those who are serious about learning. It was in a poor village, Ijero, where the average person made less than $100 a year. I once gave a young child a three pence (3 cents) coin and told her to buy me bananas in the marketplace. She brought me back 50 bananas. It was a farming town in the rain forest and no one was really materially rich. The students were dedicated to learning. It was such a privilege for them to be in school. There were rigorous national standards that they studied for. There was no electricity and no running water. They studied into the night with light from kerosene lamps. They were that deeply engaged. The thing I learned about those who are serious about learning is that certain things are occurring.

(1) Good teaching. It is good to have teachers who love their subjects and pursue them in depth. Good teaching is also teaching oneself. It is important to make one's own mistakes as well as to learn things in more than one way. Classes in Africa sometimes have no teachers and students must still take the same national examinations regardless.

(2) Rigorous and challenging work. I was a mathematics teacher and every student in the country took algebra and geometry. Some also took calculus. There were no remedial classes. All worked hard to master the toughest courses.

(3) Being around other motivated people. It is intrinsically meaningful to observe and to be a part of the mastery that others can reach in their work.

These three things were true in the African village and they are also true at Lowell high school.

I have also worked with poor black students in San Francisco who have done well in school. Last year I interviewed several students from San Francisco schools who were studying at the University of California at Berkeley. Some had lived in public housing and had excelled in school. They had lived amazing lives to have made it from the projects to UC Berkeley. They had scholarships and were struggling to complete their studies. I asked each one of them what they would do differently if they were in high school again. They all communicated a common mistake they had made. They had sometimes worked hard in school, but each said that they would have taken tougher courses, because they are in classes with students who have excelled in such classes.

Many students in school have a fascinating educational journey. As a teacher at Mission High School I saw Chinese, black, Filipino, Latino, white, Vietnamese, and others who had brilliant academic school experiences. They respected each other's minds and energy, and each made his or her contribution to learning. Some went away to the great universities, and many stayed close to home. Some are still around. Some students left to attend Stanford and Berkeley. This was important because it demonstrated that students from any San Francisco High School could attend the strongest universities. It showed that it was not necessary to graduate from Lowell to be ready to continue in a life of educating oneself. They leave the San Francisco schools to go places with glorious histories and reputations and sometimes an exciting present.

Matters of Race

What about race? We all have thoughts and experiences with race. Some say that race has little scientific or technical significance, because there is less of a genetic difference between a black person and a white person than there is between a tall person and a short person. I read an article in a San Francisco newspaper that states cells in the human body each have 100,000 genes but only about six control skin color. It stated that human height is affected by dozens of genes. We all have these six genes and each one of us can possibly produce skin as black as an African native. Melanin is the substance that gives color to our skin and protects us from sunlight. Pure melanin is like charcoal dust, but we can produce it in various shades of brown, yellow, and red. Our genes control the way melanin mixes. Some of humankind left Africa and moved into other environments where the skin needed less protection from the sun and the skin grew lighter. They never lost their genes for dark skin color; it can be activated by prolonged exposure to the sun. Race is a concept by some in society where variation in skin color goes further than our human appearance but there are no genetic differences among humans to establish a division by "races". For some the genetic evidence of race is not important but instead it is a social view used to justify exploitation and oppression of others.

Argentina.

As a seaman I sailed to Buenos Aires, Argentina. I often walked the streets alone. It had seemed a more affluent place than Rio, or Santos in Brazil, or Montevideo across the Rio de la Plata in Uruguay. I had wandered through each of those places and was hardly noticed. Everywhere I went in Buenos Aires I stood out. I was a black person, and many people seemed to wonder about my being there. They were confused as to where I was from. "Brasilero," many would say, thinking that I was from Brazil. No one bothered me. I was alone and not a threat. I become accustomed to being there. Many had not seen a black person, and were curious about my presence. It did not bother me, because I was unusual to them. It was the same when I lived in Nigeria and I would appear with a white person in a village. The Nigerians would shout, "Oyinbo," which is Yoruba for white person. Most of the whites got used to Africans seeing white people for the first time, and their acknowledgment of this event.

One American never got over it, and could hardly leave his home. Eventually he left the country. The person had assumed negative things in constantly being called a white person everywhere he went. He came to Africa as a free soul walking in a white skin, but his thoughts imprisoned him in every step he made.

For the others who got over it, they understood the unusual encounter of being a white person in black Africa and were able to move through it. They did not dwell on being different from others. I did not know how the Argentineans saw black people as a group. In Nigeria, did the American who left assume that Africans saw him as a foreigner, an outsider whom they would always doubt, or did he feel as though he could not accept and live with them? We deepen our lives when being among a different group or race does not personally diminish us, when we do not allow another person's image of us to imprison or lessen us. As a teacher in the Nigerian school I was just as black as they were, but I was still very unusual to them because I was a black American and of another culture, background, and social world.

I learned a lot from teaching and being in Africa and observing and living with others there. Observation as an outsider is not enough to understand the life of others. We must become one with them. There were joys and struggles in the village and school life. I made occasional visits to a home or a farm. They deepen my life.

And if one's race has no scientific or genetic basis what is its origin and cause of racial prejudice? It comes from human thought and invention. The mind is conditioned to see the world through thoughts which arise from such things as our backgrounds, cultures, and social practices, and do not free us. One who is free lives in the world without any conditioning. Race may be a non-issue and unreal human event to some but racism is real and matters in day-to-day life. Some tell of how America has progressed to a place where race does not matter, but it is important that we learn about life for ourselves.

One day I have a conversation with a Chinese woman who is obsessive about no Chinese student being excluded from Lowell because of race. Her passion is undeniable. I told her that the district is under a federal court order to desegregate its schools. She opposes the court order. School desegregation is hard because it challenges the highest American idea of justice and fairness against the direct self interest of the individual citizen. She cannot accept when qualified Chinese students are denied admissions to Lowell. I tell her that the school district was sued because of the black students living in Hunters Point attending all black schools with the least resources in the district. I ask why should the wealthiest, and most able students have the greatest privileges in a public school. Why should this greed dominate the lives of others? Was San Francisco capable of stopping this inequality without the presence of the court? I ask her if she advocated that we return to the situation of all black students in poverty attending only Hunters Point schools. She said that it would not happen in San Francisco because the city and Board of Education were too sophisticated.

I know she is very passionate and no one can question her determination. I express that I do not accept the existence of any school that can justify a second-class education for those who are marginalized. Why are they forgotten?

The truth was that the court had provided greater depth to the issue than the city, the state or the school district had done. The problem is more profound than the inequality in resources. For generations San Francisco sustained a state and condition of poverty and isolation amongst black people; it was maintained by the self serving interests of others, as well our own powerlessness.

I spoke to another Chinese woman who questioned the existence of a Lowell High School and how the stress there had a very devastating effect on a close relative who had been such a bright and excellent student before attending the school.

Freedom implies order. There is no freedom at Lowell. We say there is order but the student stress means there are contradictions in the lives of the students, teachers, and parents. Students are in intense competition with others and there is much struggle to out achieve others. There are tragedies and also suicides. We accept this disorder as order.

Her greatest complaint, though, is not that blacks and Latinos are under-represented, but no one advocates for the Chinese who are poor, and who are not the model minority students. No one advocates for the Cambodians, Laotians, and Hmong who are poor, and live in the downtown slums, and who face such hard language barriers, and the opportunity to complete school. She feels that the rich and middle class Chinese have Lowell and many other educational opportunities in San Francisco.

Of the 2500 students attending Lowell one year, only fifty were from public housing. Seventeen of the group was black, and they represented the largest ethnic group from public housing. The black students are amongst the poorest in the city, but there are always those who achieve at any of the schools. They are sometimes few.

It is important that all students in San Francisco have a demanding education, the rich and the poor and all ethnic groups. From its early days San Francisco schools excluded Negroes, Mongolians, Indians, and non whites. All groups have struggled for an education. Too often we settle for mediocrity in our schools. As long as we have schools of the privileged there will be conflicts. Opposition and argument will continue to exist because the rich and successful cannot sustain their achievement and accumulated material possessions indefinitely.

How can the rich and the successful feel proud? Because their way of life is as it is the poor lives as it does. Corporate greed and violence breeds street greed and violence. No one can claim this world, as it exists, is not our responsibility. The poor are the way they are because of the way the non-poor live. Each one helps create the other. The rich and the poor are words and thoughts that imprison us. We are all responsible for everything in our world. Looking deep within ourselves we are connected to all children and we share their suffering and pain in the world. When the poor and the uneducated understand their connection to all others, and that they are exploited by others in the world this truth frees them.

One year I attended a Lowell graduation. Much academic achievement is acknowledged and recognized. There are articulate and reflective speeches and students are commended for their past excellence and their bright futures. Many of the students have received the highest possible grade point averages, and a large number are accepted to prestigious universities. Many would be attending the University of California at Berkeley. Everyone seems so positive that this day has arrived; it is a marvelous event to add to the glorious history of the school. The graduation is at the Civic Auditorium in downtown San Francisco. The principal commends the students. He then tells them that there is only one thing missing. He tells the students that they have made their families and the school proud of them, and have made excellent speeches but that no one has spoken of the homeless and the poor who are just outside the doors and across the street in the civic center park. I wonder how many people understand what he is saying and are capable of living a more profound life.

Society as we know it is based on competition, greed, and envy in a aggressive pursuit of one's own fulfillment and achievement. We live in a society in disorder as there is not a fundamental transformation of the human mind.

There is probably less compassion for the poor at Lowell than at the other schools. There are those who say there is bias against whites and Chinese in our society and pursue this as an issue instead. They say they are sure most people would prefer to rise or fall on their own merits rather than depend on discredited social programs or a racial advantage to fulfill their aspirations.

In a school there are various types of students. One group is self-motivated, empowered, and transcends the school and the education system. Nothing can stop them from learning. Their revolution in learning comes as they are able to take life as it is and not have it imposed on them by government, society, and others.

Another group of students is driven by the merit system that is one of grades, awards, recognition and other external rewards that they compete to achieve. Schools perpetuate this conformity of merit and mediocrity with the professional masses of persons who are scientists, doctors, lawyers, engineers, government workers, and school teachers. They are imprisoned hostages to luxury, position, and title that give them security and governance which merit brings and protects their self-interest.

A third group of students have little self-motivation in being in school, and does not compete for knowledge or academic status. The school system justifies rewards and merit that causes this group to be sorted into a lower class education. Such students internalize failure as an individual, and are often unaware of a social problem that is self-perpetuating their condition.

Still the Lowell students are not to be disliked for a school that society has created or has allowed to exist. Lowell is not an isolated case. There are regular and alternative elementary and middle schools in San Francisco in which students are acculturated for the Lowell experience of being in an elite place with special privileges. For most of the students their state of mind accompanies them from the day they enter Lowell. They are conditioned to conform to this system of perceived privilege and superiority as well as the momentum to sustain it. From Lowell students go on to elite and private universities as Stanford and to prestigious places such as the University of California at Berkeley. From there they become scientists, lawyers, judges, and professors and continue in this life. They live in places so that their children can attend schools that know only this system of privilege, and education in which they themselves have existed. The scientist in the laboratory inquires by searching, looking, asking questions, and doubting all things. Outside the laboratory he is like anybody else. He ceases such inquiry and does not look deeply into things such as the existence of serious schools of learning for all students.

Why trash schools or demean and denigrate individuals, but see them as having energy to transform and to educate themselves and others. Why cannot all schools have a vision of doing the best they can for themselves, the students, their families and the community outside of the school?

People pursue goals and dreams because they feel that they can achieve what is valuable to them. Few poor and black students who value learning go to Lowell.

Lowell students have interesting lives also. Many are exploring, curious and inquisitive, talented and enjoy a life of learning. Some, though, use their knowledge and ability to figure out how to get an A and not spend their time thinking, exploring, and accepting whatever grade that their work may bring them. They are not lazy or unmotivated, but push themselves to get good grades and they become programmed and conditioned to this life which is hard to change. To get into the school means that they are winners of a system. Why would they want to change it? All have gotten high grade point averages and high scores on standardized tests. They have memorized and studied many things which have enabled them to succeed in the school system. They have learned to get along in a world with a point of view that they understand and are literate in, and they do not challenge or disagree with it. They accept this world and conform to it. Few poor and black students enter this privileged world, some because of how they feel it will judge and devalue them. They refuse to struggle to overturn a caste system that they feel is imposed by society.

San Francisco students have their own beliefs that divide them from each other. Their particular view of the world is an idea that lies in the superficial culture they acquire from family, tradition, and environment. The uniqueness of humankind lies in the total freedom from the invented symbols, and abstractions common to all humankind. So one is not free, and not an individual who conforms to traditional images.

Another school in the conference of the top twelve public schools in America was New Trier, just outside of Chicago. The principal was impressive in his knowledge of the school and its community, and he had an awareness of human differences in the real world. About ten years after I met him I read a Time magazine article about the school, and its struggle with students and drugs. Another person was now in charge of the school. The article expressed the problems, and the thinking of students, parents, and school officials. Unlike San Francisco and other urban areas, the students from this mainly white suburban area never confronted a culture of addiction, crack houses, mass police arrest, or hopeless despair. Almost all the students look to become successful in life just as their parents have. Those who do use drugs will still have unbounded opportunity. Probably more so than at Lowell, New Trier's graduates will go on to other elite institutions. They will become the same scientists, engineers, doctors, lawyers, and corporate directors who live in the community because of the excellent school system. The school student profile was 85% white, 12% Asian, 2% Hispanic, and 1% African American.

Their concern is for those students who get started on drugs, and are unable to stop. It is a problem the school is not able to solve. Many of the students will have a substance abuse problem all of their lives. It will be from a problem greater than drugs. It is an inability to deal with life in a society that tries to solve the drug problem by criminalizing it. The police report that many of the students are not deterred or frightened by the law. They say that they love to see the police car drive up and that having a record is seen as something to brag about. There are parents who do not care that the students try drugs or those who fail at trying to stop them. How then can the school solve the problem?

School officials say that the school should address this problem, but the students do not learn to do drugs at the school, and they hardly do drugs at the school. The article tells of how real dysfunction is in tranquil suburbs, and how students cannot manage their lives, and will do things like sell pot in the boy's room and not buy books for school. Some are sent to out of state treatment centers, but a week after returning are using again. The students are like other students in that they rebel by choosing immediate pleasure over conventional restraint. Though fortunate and well off, some select a path of self-destruction. The article said that the parents were unable to turn their outrage about drugs into a clear and compelling message. They become powerless to act effectively. How does one reverse failing schools or shattered lives? The goal is not for outside forces to change schools or individuals, but to help them learn by allowing them to see things that are true and profound in their lives. Let them change their own behavior.

The human condition that we encounter in the world is as real at New Trier or Lowell as in the schools of poor communities. The tragedy is how society acts to control and to perpetuate downtrodden classes of people, who are everywhere. A deeper societal dilemma is that no student from New Trier has been convicted of a drug felony in recent memory. The community provides the strongest legal defense for those accused and there are judges who live in the community. It is reported that they will explore every avenue before sending a suburban youth to Cook County jail. It is not that slavery, discrimination, and segregation are acts that are the fault of students now at New Trier or Lowell, but still they benefit from them. How deeply do they understand that the freedom of some is dependent on the bondage of others? In San Francisco those who are poor and economically dependent on society are usually socially and educationally subservient, which excludes them from excellent schools and from participating in a serious learning society.

It is interesting that Lowell is known as a place where serious learning occurs. Nothing seems to change as it maintains its image. One year the principal has a spirited discussion with me about how much more significant the school would be if it stood for the spirit for whom it is named. The school's publication states that its name became official in 1894 in honor of James Russell Lowell. He is described as a distinguished American poet, educator, diplomat, and abolitionist. The abolitionists were individuals who tirelessly opposed slavery and brought about its abolishment so that all citizens have full rights and are well educated.

If one is not free from the conditioning of schools maintaining the inequities of society, then he accepts the prison, and lives in it with conflict and misery, and a life where hatred may be practiced and where violence is accepted. A society is in disorder when there is no fundamental transformation of the human mind. A strong and clear mind demands freedom for itself and for others.

# 24

# METROPOLITAN HIGH SCHOOL

Of the four high schools in the school review process only one graduated. I call it Metropolitan High School. It had a new principal who was successful at a San Francisco middle school. He came into the school with a running start. His first year there Metropolitan High School was selected for the Review Process. The school was also scheduled for an accreditation visitation by the Western Association of Schools and Colleges. Many advised that the school make a special request to postpone the accreditation process. However, the school decided to face both the school review and accreditation process, and that it had the energy to do so. I had visited the school in the beginning with the new principal. It was a troubled school with some students who were tough, undisciplined, and indifferent to learning.

The school facility was the newest of the San Francisco high schools, but the bathrooms and hallways were filled with graffiti. I walked around the entire campus with the principal the summer before the school started. He decided that a number of things were needed to dramatically change the facility. The first thing was to remove all graffiti throughout the campus, and inside the building. The school covered about 15 acres. The painters started to paint over the graffiti inside the building. They were soon stopped. It was pointed out to them that they were covering up places that had been defaced, but it still looked like a ghetto school. The whole wall would have to be painted. It transformed the building and when the students returned to school it looked like a new place.

I remember walking through the school with the principal on the first day. A school is always exciting when it begins the new school year. No one is burdened with the thought of 180 days that are to be endured and dealt with. There are the great hopes and expectation for successful times. No one gives serious attention to renewing and sustaining the energy of the first day, and keeping it going each day of the year. Perhaps one of the things the school did in a serious way was to keep its walls graffiti free throughout the school year. The principal and the staff were that dedicated to maintaining a school that was totally clean throughout. It impacted the life of the school.

On the first day I walked around the school with the principal there were students with hats and radios. The school rules were no hats or radios. The new principal told students to take off their hats and most cooperated. Some of them knew him as the new principal, George Sloan. Many of the students seemed happy to be among their friends, but there was not a rush to get to classes. He asked an African American male student to take off his hat; he ignored him and quickly walked away uttering that was not the way things were run at the school. He did not choose to talk about it, even though the principal asked him to stop and wanted to talk to him. He hurried away determined to do what he wanted to do. We did not chase after him.

We continued to walk around the building and the principal saw a number of students who had attended the middle school where he had worked. So he knew a number of the students and that helped. Students respond when you know them, and are able to engage them in a conversation which furthers their meaning of being in school. This first day said a lot about how the school was changing. The school is profoundly clean which communicates seriousness to everyone. The principal is visible. The students see this and the school staff realizes it.

Several years ago I remember a different San Francisco principal who went into a troubled San Francisco high school. He also had an immediate impact. He had been a successful middle school principal, and so he too had come with something to offer the students, staff, parents, and community. I remember walking around the school with him just as I am now at Metropolitan High School. He knew students by their names and spoke with teachers and made it a point to introduce me to those whom he met. He was totally involved in interacting with everyone in the school and had a meaningful presence. He had a natural style with people. He became a successful principal for 11 years at the school and he had made an impact at the school from the very beginning. He brought a presence. He loved the school. He supported the students and the teachers and he gave attention to the community. There were 2700 students at the school so there was sometimes fighting and violence, but it was dealt with. The principal worked hard at solving hard problems. He was open and straightforward and resolved issues without aggression and force. There was also academic achievement in the school. Capable students and teachers were able to flourish in their work.

The Metropolitan High School principal is similar, but different. He is good in working with people, but he sometimes solves problems with more confrontation. During summer school an incident had been referred to him about an African American male student who was accused of cheating on a science test and of taking the teacher's grade book. He was also an athlete on the basketball team. The principal investigated by talking to the teacher, other students, and the accused student. The accused student was deeply angered that he was accused of cheating and taking the teacher's grade book. He denied everything and was outraged at how he was being treated. The principal told him that he had investigated the situation, and that he was probably not going to allow him to stay at the school. The student was furious and stormed out of the office.

The principal learned that the student was on the basketball team, but had an attitude. He was used to getting away with incidents with no consequences. His mother strongly stood behind him in coming to the school, and fought for his cause. She had always been effective in her struggle to keep him in school. This time it was different as the new principal told her that he was not allowing her son to remain as a student in the school. She and her son both were shocked. She argued about their rights and the principal told her that he had investigated the incident, thought that her son was lying as he had spoken with other students and the teacher. There would be a hearing and they would be allowed to present their case and a recommendation would be made.

At the hearing the case was reviewed, as well as his record as a student at the school, which was disastrous. He was assigned to another school. The mother fought as hard as she could for her son, but in the end she knew that he had to become more serious about his life and she told him that. That incident had been dealt with before the school term started and it had an impact on the school as the principal had communicated the serious action he would take in running an effective school. He has a strong physical attitude as he runs regularly along the city streets and hills, as well as a strong mental attitude for the job as he seriously studies and learns all of the school programs.

As we continue in our walk around the campus we encounter the student who had run away when he was told to take his hat off. We had unexpectedly come upon him and he froze in surprise in seeing us. He told us his name. I told him that this was the principal, and that students were not allowed to wear hats in the building. He still had his hat on. We were outside. After realizing this was the new principal and the new hat rule, he took off the hat and walked away. The principal told him to stop. He did. He told the principal that he had taken his hat off and wondered what the problem was. The principal told him that things were changing at the school, and that he did not like his attitude. The student was anxious to leave as we seemed to be wasting his time over an unimportant matter. He did not know why he was being held up, and wanted to walk off as he had before. The principal was in no hurry and he told him that he was in charge of the school, and did not know if a person with such an attitude should be attending the school. The student was shocked, and could not believe there was a discussion about his staying at the school. He was still anxious to leave and continue his activity.

The principal told him that we were going to the counseling office. We got there and looked up his record. He was in the eleventh grade, a good student, and a member of the track team. He said that he had sores on his head, and had worn the hat to cover them up. In the end they communicated more clearly with each other, and there were never any other problems with this student. I would see him from time to time, and always with a positive attitude.

The school was filled with students from many different backgrounds. The two largest groups were Latino and black. There were other San Francisco groups including Ethiopian, Samoan, Arabic, Russian, Asian, American Indian and white. Most of the groups generally got along well together. The school also had the largest percent of public housing students of any high school. The school seriously accepted this as a challenge, and worked hard for an environment where all students learn.

During the school year there were many fights initially, but the principal and security aides worked hard in following up on all incidents and taking action. There is a definite strategy of confrontation and follow-up. The cooperation of the school car police team and the school staff persevered, and did stop the fighting.

Other problems were with handling gangs and the students who were members, or influenced by them. I worked with the gang task force on a number of cases and was impressed with the community of people who had skills to communicate with, and deal with struggles and hard times that could happen. Often the high schools are overextended in trying to handle gang related problems. I have seen a number of incidents that impacted the entire school. The schools struggle to stop violence, death, anger, and hate. Sometimes this was the action of just a few students. I think that at Metropolitan High School they did as good a job as any school. The students most affected by gang related activities were the Latinos.

The school staff kept a clean school. The school remained clean and graffiti free throughout. Any graffiti was immediately removed without exception. Students would often try to wear the color of their gang. All students were told that Metropolitan High School was not a "red" school or a "blue" school. The administration would deal with the students immediately letting them know that they were at the school to be students not gang members. Students either were sent home, or had to remove their colors. There was no tolerance of any gang display or activity.

There were almost no gang task force resources brought into the school. It was handled internally by monitoring each student following the school expectations. In the end one discovers an interesting thing about schools: if you do what you say you are going to do it is a miracle. When the school said no hats, it meant no hats. No gang expression in the school meant no gang tolerance. None. After the first year the school did the things it said it would and there were quiet miracles.

Schools are like students in a lot of ways. Very seldom is a student poor in every subject. There is usually some subject or area that a person is interested in, and is capable of performing well. The same holds for schools. There are some activities that a school does well with. At one time there was an Arts School which was a part of Metropolitan High School. Almost 60% of the students were white, but it did not violate the court desegregation order, as they were counted as part of the total Metropolitan High School student body. The students did well academically and attended prestigious colleges. Eventually the Board of Education and the new Superintendent Rojas agreed to give the school its own site and separate facility. Some of the Metropolitan High School staff had been glad for them to leave as the program seemed separate and apart from the school. The school flourished at its new site as it became desegregated and offered a rigorous academic program to all students.

In the first year of the Arts school I remember a white parent upset because she was not able to get her child into the school. I told her about the district goal to limit the number of white or any other concentrated ethnic group of students at the school. She was upset because she had struggled in the sixties for the civil rights of blacks, and was angry that her daughter was now being denied admissions to a good school. It is the outside world that determines good schools. There are the good schools and the remainder schools, or those that are attended by many who are unable or are unacceptable to go to the good schools. My response to her was first that she should not give up if it meant that much to her and her daughter. I then asked her if she wanted her daughter to attend a school that gave poor students and non-white students the opportunity to attend a good school, and she said that she did. I told her that all students were valued and the district's goal is to help every student that we can attend a school without exclusion when possible. I told her that it was possible for her daughter to attend the school but for it to occur we had to enroll two non-white students for each white student. That goal was achieved and just about all the white students who were on the waiting list did get admitted.

Today students across all ethnicities are performing well. Recently two Arts School black female students from public housing received full scholarships to UC Berkeley and are doing well there. I have spoken with them on several occasions. At the school the arts have an impact on academic achievement as they are processing what they learn. Their mission is to provide a balance between process and product. One day I attended an Arts School dance class and I am amazed at energy, effort, and exuberance that drive the students for an hour and a half. It is profound. They take their academics in the morning and dance in the afternoons while most other San Francisco students study six hours a day in factory settings in their seats for much of the day. Just as the students in the San Francisco Ballet, they are so engrossed in the dance that the academic course work seems hardly an obstacle to them. It is for this reason that several members of the Board of Education want all San Francisco students to participate in the Arts.

At Metropolitan High School there are several programs that are unique to the school and make it a different place as a school. These programs are Alta and Urban Pioneers. Traditionally they operate as isolated programs in many ways, with limited interaction with other school programs. It seemed intentional, and it was sometimes brought on by the school administration. The new principal made it clear that he accepted these as programs with serious approaches to learning, but he communicated that it was just as important that the students in them are no more privileged than any other students, and that they should work to have a deeper impact on the entire school. This had an effect on them and the programs.

The Alta program is described by its director, Audrey Hallum, as a small humanities program which approaches learning in an interdisciplinary and production oriented manner, where students Explore—Discover—and Create. It is said to more readily fulfill the psychological and intellectual needs of certain types of learners who achieve better in a personalized and student-centered environment. The program has existed for more than twenty years, and students who participate in the program demonstrate significant academic achievement as they understand and articulate different points of view, interact well and cooperate with others, participate in self-discipline in artistic and intellectual pursuits, and take increasing responsibility for their own education. The time I spent with the program the students in it had a mission to impact the school. They changed the school and created an interest in the greater society.

They moved a San Francisco newspaper reporter to investigate their work and to write about the project that came into being called SPAM. These are the Students for Positive Action at Metropolitan High School (SPAM), and they're busy living what they are learning. They are 30 or 40 students, and no one knows the exact number and no one is counting. It is an outgrowth of the Alta program. They have a rebellious spirit. They learn that the world changes when they change. They are cleaning the campus, and leaving trash bags around the school. Some laugh at the effort and pull down and destroy the bags, but the group is relentless in its mission. The school changes with their cleaning up the campus and the building, bringing in plants, sorting items for the homeless, soliciting contributions, and writing letters to businesses and individuals to donate goods and money. They write letters of thanks to those who donate. They work with government agencies and community organizations.

"If we don't change the world, who will?" some of the signs ask.

One year there was a sting operation at four San Francisco high schools by the police department. Superintendent Rojas had suspected that the mayor had set up this operation to make him and the district look bad, as the two of them had disagreed on a number of issues. One issue had to do with the superintendent allowing a drug felon to do community service hours in the school district. I will refer to him as John Thomas. There was a newspaper and television story that questioned the school district's role in the matter. The superintendent says that it is gives John an opportunity to be a contributing member of society. I personally worked with him, and supervised his community service hours. John Thomas is determined, spirited, and conscientious about the work in the community, from projects with recycled computers and technology to the neighborhood organizing of public housing residents, and working with jail and prison reform. He is diligent in his work. I meet his wife and children and I am impressed with their support for each other.

Periodically, I meet with his probation officer who had attended another high school in San Francisco. John also attended high school in San Francisco but had dropped out of school. After the community service hours had been completed, I met a police officer whose sister is a teacher in the San Francisco schools, and is a friend of the family. He is a commander in the police department and tells me how extensive John Thomas and his operation had been with the sale of drugs in the Mission District. He says that the Thomas family was doing a multi-million dollar operation and how they had operated out of the neighborhood. I asked him what he thought happened to the money. He did not know but he tells me that a house may have been bought for a family member, but the main priority is to have enough money available to hire an attorney.

This seemed to be what may have happened in the Thomas case as I had met his attorney on several occasions. He had a nice office in a fashionable area of the city. He seemed competent and capable in representing his client's interests. In the end it had been an interesting time working with this case. All 1,000 hours of community service hours were accounted for, and we all moved on. I did see John Thomas at his child's elementary school promotion exercise. He and his wife are proud and supportive of her schooling. They celebrate as she leaves elementary school for middle school.

During the sting operation, two twenty-three-year-old female policewomen posed as students, and mingled with them at the high schools for over ten weeks. In the end sixteen high school students were arrested for selling drugs. It was thought that the drug problem in the schools was far worse than what was exposed which had surprised the police department. Six of those arrested were from Metropolitan High School. In the end, the police department said it was delighted at the job most of the schools were doing. However, the school department stated that it was dismayed by the arrests, but was pleased that out of the 20,000 high school students, only sixteen were caught breaking the law. Those arrested faced possible sentences from probation to incarceration time.

The newspaper report made heroines of the police officers, and societal outcasts of the arrested students. That was the voice of the media, but what of the voice of the students, that went unpublicized, and who were friends of the six students who had been arrested by the police?

The principal and I met with a group of students from the Alta program who were angered with how the two police women had been assigned to the school, and worked in the arrest of six students attending the school. They were told to express their feelings in writing. They did:

> As students of Metropolitan High School, we never felt a threat to our safety or well being on any type of large level. The fact that we, as students, as people, who have been watched and video recorded over the last three months enrages us. We have also learned that school officials had no idea as to the "sting" going down at the school. Imagine . . . a principal unaware of hidden cameras videotaping his students' every move. We have been taught in our classes (yes, we do go to school), that the government and legal system has a responsibility of gaining information in a reasonable, humane and fair way. This leads us to believe that we need to take a closer look at the way things are done in our city police force.
>
> We have watched our peers go down in the last few days, and have been a witness to some of the deals that landed our peers in jail. We have seen the way the "new girls" badgered our peers relentlessly for the small amount of drugs they possessed. We have overheard our peers tell the officers that they did not sell and have no intention to, dozens of times. Finally only after being pressured and harassed by these girls for three months did a few of our peers break down and do a deal with them as a favor for a "supposed friend." We understand that is not something they should have done. We are sure they do too. Another thing we are sure about is that it never would have happen if the officers hadn't ruthlessly badgered these young people. After three long months of listening to them beg and plead, you finally gain the mentality that if you get them what they want they will finally leave you alone. What we are trying to express is that these officers did not *find* drug dealers; they turned average

kids into people willing to sell. We also witnessed them smoking marijuana and supplying minors with cigarettes on school campus.

What they did was a legal term called entrapment which basically means that the drug deals that happened would not have happened if the "new girls" had just left them alone and not so fervently pushed them into a situation that they felt they had no way of avoiding. That is what happened here at this school. Probably a lot of other schools too. Our peers had no intention to sell to them in the beginning and were finally after months persuaded to do so. That is emotionally dishonest and a betrayal of young people.

We have also seen news broadcasts showing video footage of us and our peers, who never gave permission to be on camera. Although our faces are still blocked out we are recognizable enough to go down with the students who were arrested and possibly fired from our jobs. This same news broadcast also gave false information stating that this particular group of students is tied to crack-cocaine and heroin use that is untrue.

If people are so worried about a teen population that uses and sells drugs target the harder, larger criminals who are selling the drugs to these children. We personally know a number of the students who were arrested. Kids who are, or were going to school every day. Kids who were on the honor role. College bound kids who were entitled to their civil rights and the right not to be violated by secret hidden cameras recording everything they do.

We completely understand that the acts committed by our peers were wrong and they have to suffer the consequences but, at the same time we feel that our peers have a right to a fair investigation, not an investigation that is inhumane, unjust and unfair. Not to mention the right NOT to be entrapped.

Concerned students from Metropolitan High School

This letter never made it into the newspaper but circulated throughout the school district. I later met and worked with one of the six arrested students.

The other unique program to Metropolitan High School is the Urban Pioneers program. Wayne McDonald, who is an outstanding and a dedicated teacher founded it 25 years ago at the school. It is a semester course that includes a wilderness trip, a community service project, career exploration, natural history, urban gardening and urban resource discovery. I am fascinated to be involved with the staff and students in the program as I also work with the Outward Bound program in San Francisco. At the time it is the Pacific Crest Outward Bound Program (PCOB) located in Oregon with a center in San Francisco. I have participated in the program for the last ten years. It is an adventure education, and outdoor wilderness leadership program which has taken me on a number of wilderness expeditions.

We learn from adventure and the unexpected. I find they provide seriousness to our lives. I understand that the kind of people we are, and the depth of the work we do cannot be separated. In both Outward Bound and the Urban Pioneers program at Metropolitan High School I am able to see and understand the effects of both personal and collective learning. What is so remarkable about work with Outward Bound is that all the staff and members participate in the rigorous outdoor activities. It brings together people with a common mission to complete its expedition and journey. In the Outward Bound expedition, the only measure of success each day was did the group make its destination? Everyone is connected to the outdoors, and the wilderness. That is why it is such a strong program in the school as all the students and teachers have a mission that connects them, and challenges them to live serious lives. It is why the Superintendent so strongly supports the program and has helped to expand the Metropolitan High School program and even wants his own staff to participate in such activities.

The Outward Bound program is now worldwide with thousands of persons participating. It started sixty years ago in England to help British sailors handle World War II wartime stress. Using a wilderness environment, it continues to show life as never fully predictable. The curiosity, discovery learning, and skills one gets on the rocks, ropes, hills, and rivers and streams form one's everyday life. Leadership, cooperation, and rigorous challenge in adventure school programs get us beyond our "old self" that drifts through life, and holding to a known and familiar world. In selfless action, concern for others, and for the earth we change life into a world of compassion and unselfish contribution.

The students and staff of the Alta and Urban Pioneer programs heavily contributed to the Metropolitan High School review presentation. They were major contributors in the school's graduation from the school review process.

After the Review Process graduation, Prince Philip visited the school. He came to visit the Metropolitan High School Urban Pioneer program, because of the work of Wayne McDonald, and the strength of the program. What was fascinating, to me, about the visit were all the questions from students, teachers, and guests as to how to greet and welcome a member of British royalty. I did not know and said as much. America is so grounded in the individual and the ordinary person that extreme behavior for someone of royal prominence seemed questionable and un-American. There was still curiousness about proper protocol.

Prince Philip's motorcade had appeared suddenly. Before entering the building he spoke with an expedition that was leaving the school for the Los Padres National Park for 11 days in the wilderness. I was unable to hear him, but did see how relaxed he was with seeing the students off. The teacher, Les Schlesinger, was very comfortable and serious in talking with him about the students and the expedition. Prince Philip then entered the building.

I was assigned to introduce him to the guests and students. I shook his hand and told him that I worked with the superintendent. He was energetic and waited for whatever was next. I introduced him to the guests, the president of the school board, and to students and teachers. In conversation I could hear that he had mentally assigned all individuals to the correct lines of authority. He knew who reported to whom, and who was whose boss.

The prince, superintendent, and principal spoke and Wayne McDonald was introduced as founder of the Urban Pioneer program. The prince individually congratulated six urban pioneers who received congressional medals for service, wilderness expedition, and fitness. Each came forward to meet the special guest. Prince Philip had warm and personable conversation with each of the individuals. He asked them such questions as their age, whether they had received the bronze, silver or gold medal, and what they were currently doing. His presence was jubilant and authentic. Students asked him if there was gang violence in England and if there was a teen dropout rate. He said that he imagined there was, and that there are certain areas where problems are worse than others. He and his party left, and the school appreciated the attention and energy he brought to the school.

One day I was leaving my house in San Francisco and I unexpectedly met a student whom I had seen several months before. He had recently graduated from Metropolitan High School. We know each other well. We met as a result of the drug sting incident near the Metropolitan High School campus, and subsequent trying circumstances. It had been a very active time at the school as the principal did not allow any of the accused students to return to the school. He informed them that they would each have a hearing and a decision would be made on their future school assignment. I did not expect any of them to be returned to Metropolitan High School. The principal had numerous parent conferences, and was very firm about the serious nature of the charges, and the fairness that must be applied to each student. He therefore anticipated no student returning to the school despite all the pleas from students and parents. The principal was therefore shocked and upset when one of the students involved was told by the school district that he could return as a student to Metropolitan High School.

This student had been a member of the Urban Pioneer program. The principal had been adamant about not accepting his return to the school. It was not fair to the other students the principal said. He had been caught red handed selling drugs. The student was a Latino male and he had convinced the Student Placement Office that he was not directly involved in the drug incident he was accused of, and had been convincing enough to be given another chance at the school. The principal strongly protested, because the student was recorded on video tape in a drug transaction. Perhaps this was told to the principal or he may have even seen it, but that evidence was never produced.

In the end the principal, and I talked to the student. The principal told him that he did not want him to return to the school because of his documented involvement in a drug sale. He denied any direct involvement. The principal told him he did not believe him and told him that he still believed that he was dealing drugs. In looking at his transcript it was determined that he had enough credits to graduate at the end of summer if he passed all of his classes. The principal told the student that he had not been a good student, and questioned whether he was a serious enough student to attend school, and pass his classes.

The student admitted that he'd had a history of failing classes, being absent from school, and staying in trouble until he was accepted in the Urban Pioneer program. It had changed his whole life and he was now a better person and student and knew that he could graduate if given the opportunity. He was very convincing in his appeal for furthering his education at the school. In the end the principal decided to give him the opportunity he requested. I also told him what I expected from him was that he would take advantage of the chance given him, and that he be as serious a student as he is capable of being. We talked about other things, but I found that he was already totally serious about his life.

I would tell a student who had problems and wanted to turn things around that coming to school every day and on time it could change his life. It never lasted. In every case it had been my goal and expectation. It was abstract and second hand to the student. But in this case the student understood and internalized the situation. It was beyond preparing for something that wasn't there, but accepting the new life he had been given.

This student is serious about doing the things that are within him to do. He does not seem to be searching for goals outside of himself. It is very amazing because from that moment on he is a model student. He does all of his work and is genuinely grateful to be at the school, and impresses his teachers. He graduates as he is scheduled to do and after he graduates I continue to see him. He is working as a tutor in a community program with young black youth. His entire life had changed from the drug incident and he is now a contributing member of society and is connecting to a world larger than himself. The day I see him just outside of my house he is still a serious person. He eagerly tells me that he was attending college and that his grade point average is an A-. He still says that it was the incident at Metropolitan High School, the Urban Pioneer wilderness program, and the seriousness of those around him that transformed his life. His own self-discovery propelled him.

Over the years I have found students and their connection to the outdoors have given them opportunities to discover fundamental things about life and themselves. Wayne McDonald, the program founder and director, invites me to a congressional award presentation for students in their outdoor participation and community service. I meet fourteen such students who are awarded. One student in the program has an inquisitive and enthusiastic presence. One day I was in Northern California and we were just descending Mt. Shasta during an Outward Bound expedition and I meet him again. I had been on a spirited team that had pushed to the summit but I was weak from the descent and heard someone call my name from a distance. How strange it was that some one would be out here who knew me. When we met, after walking in the thick snow where he is calling from, I recognized it was David Ibarra, a Metropolitan High School student who was working with a mountain climbing group. He is glad to see me. He talks about the school system and the education of its students. I tell him how surprised I am to see him and how great it is to meet him working in this mountain world. David moved on from San Francisco to the Outward Bound Program in New York City. From Wayne McDonald and others I find out he died on the road from a disease caused by an insect bite.

Outward Bound

Outward Bound is an outdoor wilderness leadership program. It is a way of getting into nature where we are confronted with natural phenomena. We learn about ourselves and to cooperate with those on the same journey that we face together. As ordinary individuals we find out what moves us to challenging adventure. In such adventure we face struggle, are empowered, and feel truly alive. From all walks of life we learn the splendor and significance of the natural world.

There were many programs, teachers, parents, and students full of energy and enthusiasm at Metropolitan High School which all were contributing factors in the school's graduation from the school Review Process. The school was proud of the only high school to do so.

Metropolitan High School was closed six years later. Urban Pioneers became a charter school. It too was closed when two students were killed in Los Padres National Park during a school wilderness expedition.

# 25

# HOMELESS

The city of San Francisco, as well as the schools in their plans for reform for the poor, often uses social control. The poor people are vocal and persistent in a struggle for justice, and not control.

In the daily life of a homeless person, society often finds him out of place. Life is hard because of the disorder they live in and encounter. Order is important in life because it is so hard living in chaos. A homeless person is often in the wrong place in a city setting.

To those in the business community—which includes such persons as the owners, managers, and investors—the presence of the homeless impacts their opportunity to make money. Seeing a homeless person around a business is a problem to them and their property. The city uses authority and control to resolve conflicts. For these businesses the homeless person hanging around is a problem.

There are other views of the homeless. Some people, when they see the homeless, understand the dilemma involves issues such as a lack of housing, no accessible health care, not having a living wage job, or an absence of educational pursuit. Most homeless, like a lot of the mentally ill, are not citizens who are engaged meaningfully in society, and do not have their participation and contribution valued.

San Francisco Homeless Project

However homeless persons are viewed, and whatever image there is of them, they enter the city civic center auditorium, and many wonder what awaits them.

In the San Francisco Civic Center, citizens work to help the homeless who come for help. Some have been sleeping outside on the streets and in the parks. It is an incredible event as more than fifteen hundred volunteers work with almost seventeen hundred homeless persons. Enthusiastic and energetic persons come to the city center to volunteer, and to assist the poorest citizens, who are lining up around the block to get clothes, inquire about housing, wheelchair repair, or medical assistance. They come looking for services.

The event is to provide homeless persons with a multitude of services to meet their immediate needs to change their situation. Some lives are more desperate than others. Resources available to them connect them to places such as drug and medical treatment, housing, jobs and employment, legal assistance, and identification cards, along with new clothing, eye examinations, glasses, dental care, and counseling. The volunteers graciously welcome them as they enter the facility. The workers do not know which of the homeless lives are broken, dysfunctional, lonely, or disturbed. Some come enthusiastically. To the homeless these volunteer workers are people who are thought of as sane, conventional, articulate, and independent. They have lived in separate worlds. The volunteers with whom I work are selfless with all persons they encounter. They offer their gratitude, and express an appreciation of everyone's presence. Their past thoughts and experiences vanish as they enter a new world. I see profound human encounters.

The homeless themselves are sometimes shocked at the degree of acceptance they find. Many homeless have no regard for politics, bureaucracies, or government. Several persons I speak to are overwhelmed at coming to a place in the city where they are genuinely welcomed. Nobody is looking over their shoulder, or viewing them with distrust. Some of them deeply appreciate the human encounter as they move through the event. Students I have known, and people I know living on the street add to the energy and power of the event for me. They are pleased to be here, and I am excited to see them receiving services to help their survival.

As the day passes, it is interesting to see how many homeless persons have no idea of what to do once they enter the building. They are told the direction to proceed, and also where the bathrooms and water fountains are when they ask, and many do. One person asks me where the food is. We go to the food area, but his most pressing concern is that I scratch his itching back. I do. I also accompany a lady to the food area. On the way there she sees her husband waiting in line for information about housing. I ask her if she wants to join him and she tells me that she does not think so. As she stands in line for food she says that she can talk to her husband when she needs to. She shows me her cell phone, and lets me know that she can call him and talk with him if it is necessary.

Earlier a guy says that he has been in San Francisco for seventeen years but he has never been in this building before. He seems surprised that he finds himself in this circumstance. He does not seem excited by being here. It is just being here is a new experience that took so many years to happen. When I see him in the food line he has several bags of objects and items he collected. He does say that his day has been all right. He has no complaints. One person I meet after leaving the food line is leaving the building. She has so much to carry that she is unable to manage it all. A taxi is ordered and drives her to a hotel in the Tenderloin where she lives.

Someone asks me if I have seen the police around. I have not. One can wonder about their presence, because they can be harsh and authoritarian. I sometimes question their aggressiveness when they trample and remove street dwellers' belongings, handcuff, and arrest them. Sometimes one needs caution in involving the police in the lives of the homeless. I am told that a person forced himself in, and threatened to hurt those who got in his way. I come upon him in a confrontation with a woman police officer. He is attempting to explain his actions to her. In the end I learn that he has a switchblade knife in his possession, and is taken away by the police. One person has back pain from an irregular heartbeat. No one knows exactly what to do to help him but he gets through the day all right.

There is a black person with a neck brace on. He asks me several times if he needs to show his passport as we walk to the medical treatment area. Once there, he asks about getting a new brace. I ask him where he is from. He tells me Russia. He has a wife and two children there. He says that his name is Latiner, and that it is a Russian name. He says that he lives in a suburb of Moscow. I later try to look up the place but I am unable to recall the name of the city.

Outside on the street corner is a lady begging for money. I give her a quarter. She is very grateful because I am the first person to give her money. She feels that this is what she needs to get her started with collecting more, but no one gives her money as I stand there. One guy walks by in a t-shirt that says Wild Horse Bar and Salon. He does not give her any money. She asks him if the bar is in Washington DC. He tells her, "No," that this place was in Las Vegas. She says she knows a place with the same name in Washington DC. She says that she use to be a dancer there.

I go back inside and I talk to several of the volunteers about school. A second grade teacher tells me she had students sit in rows, such as 2 by 5, so they can practice their multiplication together. An interesting question to me is does every child in the group know that 2 times 5 equals 10? She says they do. Another person says she runs a day care center. I ask her if all the children learn to write their name, count to ten, recite the alphabet, and know their colors. She says they do not. She realizes not all persons can master the things taught to them, and adds that she took algebra four times and only passed it once. She gave me the name of a book that helped her learn it.

Another volunteer is a stay-at-home parent. She has two children and they both attend a Quaker school. The school has kindergarten through third graders. They plan to add grades until they become a kindergarten through eighth grade school. Her two children are in the third grade and kindergarten. She says that the kindergarteners sit in the innermost circle, surrounded by the first graders, then the second graders, and then the third grade students. The kindergarteners are expected to remain quiet and silent for fifteen minutes. They then leave the circle. The third graders the school tries hard for them to have the self-discipline to remain silent for forty-five minutes. I tell her it seems like an interesting and meaningful place for the children. She says that it is worthwhile for her children to engage in such a world.

As I talk to them about school a homeless person asks me if he can get a haircut. I tell him, "No." He says that he wants to make a recommendation that such a service be provided. I learn there are no haircuts because of water sanitation and the possible spread of infection. I tell him that the service is not likely to be provided. By noon some of the persons coming in are hot from standing in the sun. Several of them come in, and take a bottle containing a liquid and spray themselves. I see that the bottle contains a chemical cleansing solution, and move it away from those standing in line. No one is reading the contents of the bottle, only following what they see someone else doing. I see a person who is a heroin addict still waiting in the same location for more than an hour. He tells me that he is unable to seek help from inside the civic center because he is awaiting a fix. He waits for his friend who never comes. He waits and waits then he leaves, unable to function. He never receives help.

One person faints after entering the main service center. She says that there are too many people around her and she has trouble breathing. Few people actually notice her as there is a multitude of people and activity. Someone finds a chair for her to sit down. She says that she is going to be all right. The paramedics come and ask her questions and give her oxygen. This calms her down. I am impressed at how quickly the paramedics arrive, and how focused and deliberate they are in doing their job. They are impressive in that they know what to do, and proceed to assist her to recover. They come with a clear mission, and complete their task and remain with her until the woman is clear headed and is able to participate in the activities. The paramedics stand in readiness if any other event occurs that calls for them.

When I leave the city center building I see a group of homeless people who did not attend the event. A man has a shopping cart filled with his belongings and I hear him talking to those around him. He gives them this insight "Nothing is free."

I am not certain to what he is referring, but I know of a couple at a previous event who are among the first to arrive and receive services. They receive free subsidized housing. They are elated. A week later they are evicted from the hotel, but they both have been bitten by bed bugs and their bodies are infected with sores. I think about what the homeless man says about nothing is free. How fortunate the couple seemed in getting subsidized housing, but how miserable it really makes them.

If society is really concerned about all of its citizens, it creates an environment where we can all participate. It is not one that is dominated by authority. An example in this country is curb cuts or cutouts in sidewalks where people in wheel chairs can navigate city streets. The disabled community, those pushing young children, and all others can use such sidewalk access points. They impact all of us as we move through our lives as participants in society. Unless one is free, he or she cannot explore, investigate, or examine life or the world.

For many of the homeless life is not beyond the day they are in. Night comes and some wander off to huddle in doorways, find shelter beside a building, or somewhere in an alley to sleep. Some are in wheelchairs. Others are sick from not being able satisfy a heroine, or crack habit. They tremble and shake as they face another night alone on the concrete, or a piece of cardboard. Some eat leftovers from other street people. Some have no possessions, and others have overflowing shopping carts. They realize how miserable they are and that nobody cares. While they kill themselves wasting away, those who pass them on the street often feel helpless to do anything.

Another side of homeless life is that everyday some person on the street is hitting rock bottom, and finding a way to recover, and step out of their desperate life. They use what resources are around them, and they transform their life. Each day there are those who refuse to deteriorate further on the street. Every day someone finds it possible to step out of this cycle of drugs, crime, jail, and poverty to another life. Some never give up, and others revolt against the patterns that have sustained and imprisoned them.

Rare is there the energy to stand alone against a system of greed, human disregard, and corruption or to defy a way of life that destroys human respect. A dominant class that lives a materially privileged life while others have nothing is routine in our world. Poverty is real, but what brings the energy of protest or self-sacrifice is the marginalization of those who live on the forgotten edge of society. Such situations exist in America, China, India, and elsewhere. One person in Tunisia sacrificed his life that started a human revolution that suddenly spread across nations and challenged the systems of greed, violence, and corruption that denies life and regard for all human beings.

When will such urgency reach America?

America lives under the illusion that it is a selfless and caring nation dedicated to promoting democracy and freedom but is really a plutocracy or a government of the rich. It has never been a democracy. There needs to be a planetary revolution to empower the well being of all.

# 26

## ONE LIFE

Accidents

Though much of my life is spent in schools, life is happening everywhere on the planet. It is why I write about things that occur in such places as New York, India, and the wilderness, as well as in my own neighborhood. I run through San Francisco streets around our house and in the parks. I have been running for almost as long I have been a teacher in San Francisco. Over the years I run for thousands of miles through San Francisco streets and over its hills. Some places I run through hundreds of times without thinking much about them.

Usually I run in the morning before I start work with the schools. One place I often run past is three blocks from our house. Streetcars had once run down San Jose Avenue by our house before we moved there. They have been brought back with all of their noise, mass, and vibrations to the street and impact the houses and the people they pass. They are massive and sometimes move rapidly along. People are cautious and careful to stay out of their path. One morning, an eighty-eight year old woman was on her way to see a relative. She is struck and killed by a streetcar only a few steps away from her door. It is three blocks from our house. She is rushing to catch a streetcar going downtown, when she steps off the curb to reach the safety island and is struck by a streetcar going in the opposite direction.

Neighbors and friends look on for more than an hour as firefighters and streetcar workers labor to raise the streetcar on to wooden blocks and remove the body. Service on the streetcar line is disrupted for two hours. When it is resumed the streetcars move slowly across the spot where she died. They are almost at a standstill. Life sadly goes on. No one thinks about or expects her to die in such a way. The world is not dominated nor controlled by our thinking, or our thoughts. Some things we survive or live through, and others we do not. Our thoughts are of a known world are of the past, but we exist now in a world that is new and unlived.

One day in San Francisco, when I am sixty-two years old, I step out of a building and run to cross the street before the oncoming traffic arrives. As I run, a truck is quickly backing up. The driver never sees me. I am unaware of the truck, or any impending danger. But we are heading into an unavoidable collision. The instant before the encounter, my mind quickly tries to reverse time, and to undo the events that now confront us. I cannot stop this mishap that is happening. It is not possible and it is too late to escape the crash. Nothing can cancel the moment that is already here. It is an impact of two forces. The intensity moves through me as I wonder at the extent of damage to my body being struck. I am in the path of the truck, and bounced off into a course I am unable to calculate or predict. The impact alters my direction and sends me spinning to the street. Emerging forces twist and take me. I hit the ground and black out, but I somehow recover and jump to my feet.

The driver descends from the truck and is concerned about my condition. I am somewhat in a daze, but tell him that I am going to be all right. I say this not knowing what devastation, if any, my body has gone through. I can hardly speak as my breath has been taken away. I eventually realize that I am light-headed, and hardly able to stand. There are bruises to my knee and arm. I convince the driver that no one is at fault and that I am all right. My own sense is that all my running through the streets of

San Francisco over the years has my body able to move through such moments. I feel fortunate to be able to walk away from the incident, and I am able to find a place to sit down and rest. I know that life is getting through such times and going on to another adventure.

Another Moment

In our human journey we traverse the planet and move into space learning that we can take no thing for granted. Yesterday I travel south from San Francisco for a meeting. It involves San Francisco schools and Stanford University. During the meeting I have to leave and walk to the car. On the way back I am walking along the sidewalk, careful to move to the side for those walking along the way in the opposite direction. Suddenly I find myself falling and stumbling forward and I am unable to maintain my balance. Again I know I am entering a situation that awakens my mind from a prior moment and I know this can be a traumatizing occurrence. It is certain that I am going to land in a hard collision though I stretch forward and try to lessen the impact of the fall. I know that the angle of the impact can sometimes be critical. I learn this from the more than a thousand people who have jumped from the Golden Gate Bridge and the few who have survived. My body and face severely collide with the ground. I do not seem to black out but I am unable to know any sequence of events. The universe changes from moment to moment. Every time I collide with another object or mass it is an unreplicable moment. The universe does not stay the same in its moment-to-moment existence. Another person witnesses the fall and covers my head that he says is bleeding. He is Asian American and says that he was once a paramedic and a solider in Vietnam and had carried fifty-pound loads on his back. He asks someone to call for medical assistance. I tell him that I want to return to a meeting I am attending. He says that I need medical attention. The medical emergency unit arrives. The promptness of their arrival lets me know that I am not in the wilderness or in some poor San Francisco neighborhood where life is less organized. I am impressed with the team that comes to determine the situation and to respond from what they learn. One of the emergency workers is the son of Wayne McDonald, a retired San Francisco teacher, with whom I once worked. I am checked out and sent to the emergency room of the hospital. The staff and doctors are dedicated workers who do an outstanding job of attending to the wounds. As I travel through Stanford Hospital I notice the different races and backgrounds of those acting as one team and all contributing to the life of the system. It seems a natural result as to how the hospital is operated. Everyone has a seemingly clear role of assisting the afflicted and seems capable of doing the job. A cut to the head is sewed up with seven stitches, and three hours later, I am sent home. I never get back to the meeting.

The Stairs

It is interesting to step to and from our house into our back yard. The stairs from the house are built by a friend. He had been a substitute teacher and sometimes did work at our house. He had never built a set of stairs, and he was so excited when he took on the project. He enthusiastically faced the questions he had to solve and work through. He diligently conceived and constructed them. The staircase is a good and sound structure. Surprisingly, shortly after our friend completed these stairs he committed suicide. His voice is in the work as the stairs still stand strong.

What is it we are to do when we are living? It is not building things to glorify ourselves. It is doing things in life that profoundly involve us, the things we seriously pursue in school, and elsewhere. Sometimes we surpass the goals and expectations we have. Sometimes we never seriously enter any world. Life is not a quest for wealth, objects, or achievement, but a way of discovering the world and universe. Walking the stairs I move in a world where there had once been so much interest and engagement. In the end we do but our best, and work our hardest, but nothing stops the impermanence of life and the vanishing and transformation of matter and energy, back and forth.

Oneness of Life

We each have unique journeys on this earth. One day I meet a high school student whose family six years ago make a journey from East Africa and the Rift Valley to San Francisco. America is a new world for him. He loves learning and in school he is introduced to an organization that is building schools around the world. In working with this organization he goes to Nicaragua to help build a school there. It is a meaningful experience as he learns things about himself and another society. I also meet rich business leaders who work with this organization who are involved with school construction programs in places such as Haiti, Nepal, Mali, and Malawi. One young and enthusiastic leader talks to a San Francisco audience about the work of building a school in Mali, West Africa. He himself works in the desert where he sees people he is working with who walk for two miles to the nearest water. They labor hard throughout the day and he shares how much it means to them to build a school where children can learn. He lives amongst the Malians for three weeks sleeping on the ground and seeing how daily life is such a struggle for survival. He is inspired to see the human spirit and how it endures such hardship for existence. One realizes the oneness of life. A poet once wrote that every atom belonging to me belongs to you as well. It is interesting to me to learn about the closeness of a life of extreme poverty and that of fortune and wealth. An existence on this African Road transforms how we understand each other and ourselves as we traverse the planet and observe such a oneness of life.

# 27

# DALLAS

I am in and out of Dallas quickly it seems. I see much and I learn some new things. I stay in a hotel near the Dallas Public Library. I look for books about black people in Dallas. I do not find much. The librarian shows me several things but I find little of what I thought that might exist. I am not surprised or disappointed. In San Francisco there are books I find, but there is not an abundance of materials in the library. I learn much by walking around the city and running through the streets in the early morning. I have come here to observe the public school system, and study student learning. I am interested in the education of all students, and particularly that of the poor. I have been given information on the schools, and how students are performing by income and race. From the disaggregated information I know exactly the schools and neighborhoods to visit. I go to a public housing development that seems similar to the projects in Oakland, San Francisco, Los Angeles, or New Orleans that I had seen. My visits to the schools are fascinating.

In the early morning I run through the city streets. One day I fall and bruise my knee. It is bleeding so I return to my hotel room. When I enter the building I ask a black guy who works there if I can get a towel and a bandage. I follow him through a seemingly twisting path around several hallways. We pass several other black men who work for the hotel. I completely forget about my leg that still bleeds as I become aware of the distinct southern cultural thought and way of life of those whom I encounter. They are service workers in the hotel, and do everything to help me knowing that I am staying there.

I am reminded of the subclass life that they accept as part of the job, and of a second-class existence that they never question. I think about a similar life of black people I observed as a child living in Memphis. I am grateful to these men for their earnest and unpretentious help. I appreciate their unassuming manner but I am troubled by the place in this society they have accepted, and adhere to. They allow themselves to be controlled and dominated as people on the fringe who are almost meaningless and irrelevant to the dominant society that oppresses them. There is contempt for them and their status by this society.

I am in Dallas to work with Waldemar Rojas who left San Francisco and is now head of the Dallas schools. I am here to observe schools and to work with those in the Dallas education community. I have been given a great deal of information about the schools. It is a serious visit for me. There are 150,000 students and more than 200 schools. I work with the superintendent, and his staff, and all of the data and information they provide me. I focus on the performance of black, Latino, and poor students, looking at such things as test scores, attendance, and dropout rates.

The Latino students have the largest number of "No Show" students or those who never enroll in school. The blacks more than any other group give that they "dislike school" as their reason for dropping out. These two groups are also the lowest performing in reading and math. The blacks, Latinos, and American Indians performed worst in the national examinations, and were well below the national average, but whites and Asians exceeded the national average. The District expects all groups to exceed the national average within one year.

How will they do and will they deepen their learning experiences? The truth is that there would be no next year as the Superintendent would lose his job, and would not be there but this is not known at the time.

It is evident from being at the schools, and seeing academic performance of some students that there are groups of poor and black students capable of high academic work against great odds. Of the two hundred schools I visit five. I am impressed at being at each place I see as they are all very cooperative in presenting their schools. Three schools stand out. One is the high school for the gifted and talented. It is a small school of 150 students. One third of the students are reported as black. I look forward to going there. The principal is very open, and speaks of how accomplished the students are. I observe several classes. The students are inquisitive and highly engaged. Their conversation in the class and my individual interaction with them is serious and profound. They are each very impressive. They are all seemingly driven to learn. Of the many students who work hard and have much academic success, only few make it to this place.

I once visited Blair High School Math and Science Magnet Program in Maryland. It is a place of highly able students taking the most rigorous of courses. Only a hundred students are admitted in the ninth grade. The coordinator of the program is unassuming in presenting a spirited and strong school program. In the Dallas school, when I am there, I see very few black or Latino students. The principal assures me that all groups of students are equally represented, and do excel at the school. I think that it is significant that students with greatest interest and motivation are served by public schools. It is equally important that students of the greatest needs are served and are able to live serious and profound lives. In Dallas, just as in Maryland, I am immersed in great and serious dialogue and student work, but I encounter few poor or minority students. In both Dallas and Maryland schools I find middle class children's work and education in the absence of poor and black students.

I visit two elementary schools. Both have black women as principals. The first school I speak to the principal by telephone, and she tells me that she has an emergency absence of a teacher whose class she must cover, but I am welcome to come to the school. As I enter the building, she is walking the class upstairs.

She has to pull one student aside, and make it clear to him as to what behavior she expects. In the classroom she does not begin until there is silence in the room, total silence. With their complete attention she tells them that she expects nothing, but the best work they are capable of performing. She is clearly competent, focused, and fearless. From the academic achievement of the students they seem to internalize her seriousness. I leave her as she teaches the class. The school is more than 76% black, and on a nationally normalized test given by the school district the school is first out of 149 schools, and significantly exceeds the national average.

The other school that I visit is also unusual. Many of the students are from poor families, or living in public housing projects. On the nationally normalized, standardized test given by the school district, the school is second out of 149 elementary schools, and significantly exceeds the national average. The school is more than 98% black. I am accompanied by the principal, who tells me the school has exceptional parent cooperation. Many parents themselves attended the school, and are committed to sustaining its strong academic nature. I visit a computer lab in which all students are quietly engaged in completing their assigned work. The students throughout the school are expected to complete certain critical standards such as having a number sense, to the understanding of place value, and automatic familiarization of multiplication tables, as well as spelling correctly, rules of grammar, and narrative presentations. The computer is used as an empowering tool.

I learn that the school will be changing to another form of the national examination, and ask the principal if this will have any impact on the school performance. The school welcomes the new test. She says that she expects no decline in academic performance because the entire school works one year ahead of grade level standards. They welcome change. When I look back at the performance of the school eight years after I leave the Dallas schools, the school is listed by the district as being exemplary in the state of Texas, and has been recognized and awarded for its performance.

Hundreds of people attend a community forum on schools and education. It is about the educational world of black and poor children. I am impressed by the depth of understanding of some of the individuals whom I meet. They express a need for competent adults and qualified teachers with demanding and rigorous work for black students and all others. They want to support good teachers. They state a need for quality teachers on a yearly basis. It is essential that learning is continuously renewed. As to dropouts and student attendance, they express the need for student-motivated attendance.

I find their understanding to be insightful, as compulsory attendance works to produce schools that are irrelevant. It uses force and conformity, whereas life itself is driven by self-direction and creativity. The individuals demand to see a society where people show that they care about others and that we provide a coherent and consistent program to stop student failure. I am inspired by my work with them.

# 28

## SCHOOL CLOSURE

Of all the days at a school often the most serious day is graduation. In elementary school those who leave are fifth graders. One year the San Francisco school district announces that it is closing six schools. Five of the schools are in poor neighborhoods where they are in a struggle to offer a worthwhile education to the students. I worked with two of these schools over the years. Low student enrollment and academic performance were reasons being considered for their closing. In the end the schools closed were predictable yet tragic.

In the United States it is said that no one person is more important than another, but not all the schools that the school system said should be closed were closed. My wife told me in advance that the schools in the neighborhood of wealth and power would never allow their schools to be closed. She is right in every case. In the end only the poorest schools, in the least served communities, are done away with and eliminated. Those in them are unable to challenge a system of greed and selfish interest. My wife and I have been at one of the schools that were closed. I work with the fifth grade class as a math teacher and I am asked to be the graduation speaker for the school. My wife works as the part-time school librarian. The closing is tragic for some people, because each day as the sun always rises and sets, there is coming for the school a time that the sun is going down for the last time.

The school has students who are mainly black, but also there are Asian, Latino, and two are white. The fifth grade class reflects the overall school enrollment. The total school enrollment is 96 students. Last year there were 120 students. It has a declining enrollment, just as the school district does. However, the school's increase in academic performance was amongst the highest in California in the urban school districts. The increase in black student performance was particularly significant. Over the last several years my work with the school is with the teachers, students, and parents. The school is situated across from a public housing project. There is a great effort to get parents involved in the school.

Two years ago I work with several black parents in a math program. For them it is engaging work to construct congruent geometric figures from varying arrays of dissimilar points. I am surprised at their deep interest and their ability. They do well. The next day one of the parents, who lives in the public housing project near the school, goes on a field trip with her son's class. One of the students in the class gives her money to buy him something at the store. He gives her fifty dollars. She buys the inexpensive things he wants and does not give him any change back. The boy's mother who is a neighbor in the same housing project is furious that the woman took her child's money, and the school is left to solve the problem. Such situations never go away. In solving some conflicts one does find out unexpected information about the persons involved, such as a parent who sells crack cocaine to another parent who is a user. In this case the situation prevents closure on a case arising in the school and the community.

It is often said that urban inner city youth are isolated and are unaware of the places and things that are commonly known to the residents of the city or of the world. It is not that a youth's mind is less probing or curious as the older citizens, but the technical knowledge of streets, landmarks, or countries is not needed or valued by them. One week I run the Bay to Breakers race that passes on a street near the school. It is Hayes Street with the well-known Hayes Street Hill familiar to the 80,000 runners and the thousands of spectators. When I ask the students about Hayes Street, which is three blocks away, they know nothing about it. Why had I assumed that it was important that they know about it when it is never a part of their lives or information they ever need? They all go home in the other direction.

The school does take a lot of field trips. It is good that the students are able to go to places away from the school. They can journey into nature, and do such things as the clean-up work of Ocean Beach. The school is not far from the sea. Both nature and the sea are great places for students to reflect. This makes life more meaningful to them, and the teachers. A lot of people in the schools are not connected to nature or saneness, but are dominated by discipline and classroom management problems. Some students and their families feel rejected by the school, and that the school is against them. They feel themselves to be a problem. They give up on trying or cooperating in being a part of the school world. School rules and procedures are sometimes set in stone so that these persons are excluded. Such a system does not work for them.

Racial and cultural bias in disciplining students can mean some students are caught up in life in a system of personal destruction. School discipline that frustrates, alienates, discards, and eliminates students of color demonstrates they are not wanted in schools as they exist. The exclusion and isolation leads to personal and societal failure. The principal and the teachers at the school are aware of this and refuse to give up on letting students know how living intelligently and responsibly can change their lives. It is understood that each student's journey through the school is unique.

The life in the classroom is lively and energetic. From the first day the students are serious. Nothing is too hard for them to eagerly pursue. Over the years I converse with Don Cohen about his work with young students. His ideas and materials in teaching calculus to young children is a focus of my work with them. I work with the class two days a week, thirty minutes each class. There is seldom deviation. I start the first day with partial sums of a diverging series. Later on we cover the limit of a converging series and the rational (fraction) expression of infinite repeating decimals. Their openness to new things stays alive. Their enthusiasm is strong and the capability of a number of students is evident. No one is excluded from the mathematical conversation and the lessons we all work on. There is a need to always return to elementary facts about the number system. For some it is a long journey going from working to master adding, subtracting, and multiplying to the more technical symbols and formulas that generate elaborate mathematical expression.

It is a great time to think about how we learn things. It is important that students construct their own knowledge. However, can they be expected to reinvent 5,000 years of mathematics all on their own? Over the years I find that some students do connect to the collective genius of humankind. They understand mathematics at a deep level. In this classroom I want them to know that anything they get from me that they are better off learning it on their own, which is really a matter about knowledge itself. How long technical knowledge or knowledge in general has existed is unimportant. It can disappear at any moment. It is why content and knowledge are illusions. Things are profound and interesting to us because they exist and are before us regardless of the path they have taken. There are no actual paths to truth. Getting there does not depend on any pathway.

Elementary school mathematics is not really about explaining things. It is a much more serious and deep matter. It means discovering a world of subtle and sometimes hidden assumptions and rules, and it is a hard journey for some minds. It is because ideas that look obvious must be internalized and verbalized.

In elementary school students learn the operations of addition, subtraction, multiplication, and division. It is hard work for some students to master them because they must be able to use the operation and then express the results in the decimal system, where a power of 10 is assigned to each place of a number.

Addition and subtraction are too simple to describe the world. When things become more complex multiplication and division are used. Multiplication is taking a set of objects (which becomes a unit) and repeating it. Division is taking a set of objects (which becomes a unit) and subtracting them from a given value. It is also the inverse of multiplication, just as subtraction is the inverse of addition.

Division is the most difficult operation to use and can deal with more complex questions such as ratios and fractions.

Understanding the principles of mathematics makes it meaningful to students rather than our assuming they understand them or having them think that they do.

One does not know when one is coming upon an interesting mathematical idea. I read about a calculator problem given to a second grade class by a professor from the Massachusetts Institute of Technology. It is a problem that questions the understanding of place value and gets the attention of the students. The problem is to use a calculator with only three functioning keys: 0, +, and 1. They are told that with these three keys they need to display the number 2,314. A number of students are able to perform the problem and are eager to express their discovery to others. They show that they understand the place value system. It is significant for me to observe who understands it as something they discover for themselves. For others it is still unclear and abstract. We work among ourselves so that all can find a breakthrough to understanding the system.

The last day comes and I speak to those at the school.

As Golden Gate is now ending as a school, it is important that I acknowledge the effort of the entire community who fought to save it from closure. Nothing lasts forever and the impermanence of life and things is certain and evident to us all. What is so tragic in this event are those who used money as the major reason to close the school. It is true that the school struggled to sustain a high enrollment of students. For me in a city such as San Francisco it is unforgiving for those of authority and title to destroy and eliminate a school with exemplary academic achievement in the state of California, achievement attained by some of its most deserving students. To the students and this neighborhood San Francisco is not a great city, but is a place that does not care about all children or the quality of life and education in every community.

The school staff expressed this fact in a joint statement, "As a school community, we at Golden Gate Academy feel that we have become invisible in the eyes of the district, and therefore invisible in the eyes of the public."

Mr. Pirrello, the fifth grade teacher, stated, "We feel like the district instead of closing us should be copying us. We've taken some kids who would be considered challenging and shown them how smart they really are. They like reading. They like math. They like learning. It goes against all the stereotypes."

The school has had a great staff that is able to provide a relevant and rigorous education for its students. The principal, Ms Wheaton, articulated a vision of high expectations for every student and never gave up on the school challenging each student's mind at the highest level: "I thank the parents and relatives of the graduating fifth grade class for being here on this occasion as well as school staff which has supported these students from kindergarten through the fifth grade. It is also a privilege to have all the community members and school supporters here today."

My wife and I both worked at the school this year. My wife taught reading and worked as librarian and I taught Calculus and mathematics to Mr. Pirrello's fifth grade class. Like all classes in the school these students were special. Each day I came they were an enthusiastic and bright group. Whether we were studying partial sums, infinite repeating decimals, the binary system, or Rubik's Cube, their fascination shined.

I begin by congratulating all eighteen of them in leaving the school to attend six district middle schools and one private middle school:

"All of you will be starting lives with new beginnings," I tell them. "The world will be greater and larger for you as you meet students and teachers at these new schools. You are going to study new subjects in middle and later in high school such as algebra, economics, and literature. Some of you will become poets and writers, scientists, and teachers. You will learn about things that your parents never studied. So the world will be larger and filled with new adventure.

"At the same time the world is also is going to get smaller for you. As you go to middle school and then high school and to work or to college you are going to be able to travel to places that once you could only read or hear about in books or see on television. These new places will be possible for you to reach because of all the air travel where people are daily going to China, Mexico, South Africa, and India. In one day's travel we can touch the Great Wall of China, or observe the Taj Mahal in India. Some of you will possibly travel to outer space. This is the newest frontier or newest beginning for humankind.

"When you go to middle school next year it is going to be important that you are serious about your new life. Reach as high as you can in your work.

"I want to share with you a personal adventure that allowed me to reach as high as I could. Not many years ago I traveled with my wife and daughter to Tanzania, East Africa to climb Mt. Kilimanjaro. The Africans call it Kili. The mountain is very near the equator and is 19,000 ft high which is about three miles. I traveled with an African guide, Richard, who was 22 years old. I know it takes three days to get to the top and that the air is very thin and it is hard to walk and to breathe there. It is also very cold. After three days of climbing and hard work we made it to the highest camp that was closest to the top. We left the camp at

1:00 am in the morning on the third night and struggled for five hours to get to the summit or top that is called Kibo peak. After getting there and resting there for fifteen minutes it took us an hour or so to climb back down the peak. It took us two days to make it back down the mountain. So it was a five day expedition: three days up and two days down.

"So as you move through middle school, high school, college, and the work world explore serious and difficult subjects and problems."

The students are not looking back. They are still energetic about life and going deeper into its adventure.

# 29

# SCHOOL ROUTINES

Parents

In a school of mainly Latino and black students, the principal is dedicated to the lives of poor children. She is Latina, and is concerned about the voice of black parents in the school. In an effort to involve black parents at an elementary school, she sends out several hundred letters and distributes a multitude of flyers. Six parents come. They all love their children and are interested in their learning. It is expressed in many different ways. One parent says that she comes to the school every day, and the times she walks by her daughter's class she sees that her daughter is not really interested in the lesson. She feels that the teacher is not aware of the attention level of the students, and is not doing enough to involve them in learning.

Another parent says that she does not know how long her child will be at the school. She does not think that her child is being challenged enough at this school. Last year the child had gone to school in Chinatown and there was harder homework with vocabulary words, and repetition, and use of words in sentences, and that the students at this new school did not have field trips to the library. When I talk to her after the meeting she says that her main goal is to get her son back to the school in Chinatown. She is now living in Hunters Point and the bus trip is too far right now. Another says that she does not read to her daughter but has her read and she listens. She says that it is important that her daughter practices to read because she already knows how to read herself.

The lady next to her says that every night that she reads to her daughter for an hour. She is in kindergarten and is excited in hearing new things. She seems very organized and understands what she is doing. One mother says that she has so little time to read after school and that she works on the weekends so she does not read to her child very much.

There is one father at the meeting. He seems very knowledgeable about the school, and the classroom. He understands what others are saying and going through. Everybody is trying hard he tells the group. He says that the teachers are like the students and that some individuals are better teachers than others just like some children were better students than others. In families there are differences among siblings.

We all agreed that it is necessary to support some teachers more than others, and that we needed to recognize that some teachers are new to the school. It is agreed that all the teachers needed feedback about the parents' observations. The gentleman goes on to say that some teacher's homework is better than others. Some teachers are more serious about it than others and it is important to them to have students penetrate further into subject matter. He also articulates that the students need to achieve results at a faster rate. Fundamental to his work with his daughter is vocabulary building, and mastering the use of words. He says that he was born in Detroit in an almost all black school district. He says that the school system was bad, but that the students did do well and that those who now run the city were the students then.

Recently I have a conversation with the superintendent of schools, Bill Rojas, whose son is with him. The son is in kindergarten and is very enthusiastic and involved with the world, and new objects he discovers, and people he encounters. While he is busy studying the construction and flight of paper airplanes, the superintendent tells me that soon his son will be challenging me to a chess game. I am impressed with their energy. I know that being a conscientious parent makes Bill Rojas a serious and more effective educator. I have a similar feeling when I meet and talk to Chancellor Chang-Lin Tien when he is in charge of the University of California at Berkeley. He tells me how he would go to the Berkeley school board meetings as a parent and pursue student and community issues in public education. I am certain that such experiences as a dedicated parent made him a stronger college teacher and a great and serious university leader. Both Rojas and Tien deeply question public schools and what they offer to all students.

Participation

School and classroom interactions among students and teachers differ widely. In school some classes never get started in learning. Some teachers do not reach a beginning to learning. Some are frustrated. I tell them about a high school physical education teacher who says when she starts with a new class she never begins until there is quiet. She waits until there is total stillness. During the first few days it sometimes takes several minutes for them to understand that she is communicating to them that she has to have the complete attention of the whole class. She does not teach over noise or to students who are not paying attention. Ninety percent, or even ninety nine percent, cooperation is not acceptable. After several days the total class gets the idea that total attention and silence have to exist for the class to begin. The students appreciate themselves, and the class, more as they understand the seriousness of the teacher. Once she has their attention she tells them exactly what they will be engaged in. She knows that uncertainty decreases their interest. It is an urban inner city school and the students participate in a learning environment of the highest quality. As a coach she has guided her teams to win all city championships in track and volleyball.

The teacher starts a school wide intramural program. Previously there were few students involved, and they mainly played unsupervised basketball and football games. Her goal is for all students to be able to participate. First they organize basketball teams. Each homeroom in the school has a team. Each team is coeducational with boys and girls. It is difficult having mixed teams, and working with new people, but that is the purpose of the program. After initial misunderstandings, it runs smoothly. It is clear how the program functions. Everyone understands. Students of different ability, gender, and ethnicities play hard together. After basketball a volleyball program follows. It is coeducational also. The students eventually organize their own programs, and their own supervision. They were able to create their own standards, games, tournaments and a school wide system of play. Students are given the opportunity to participate and in doing so they discover their ability to self organize. The teacher believes in the students and they perform at a serious level.

Lincoln High School

One of the first jobs I work on with Bill Rojas, when he is the new superintendent, is a high school principal selection. It is with Lincoln High school parents and teachers. It is interesting as I have worked with this team of school staff and parents before Bill Rojas was selected, and the group had already selected two candidates. They are both male and both are working in nearby school communities. Both of them seem articulate and are experienced educators. Bill Rojas interviews the candidates and decides that he is not interested in selecting either as the school principal. He tells this to the team. They are all shocked.

Some have probably looked forward to working with the superintendent in completing the job that had already taken months of serious work. One parent says that she is amazed. She cannot believe what he is saying. She wonders how he can get any other parents to take time from work and their lives to participate in a useless process. She cannot figure it out. She makes it clear that she will never give up her time for anything like this again. How is he going to get parent involvement with this way of treating people? It seems to be such a fundamental disrespect of working with and appreciating what others give to a school.

Bill tells her that he does appreciate what she has given to this process, but unfortunately the process did not work in this situation. He had interviewed the candidates, and they did not have the leadership and academic depth that he felt that the school needed. He tells the parent that this system of principal selection does work maybe ninety five percent of the time. It did not this time. A representative from the teacher's union who was on the committee was appalled that the new superintendent, who did not know the school or the teachers, and was exhibiting this kind of authority. Who was he? He tells Bill that his act was a disgrace that dishonored teachers and the school. He tells the superintendent how he despises what he is doing.

The superintendent is unfazed by the comments and allows him to get out all the caustic, bitter, and scathing disgust he wants to express. I know that Bill Rojas is not bothered just as in his early struggles he faced with the superintendent's job. There was a loud community force who wanted a black finalist to be the new superintendent. Though told he would be followed wherever he goes, he lives with the threat and is unbothered.

When the union representative is finished Bill Rojas tells him that it is his responsibility as superintendent is to select a capable instructional leader who can move the high school in a new direction. Neither one of the two candidates is that person. He states that the question is: does he appoint someone who does not have the background and would not do the serious work needed, or select someone else. He is going to select someone else.

Another parent speaks up and admits that there is much that he does not know about the academic background required for the position. He is a parent, and he has spent a lot of time interviewing a lot of different people. He wonders what it is he is missing. He does not understand what he is not observing. He says that using the process that worked for the group he would feel comfortable, as a parent, selecting either two finalists to be the principal. He does not have a technical, educational background, but why is this a complicated process? What is it that he is not seeing? He wants to know!

The superintendent talks about the ability to lead a school, an instructional vision, and the academic achievement of the students, and other things. It probably does not seem convincing. Is it education jargon, or does he really know about education at some great depth? In the end the team is still not happy. It will take other situations and educational leadership for others to see Bill Rojas' impact on the academic achievement of students throughout the district. The only question left is the next step.

The superintendent says that the process works ninety five percent of the time. He says that the process would be repeated. No one there seems willing to participate again, and besides there is no more time before the start of school. Before this meeting, the superintendent had already asked me who I thought was the strongest candidate in the district. I mentioned an assistant principal at another San Francisco high school who had not applied because she wants to be principal at the high school she is working at. He announces her name as the acting principal for the new school year. The group is shocked again. First they do not know the person, and secondly she had not even applied. How unbelievable it just all seems. It is a disgusted group. In the end a compromise is reached. They would give a chance to this person who had never been a principal and who they knew nothing about, if they could have a school counselor who was a member of the selection team be an assistant principal at the school. The superintendent agreed. It was done.

The new principal, Gwen Chan, was energetic and serious. She had some struggles but she did turn the school around. She was as strong a principal as the superintendent probably ever selected, as she was later promoted to an Associate Superintendent. In time she became the first Chinese superintendent of San Francisco schools. The parents had been part of getting the school leadership they worked for but not within the usual process.

Student Achievement

To a great extent what schools hope to achieve is symbolized and expressed through promotion and graduation events. To me, however, they are a way of mass conformity that institutions and society perpetuate. In the absence of such ceremony of artificial importance, institutions and our present society see themselves as less significant places with a diminished purpose. What is the purpose of our society?

I have attended and participated in numerous graduations and student promotions as an educator. I have always taken seriously the dialogue with students and all others who attend. There is still uniformity with all promotions and graduations though I recently attended an unusual eighth grade promotion program.

It is the first promotion event in the history of Alice Fong Yu Alternative School, which is the first Chinese immersion public school in the United States. It is named after the first Chinese teacher in San Francisco. The principal, Liana Szeto, personally invites me to attend the program, because I was at the school three years ago and was moved by the learning and the enthusiasm of the first sixth grade class in the school. Two years later would be the school's first eighth grade, making the school kindergarten through eight. What so impresses me about this first sixth grade class is that it is a Chinese Mandarin immersion program. This differs from the Chinese Cantonese immersion program in grades kindergarten through five.

I visit this new sixth grade and observe the students in their study and find it very interesting seeing them learning Mandarin. What makes it unusual and different is that more than half the class is composed of black students. I am impressed with the energy and vision of the principal who is so proud of all the students and how they perform in their work. The school itself is a serious learning place and the sixth grade class seems academically and socially productive.

The principal, Liana Szeto, is a young Chinese woman who displays enthusiasm and concern for the students and the direction of the school. There is a clear effort to desegregate the school. The largest ethnic group in the school is Chinese (33%), the next largest is white (22%) and then black (12%). The sixth grade class started with over half the class black. Three years later half the class leaving the school as eighth graders are black. This indicated that the black students had worked hard and successfully at the school and did have a valued presence.

In the graduation, promotion, program there are twelve graduates, six are black. In the program each student stands and makes a presentation in Mandarin, no English is spoken. Students do not read from any material, but seem to present themselves as fluent Chinese speakers addressing the audience. Each student is impressive in his or her presentation, but how much did the audience know about what they were saying, and how well and accurately were they saying it.

After all of the students had spoken, the principal told us that they had all done well. Liana Szeto says that she speaks Cantonese and knows very little Mandarin. She is very proud of the students who have surpassed her in their Mandarin. She introduces two members of the Chinese community who had come to present awards for academic achievement. One was a woman who speaks at the ceremony. She is from a Chinese civil rights organization that had existed for over one hundred years. She speaks eloquently of the struggles in this country for the human rights of Chinese who had settled in San Francisco. She then presented the academic awards from the organization to the two highest achieving students in the class. Both of the recipients are black. She commends all of the students on how well they had presented themselves and what a serious and worthwhile occasion this had been for her. All of the students had come to the school and benefited from and contributed to a profound learning experience and a significant education.

Years later I attend a program where students from Beijing, studying English, come to Alice Fong Yu, and they speak of their American experiences in English. They are enthusiastic and grateful for the opportunity to share their life in the US. Their English seems near perfect and they are all serious, energetic and gracious for the chance to be here. It is interesting later visiting their school in Beijing.

# 30

# SYSTEMS OF KNOWLEDGE

Knowledge and Freedom

Knowledge is impermanent and vanishing.

> No one is an expert in everything. It is only so in specialized areas.

> Technical knowledge is that which is specialized and possessed by an expert. Everyone is ordinary in most things and areas.

Even if one is a known expert or authority, one is ordinary outside of one's realm of expert knowledge. And even in areas where one is a known expert, one can be wrong in his or her own field, and can be corrected by someone less expert than he or she. A student may correct mistakes a teacher makes, a nurse may correct those made by a doctor, a passenger may correct those made by a sea captain.

There are some interesting things that happen in schools that are often hardly noticed. Some elementary school students understand mathematics more than some high school students do. I sometimes find students in strong academic elementary schools often studying more rigorous mathematics than those in poor academic high schools.

One day I walk around a school with a teacher's aide or classroom assistant who knows more than anyone in the school about the students, teachers, and staff and how they are educating themselves or others. She knows more about how to run a school than anyone there. No one cares more about the school than she does. She is the most serious and energetic person there.

Many of us are obsessed with titles and position and not in questioning or examining the absence of learning or the self-transformation of others and ourselves in a school.

Much of the time one may operate successfully in one's own area. This is because of the way the world is divided, fragmented, and isolated. It is the way we live and a life we sustain. It is also a way we condition ourselves for self-importance. The world gives significance to certain individuals who master their domain or area. A ship's captain does not let the ship's crew navigate the ship. The reality, however, is that a sea captain's life on the shore is often ordinary in a lot of ways and areas. However, in a crisis situation on the sea the captain may save those in distress, or he may not. His knowledge may be fragmented or incomplete.

In a society ruled by experts and authorities, and even by the assumed best people, life can go spectacularly wrong. What about the September 11th tragedy?

One must find one's own way. There are no experts to instruct a person in living one's own life. We often look for an algorithm, formula, or pattern to know our next step. In life there is no next step. It is an indeterminate sequence. I record the sequence 12, 12,12,11,11,11,13,12,13,9,9. Over the years I add elements to the sequence. There is no formula as the next element is always indeterminate. I construct the sequence from the observations I make whenever I am jogging in Golden Gate Park. I count the number of buffaloes. Sometimes I may be away for months or longer but I sustain the sequence.

Often societies do not examine their laws and practices and sustain a way of life where school, education, and authority make slaves of people who ought to be free. Individuals should not only be free from bondage, but should be able to participate in society and the world. In a healthy society there is no need for imposed laws or for second-class citizens.

I discuss what to do about the severe dropout problem, the devastating crime, the rampant drug destruction, the failing schools, and the absence of an academic quest with persons who work in the community as leaders, parents, and concerned citizens. I realize, as blacks, we live at the bottom of society. From a life lived in the schools, I know of our failure to learn. I know to live in a society where we are all empowered I cannot conform to a world that perpetuates a downtrodden way of life.

What deeply engages and awakens us? In what environment do children find out about themselves? It is living a life not of knowledge but discovering who we are and understanding ourselves.

When we are learning there is no violence, and no fragmentation, or division of persons or the world. As a teacher in Africa and San Francisco I find there are interesting problems that excite us as individuals, and as a class. Serious problems that produce our best thinking deepen our lives.

Schools are places where knowledge is refined into routines, scripts, and formulas. Our use of knowledge challenges and imprisons our minds and lives.

Schools that fill, overload, and confuse students with knowledge do not empower themselves or the students.

Schools educate students through a system of knowledge. This gives those successful in this system societal status. They do not question the system but seek its rewards. The system is perpetuated. It solves problems through its own closed structured organization. Problems are solved and people are judged by conclusions derived from the system. Who can bring about radical change and a revolution to this system of knowledge? Who stands against such a society? The revolution to change it is through oneself. One who seeks a reward is never free. Who are those able to stand-alone in the world?

What do we make of our lives on this planet?

We on earth must understand the greatness of the planet and empower ourselves to pass through the natural worlds we encounter.

Sometimes there are interesting things in unlikely places. Recently I discover this as I am sitting in the terminal building with my five-year old grandson, waiting for the Staten Island Ferry. A large sign on the wall above a drinking fountain reads $H_2O$, the chemical name for water. It is interesting discussing with him how the two hydrogen atoms and a single oxygen atom combine. It is an atomic theory of matter where elements, molecules, and compounds dwell. The theory extends itself to subatomic particles that sometimes turn into energy and also energy turns itself into matter as they exist in unknown and new worlds. An interesting question my grandson asks is, "What is energy?"

It is a fundamental existence in the universe that is characterized by vibrations, waves, and movement. There are different kinds of energy such as chemical, electrical, and nuclear. Motion, heat, sound, and light are all forms of energy.

When we are learning there is no conflict, but technical knowledge can imprison us. It can also sometimes help us to survive. Those with youthful minds sometimes move through a world of knowledge with discovery and curiosity. My grandson's mind and interest moves through the wonder in the universe, like those of other youth, in science, language, mathematics, and technology. The presence of such worlds deepens all of our lives.

I realize that learning is more important than knowledge, therefore whatever my grandson learns from others, or from me I know that it is always better if he learns it on his own.

"What day is it?" he asks.

"Monday."

"When am I leaving California?" he wonders.

"In three days. It will be Thursday."

"I know," he says. "I know it's Tuesday, Wednesday, then Thursday. Then it's Friday, Saturday, Sunday, Monday, Tuesday, Wednesday, and Thursday again. It just keeps going around."

"It is just like the moon revolves around the earth, or the earth around the sun. Over and over they travel through space repeating their paths," I say.

"Have you been on a rocket ship?" he asks.

"No."

"Then how do you know about how the moon and the earth travel around in space?"

He questions the assumption that the moon is traversing the earth in space. I tell this to him,

"I read, talk, and have conversations with other people who are interested in what is happening. No one knows anything. It is just what we observe, explore, and talk about."

This theory seems plausible to me because humankind propels satellites into space, and they move through the universe just as the moon and the earth do. There are also planets, asteroids, space stations, and debris. We accept as truth those things that are not yet disproved. Humans are also engaged in space travel.

My grandson is five years old. My mother, his great grandmother, is eighty-five years old. They inhabit interesting worlds. My grandson explores life and ideas. He looks for secret worlds, games, and innovative invention.

My mother has dementia. She lives with a mind forgetting and wondering what preceded the world as it is now. For her it is a struggle to make sense and understand her own life. There is not a voice that can be contained in time, reason, or thought. Where does her mind reside? It is locked in turmoil, tension, and illusion, seldom free. Her mind is in a headlong journey back to days gone forever in Memphis that it is looking to fit into a current world. It is overwhelming. Previous knowledge is pursued in a mind that it can seldom sustain. There are names, words, and events that drift surprisingly in at times. Everything she knows is always on the verge of slipping away and vanishing. Her life is made significant through the struggles of her mind. Some days she does things on her own, other days she needs more help.

I am at times amazed at her presence in the world. The other day a nurse spoke with an accent and my mother was unable to follow her.

"I didn't understand a word you said", she declared.

The nurse does not seem to hear her. Much of the time my mother looks to be an ordinary individual and not one unable to sense the world.

The sound of language from others seldom matter to her from near or from far out in the universe.

How earthlike they all seem.

Even traveling light-years to get here does not matter.

For my mother and my grandson, the solitude of the mind and the desolate boundaries within us mystify life.

For all of us the universe is what it is at the moment—great, adventurous, and free from time and the known.

# 31

## DISRUPTION OF THE FAMILIAR

There is not a time in the United States when every child is well educated. We turn our backs on a large majority of students.

It is a familiar and accepted way of life in American society. How do we disrupt this tradition of life that we perpetuate?

I discuss with some people that the cohort of black students who enter San Francisco schools as ninth graders and who graduate from a San Francisco high school four years later is 34%. Some are shocked and surprised that it is so few who graduate, while others are surprised that it is not less. It is a fact however that black students perform as the lowest group in many school performance indicators in San Francisco.

For many students in San Francisco they exist in a world of change; for many blacks it is a world of survival. Why do we sustain this way of life? Who is working to transform themselves and society?

One day I meet Henry Safrit, a retired endocrinologist. I learn he has had a well-known career as a San Francisco physician. In our conversations I am amazed at his profound interest in the educational performance of both poor and black students. I share some data with him. I am surprised at what information he already has and I learn that he has been working with San Francisco students and teachers over the years. He began a program that annually awards scholarships to students for their academic achievement. The program has been in existence for more than fifteen years. The students receive financial support for four years as well as additional support if needed for their college completion. Over the years he sees that the group least represented is that of the black males.

Though the original scholarship program continues, he decides to establish a new scholarship program for black male students attending San Francisco high schools (Achievers Program). They are awarded the same scholarship amount as the original program. In fact he becomes so dedicated to the Achievers Program that that he leaves the board of the original program he started. He raises money for ten students a year for each student who reaches a C plus grade point average. Several people ask him why he is so dedicated to this problem. He responds with what he knows about such youth. He has learned many things. **He states that the black male who drops out of high school is sixty times more likely to go to jail than one who has graduated from college**. He wonders what kind of society are we perpetuating and what kind of nation do we tolerate. He is determined to work for a different world.

He is doing something to change it. After three years there are now thirty black male youth now in college. I have worked with him since the program began and I have had the fortune to interview most of the students. Many are the first in the family to graduate from high school as well as the first to attend college.

The students and their lives are very inspiring to me. They are from all over the city but mostly from areas of concentrated poverty. One is from a family whose parents are both drug addicts and they live on the streets. The children love their parents but they are not able to live with them and are moved in and out of a number of foster homes. Another student had spent time in jail and some have been homeless.

One student grows up in public housing. In the unit he lives in are ten people. There are two families living there as an uncle was sent to prison and so his family is also staying with them.

Several of the uncle's children are in and out of jail. The student being interviewed says from an early age that he is determined not to go to jail, be on the run, or get into any trouble. He always played sports. It teaches him discipline. He is motivated to do his best in school and in athletics. He had successfully been an honor roll student as well as captain of the basketball team. He is among the highest academic performing students of those interviewed.

I am impressed with the students who excel in college level courses and demonstrate outstanding athletic talent.

Some of the students are from Africa. Several of the students are from Eritrea and Ethiopia. There is one student from Mozambique. Another is from Nigeria. I tell them about my life and journey in Africa.

The Nigerian student tells of his situation of once being a good student. The American system of education he found easy and did well in all of his subjects. He says that he then became more Americanized in studying less and not taking school as serious. His father is very annoyed and demands that he performs at the highest level in his subjects or he is going to send him to Nigeria. His older brother was an exemplary student at the school and received a scholarship to UC Berkeley. The student is shocked that his father would actually do this. He tells his father that he was reared in America and that village life in Nigeria would be too hard for him. He feels that he would not be able to handle it. His grades do not get any better. His father sends him to Nigeria to study. At first he finds it hard living there but he works hard in school. When he returns to school in San Francisco, he receives A's in all of his courses. He has a 4.0 grade point average in his course work. He receives a scholarship. He finds that the students in Nigeria are much more serious about their education than in San Francisco. He says that he does well in school until he gets caught up in the American lifestyle.

In meeting Henry Safrit I discover a person who questions society and who acts to transform it. He is serious in his work and he has goals that are clear to us all.

# 32

# SELF EDUCATION

The serious person is the one who finds out what freedom is. He inquires into his own conditioning and what imprisons him. Why does he exist in a state where he is not able to completely stand alone?

In the absence of a free mind one cannot inquire into the things he holds on to and belongs to. One holds on to a religious belief, or a political philosophy, and is a follower of some cause, party, or individual.

It is in us to understand the things that empower us and discover freedom for ourselves. This is not freedom offered by another, where often one merely repeats what others have said. We do what others express and not seriously respect life and discover the truth. As followers and conformists we do not learn.

In the 17$^{th}$ and 18$^{th}$ centuries the English government, trying to understand the earth, worked to figure out longitude at sea. With ships being wrecked and cargo not being delivered, a huge money reward of twenty thousand pounds is offered to anyone who can solve the longitude problem. An ordinary citizen with a deep passion for his work finds a momentous breakthrough over the course of a half-century of tireless dedication. He is John

Harrison who is an unschooled, village carpenter. He lives at a time when literacy and education are owned and controlled by the upper class of society.

Knowing where one is on the sea is a matter of survival. A position north or south on earth (Latitude) presented no meaningful problems, but the measuring of distance east and west (Longitude) perplexed the minds of the time. Ships were wrecked and lives lost for not knowing such things as where land was located.

These events are interesting to me as I one day read about slave ships leaving Africa and journeying across the sea. Some are lost and all aboard die, because it was impossible to determine longitude or distances travelled east or west. John Harrison was a self-educated clockmaker who invented chronometers that revolutionized safe and distant sea travel. The devices he made allowed one to express time and the earth's rotation clearer than anyone else in the world.

It was such energy that empowered that part of the world for its colonization of other places, industrial advances, mass communication, and global commerce.

John Harrison is like others I read and learn about who are self educated such as Bobby Fischer, the chess player, and Malcolm X, the revolutionary.

All three by reading and practice became literate and passionate in their work. What counts in life is our understanding of things. None of them ever graduate from school.

They do not follow the known world of who are the authorities, experts, and the recognized educated minds. They do not accept the world without question.

They learn in a natural world that is through self-discovery and self-education. They are able to start over when they have to.

As learners they are no better than anyone else and seek no special privilege. There are no second-class persons that they are socially above. They do not work to leave any group of people behind. They are all poor much of their lives.

The known world values profit and greed rather than a world that is hard but fair.

Malcolm X asks for justice no matter whom it is for or whom it is against; no matter who speaks it.

Bobby Fischer is described as sometimes feeling that he is the only honest person in the world and everyone else is an actor.

They are able to express their work in their own way. They each express insight and brilliance. They are a light unto themselves and are able to stand alone.

Those with the intellect, the heart, the courage, and the energy to change the world, transform our societies.

# NOTES ON
# SEPTEMBER 11, 2001

# 33

# THE ATTACK

The Attack

Tuesday, 11 September 2001

My wife and I are engaged in viewing an unbelievable event. I do not know the time but the plane is said to have struck the North Tower of the World Trade Center at 8:45 A.M. in New York. We now watch the event in San Francisco about a half hour after the plane strikes the building. I, like others, want to sort out and understand what is reported, and observed. I am immersed in what occurs. Though it seems astonishing that this is happening, it is not entirely beyond belief. In 1993, attackers struck the World Trade Centers for the first time, which killed six people but the towers stood firm. On August 7, 1998, the nearly simultaneous bomb blasts in Nairobi, Kenya and Dar es Salaam, Tanzania killed 224 people including 12 Americans and injured more than 5,000 people. My wife and I were in shock as we had been to the Kenyan Embassy several times, much like those who had so surprisingly been killed and injured. The incident seems so unbelievable, and yet, so real to us.

A river of grief, anger, sadness, disbelief, compassion, and wonder flows through me as we take in this devastation. What do we make of this world as deep in our soul we see the human annihilation of those in the ruins who fought for life. The extreme act of violence and terror tests the depth of our spirit, and that of those who are attacking us. What do we make of this earth; what will come of us?

One observes attackers seizing, and using known and familiar objects to destroy us as they destroy themselves. In shocking bombardment, explosion, and fire thousands perish as they struggle for life. Some flee; others die, and destroy themselves by falling, or jumping to their deaths from the buildings in desperate hope. There are those crying and running. It is a disaster. People are still in the buildings. No one can protect them from a world that is tilted from its course. They are innocent people. Policemen and firefighters enter into the area before the collapse and many die in the search and rescue. Their spirit lives on. There is a quietness and stillness in us as we see things that seem to be happening for the first time ever in our lives.

Clouds of matter from the disaster form a dark world that is uncertain and unknown. Those who are within it scramble from death and fright, not knowing when and from where the next wave of destruction is coming.

The next moment is only in our mind and exists nowhere else. We project thoughts which may never come to be. We grieve and celebrate the past while we also wonder in trepidation and look for salvation in a future.

In our ordinary reality we take our life and existence for granted by seeing in our minds known and predictable events, but in the actual universe itself all past and future events, objects and thoughts vanish. They are nonexistent.

We live in a universe that does not conform to our thoughts. It unfolds as an unthinkable event.

We must live with no past assumptions and with no authoritative forecast.

In the attack we learn that the army is obsolete, and only serves as a symbol. It is unable to save civilian or military places that we assume it to be protecting. It has to quickly transform itself to be effective in ending such an attack.

What we learn from the attack is that we are all individuals existing on our own. We are responsible for our own lives. We are reawakened to the reality that the world itself is impermanent where nothing stays the same. It is not until the airplane crash in southwestern Pennsylvania that we understand that we must be as willing to die as our attackers are.

And though the earth is like other bodies in space in its rotation, revolution, gravitational field, and reflection of light, we now find ourselves on a planet that is seemingly traveling alone. Through inquiry and discovery we move deeper into our existence, the world, and the universe.

Until the attack America had seemed safe for us in our daily lives. We must now adjust to a life where we will never be safe again. Can military strength and weapons make any difference in the existence of hate or in an unanticipated attack?

From this attack is there not a deep wound in the heart and soul of all of humanity? Generations of suffering, war, and death have long existed in the world. Now it is being seen globally and not as tribal conflicts. Can these conflicts be brought to an end? Can we transcend the past and obsolete life of humankind?

How meaningful is nationalism, patriotism, and tradition except to condition our lives and imprison our minds. This is not an attack on a country but an awakening of our collective soul.

# 34

# INSIDE

My wife and I watch in disbelief the destruction to the World Trade Center from the two planes, then learn of the airplane flown into the Pentagon, and of the plane crash in Pennsylvania.

From the outside one wonders what is going on inside the Trade Center towers. How serious is it inside?

In the 1993 bombing in the underground parking garage of the North Tower, the evacuation time was from one to seven hours depending on how high you were in the building and what your disability was. No one knew if people could have evacuated in less time if they had to. The bombing killed six people and injured over a thousand. The response after the 1993 attack provided changes that helped in the evacuation of the towers on September 11th. In 1993 nearly everyone who could get out did so.

It is estimated that 16,000 people were in the two towers on the morning of September 11th when the attacks happened, which is much less than the 40,000 that would normally be there later in the day. Flight 11 with 87 passengers aboard and with 5 hijackers crashed into the North Tower at 8:45 A.M. It was a clear day that meant that the towers may have been seen 60 to 70 miles away. The plane struck the tower between the 93rd and 98th floor. Many people were killed immediately. The tower lurched back and forth a number of times, but when it was over the building was still standing. The tower stood firm.

For the thousands of people below the impact the stairways were clear and people quickly began evacuating the building. The fuel from the plane quickly burned itself out. However, it ignited combustible objects and materials that spread the process of burning everywhere at once. The water sprinkler system had been completely destroyed, as were the three emergency exits.

More than 1,300 people above the impact became trapped with no way out of the burning inferno. With such intense suffering some jumped, only escaping death from the extreme heat and smoke inhalation. In the early stage of the fire all attention was on the victims stuck high in the tower. It is reported that almost all of those below the crash area survived.

With the fireproofing blown off the steel, the bare steel softened, which was the beginning stage of the tower's collapse. Many people below the impact were descending stairways and evacuating the building. The firemen have a brutal climb to ascend the 93 floors to the top. They have heavy gear, which slows down the evacuation of those descending the stairs that are narrow and crowded. They proceed, not knowing the danger and the devastation to the tower, and not knowing that those at the top are already lost, and even if they were reached the equipment they carried would have made very little difference.

More than 2,000 people had managed to escape from the North Tower. Also many occupants left the South Tower that was not damaged. This is said to have saved many lives. Not everyone left the South Tower. An announcement was made in the South Tower, "If you are in the midst of evacuation, you may return to your office by using the re-entry doors on the re-entry floors and the elevators to return to your office." It is not known how many people returned, but minutes later the attackers struck again.

Flight 175 with 60 passengers aboard and 5 additional hijackers crashed into the South Tower at 9:03 A.M., hitting between floors 78 and 84. There was a great sway in the building that gave some of the occupants the feeling that it was going over.

When the second plane struck there were about 2,000 people still in the South Tower. There were 600 people above the level of the impact and 1,400 people below it. Two of the three staircases were completely destroyed and a fortunate few above the crash site found the stairs where it was possible to pass through. Eighteen people were able to escape the towers from the impact areas and above. In the South Tower 630 people died.

Because the site of impact of the plane was lower in the South Tower, the huge weight of material above the crash site bore down harder on the weakened structure below than the North Tower and the intense heat that had softened the steel and leading to the tower's collapse.

The South Tower burned for about an hour before its collapse. It collapsed at 10:05 A.M. The North Tower had been burning for about an hour and twenty minutes before the South Tower collapsed.

As many as 600 people were killed instantly or were trapped at or above the floors of impact in the South Tower.

After the South Tower fell, the North Tower was also likely to fall. Urgent messages were radioed to all firemen in the North Tower to evacuate immediately. One company of firemen had reached the 27th floor when they received the message that it was time to start back down. The message was troubling because they had worked, and trained to save people, and to go out into dangerous situations. To be told to abandon the mission seemed very strange and odd to them. By this time most of those who could have gotten out did so. One fire company had made it down to the fourth floor. At 10:29 A.M., the North Tower came down.

Over 1,400 people died in the North Tower but miraculously this fire company survived.

More than 2,700 people died, or were reported missing, in the attack of the towers. Some person's remains were found, but others were not. Four hundred eleven were emergency workers. One hundred-forty seven were on board the two planes. Most of those who perished were office workers who had been trapped in the falling towers.

Some of the earliest reports and stories written about the attack overestimated the number dead. Clearer information came as duplicated and inaccurate missing person reports were produced. Also there were records of companies located in the towers that were able to determine their survivors. Some events were originally underestimated such as those who died from jumping.

The intensity of the catastrophe deepened the human sorrow and tragedy, but showed our transcendence from desperation and doom.

# 35

# EAST AFRICA

Students everywhere are expected to use their minds to further their lives. Recently I talked to a college student who was visiting an urban inner city San Francisco high school. He was so disappointed because the students have no idea of what they want to do with their lives. They have not thought about it. We have accepted the idea of students coming to school, every day working hard, understanding their subjects, using their minds, completing their education, and leaving to contribute to society. Some students live within these expectations; many students live outside of them. Even though it is unknown how, or what one will one day contribute to society when one is in school, the visiting college student finds it disappointing that some students seem hardly able to deal with the question and have meaningless responses. The reality is that for these students school is not a place to challenge their lives or their thinking.

And just as these students were not challenged, America as a nation, and much of the world, has not been challenged. Deep in our souls we understand that we are called upon to be the greatest global citizens that we are capable of being. The world changed for a moment on September 11, 2001. The attacks bring an unwanted education that we struggle to deal with. The army quickly becomes obsolete and only symbolic. It is unable to protect its own headquarters.

From horror and tragedy we learn that we are responsible for our own lives. What becomes clear to us is that we must be as willing to die as those who attack us. America has never been attacked like this before. It has always been from a distance and not here and now without warning or anticipation. For some there had been warnings from the previous World Trade Center attack, and the attack in East Africa.

East Africa

As a youth and later as a teacher, I never know where life is taking me. I am unable to foresee places or events or boundaries of the mind. Travel and adventure stir me to discover new places. I do this by going to sea, and by being on the road in the US and in Africa. When I am twenty-five years old I live in Ijero, Nigeria, which is in West Africa, as a teacher. One school break a friend, Willie Ellis, and I leave Nigeria and travel across Africa to Kenya and Tanzania. We do not know what we are to encounter in these countries just as we do not know what or who we are to meet in coming to Nigeria. Indeed, from the very beginning in Nigeria we are in Oshogbo near the rainforest and the Asu River. Africa is a new, strange, fascinating, and exciting land. We are deeply surprised to be there listening to a European priestess who is married to a Yoruba drummer. Someone says that she is his 16th wife. It shows the extent that outsiders come and are unknowingly transformed by the African land. West African life inspires many passing through it in deep and serious ways.

In our days in East Africa we see that there is not such ceremony and human expression, in contrast to West Africa where there are rainforests, and the many gods in Nigeria. East Africa is a quieter land, unhurried. We arrive in Nairobi. I am struck by the wildlife that is so abundant, and how timeless and vast the land is. I have never been in such ancient countryside with baobab trees, scrub brush, wildebeest wandering through tall grass and quiet giraffe on the horizon. It is a land of lakes and craters. There are urban businessmen, subsistence farmers, and nomads. How close we are to earliest human beginnings as well as to lions, ostrich, impala, cheetah, flamingos, vultures, and oryx.

Serengeti

We leave Nairobi and travel south to eventually reach Dar es Salaam, Tanzania. On the mountain road to Kilimanjaro we pass through Serengeti to get to Arusha in Tanzania. Spectacular and awe filled is the road through Serengeti, seeing the largest concentration of wildlife on earth. Vast numbers of herds that have through countless seasons made millions of migrations searching for grass, water, and food in the 500 mile journey between Tanzania and Kenya. We sleep in Arusha next to Mount Meru. We leave there and travel around Mount Kilimanjaro to Moshi and on to Tanga and then to Dar es Salaam.

Dar es Salaam

Dar es Salaam is a busy place with more than a million people. It seems a world away from Ibadan and Lagos in Nigeria. Even further from them than Nairobi had been. Nairobi seems more western and has a European influence in its language, dress, schools, food, hotels, restaurants, automobiles, and businesses. Dar es Salaam is a big and daunting place for the Africans coming from the countryside. The African, Arabic, and Indian contributions to its life are evident. We meet Americans there, as we had in Nairobi, but our stay is a hard one. Our African teaching jobs do not pay us a salary to afford the cost of such a journey. We have very little money, and are total strangers in a distant place on a vast continent. It is such a hard time that before we leave Dar es Salaam, we are sleeping on the street. Who would have thought that two Americans would be so poor and so far from home? The amazing thing to me was that we were there at all.

I meet a Danish fellow there. He speaks with an accent, wears glasses, short pants, and brown sandals. He is always talking. He has red hair, and has worked in Dar es Salaam for five years as a chemical engineer and knows Swahili.

"Have you been in Dar long?" he asks me.

"No, I haven't."

"You should stay a few months so that you can come to feel the city. It lives its own life. Then there is Zanzibar. You should visit there. It would be worth your while. It was famous during the slave trade days. (I never make it to Zanzibar.) In Dar everybody takes his time here but things seem to go on. It's really quite an interesting place, you know. There is not a lot to do, but one adjusts to that. I tell you that you must be patient and stay here a while then you'll see."

I say to him, "This would be an interesting African town to spend some time in and maybe settle down for a while, if there was not so much Asian and European domination."

I had met a Belgian woman in the Congo and had an engaging conversation with her. She tells me about the Belgians as colonialists in the Congo, and the practice of paternalism and their attitude toward the Africans. She says the Belgians thought it would take 150 years before Africans were ready for independence, and capable of running a nation. The educational opportunity of the Africans was often violently prevented. The unchallenged European hegemony was so oppressive that at independence the Congo descended into chaos. I think about these things as I speak to the Danish fellow.

He says, "Well you could try to start a revolution here, but it wouldn't ever really work because after the first month you would find that you would be the only one working and you would grow tired. Then you would join the rest of us and take things as they come. That's the way it is here. That's the life. If you live here long enough you'll see."

I do find the Europeans observations of Africa to be interesting, in both the Congo and Tanzania.

We leave Dar es Salaam, and travel by bus up the coast to Mombasa in Kenya. We were fortunate in reaching Mombasa to find a truck going to Nairobi. We are offered a ride. We sit in the back with the heavy cargo in the freezing cold and wind. One never knows who one will encounter on the road. We do not expect another passenger, but a prisoner joins us, bound in chains. He seems a hard person, and is not seemingly bothered by us. He is in the custody of a policeman who unlocks his handcuffs, which allows him to climb into the back of the truck with us. The policeman sits up front with the driver. Sometimes we are also invited to sit there. The prisoner is quiet, and sits by himself. We never speak. The windswept plain that we are crossing is a quiet wasteland.

About fifty miles up the road the truck stops. The prisoner descends from the truck. The policeman handcuffs him and the two of them walk off into nowhere. There is no sign of life anywhere. It is as desolate a place as I have ever seen, or have even imagined. What was the truth about the prisoner? We would never know. Both Kenya and Tanzania at times seem like the poorest countries on earth, and as desolate as any places on the planet. I watch the two of them, the policeman and the prisoner, as they walk to the end of the earth and vanish.

We reach Nairobi and its urban worlds of African, European, Arabic, and Indian lives that compose the city. We leave to return to the schools in Nigeria.

Almost thirty years after I first visited Nairobi and Dar es Salaam, terrorists bombed United States embassies in these two cities. On Friday, August 7, 1998, suicide bombers had attacked, just after 10:30 A.M., with truck laden explosives. It is a shocking, unanticipated, and profound event against humanity.

In Nairobi, more than two hundred Africans are killed and twelve Americans are killed. Almost five thousand persons are injured.

Four minutes later and 600 miles away in Dar es Salaam, eleven persons are killed and eighty five are injured. No Americans are killed.

The near simultaneous bomb blasts kill more than 200 and injure more than 5,000. At the trial of captured suspects, who are involved in planning the attacks, it is ironic at how they, and others, plead for their lives as though their lives are more important than the innocent people they planned to destroy.

A survivor at the United States embassy in Nairobi says, "Those involved never need to see a sunrise, sunset. They should never be allowed to touch another human being. They should never be able to hold their wives, their relatives, their friends."

In Nairobi the survivors fight their way down stairwells filled with dead and those dying. Many see their colleagues and friends eviscerated or dismembered. The rubble buries many. Some take several days to be dug out and many never are.

The attackers bring great pain and emptiness to the cities of Nairobi and Dar es Salaam.

Though the targets of destruction were the US Embassies, the reality is that mainly Africans are dead. Their hatred and view of the world diminishes us all in the killing of mainly innocent African men, women, and children.

# 36

## SEPTEMBER 11TH

It is a monumental event of our time. Why does it happen? It is because the attackers are driven with single-mindedness.

When the passengers on Flight 93 learn through communications with others that the plane is to fly into a building as a suicide attack, they understand that they have to be as willing to die as the attackers. They are then more mission driven to take back the plane than the attackers who have been dedicated to their death and destruction and possibly the death and injury of thousands of others.

At 9:37 am the Pentagon in Washington DC is hit by Flight 77. All 64 persons ( the 59 passengers and the five suicide hijackers) were killed, as were 125 inside the pentagon. It was estimated that there were close to 2,600 people in the pentagon near the impact site.

The pentagon incident would have been a story of highest magnitude, and extraordinary occurrence if it had not been for the catastrophe at the World Trade Center which imperiled tens of thousands of people.

American Airlines Flight 11 hit the North Tower of the World Trade Center at 8:46 A.M. on Tuesday morning. It was an attack worked on years in advance and was not deterred by setbacks. The United States military forces had never mobilized against such a threat. They had no clear direction or plan to follow. The attackers had been patient, dedicated and deadly.

The government and those who were to protect the nation and its borders did not imagine, or suspect such a deadly attack could ever happen. Its defense had been built in another age dealing with a world no longer there. They never expected suicide hijackings of American planes. When AA Flight 11 crashed into the North Tower all board the plane and an unknown number of people in the tower were killed instantly. The plane had brought to the tower mass murder without warning. There was so much hatred that the attackers had killed themselves to kill others.

I read about a young son on United Airlines Flight 175 who spoke to his father by cellular telephone. He told him that men had taken over the plane, and that they intended on going to Chicago or someplace and fly into a building. He told his father not to worry because if it did happen it would be very fast. A woman screamed just before the conversation was cut off. The father turned on the television, and saw the airplane hit the World Trade Center. UA Flight 175 hit the South Tower at 9:02 am.

On Friday, February 26, 1993, at 12:18 pm, the World Trade Center is bombed. Six people are killed. All are in the basement and not far away from 1,200 pounds of explosives driven by van into the basement and set off by terrorists. A number of cars catch fire and the burning tires produce large volumes of smoke. There is a loss of power. For thousands of people it is a slow, demanding evacuation, without a communication system. It takes more than ten hours to evacuate everyone from the towers. It is an uncontrolled evacuation that is extremely laborious as everyone clears the building on their own accord, and there is much duplication of searching the same floors by different emergency rescuing agencies.

On September 11th the prospect of an air rescue exists in the minds of some of those who are trapped on the upper floors. In 1993 a helicopter settles on the roofs and carries people to safety. They help people who cannot make it down the stairs on their own.

From the beginning moment each person, company, and rescuing agency has but part of the knowledge or information of what is occurring.

We often take each day for granted, and seldom question the things we routinely do. Many of the things we do are trivial and mundane. What changes this? What makes life serious for us? For some of us it may be the work we do. When firefighters find themselves in a life and death situation it makes life serious. It is what some of them live for.

For those of us doing ordinary things life may not be serious to us because it is unchanging, and comfortable, and we tolerate many of our problems, and conflicts. As one enters into any activity it becomes a serious adventure for us when the possibility of dying exists. It is a reason we are so engaged in such encounters. It is what makes the stakes high and life serious. When we are in a high stakes situation, everything matters. It is why the survivors of the World Trade Center destruction understand how little separates their actions and lives from those of friends, and others who die on that day. Everything matters.

On September 11th in the North Tower more than 1,300 people in the impacted zone, 93rd through 98th floors and above, have no escape. They all die.

In the South Tower 2,000 people in the impacted zone, 78th through 84th floors and above, have 16 minutes to leave before Flight 175 hits the building. The moments matter.

Fourteen hundred people escaped from the top floors to the safe zone below the 78th floor. Six hundred did not make it. **Over 90% of those who died in the two towers were at or above the impacted zones.**

As I read the stories of the survivors, witnesses, and others, I see the question of life and death is uncertain yet undeniably real. Dying and surviving are actualities that come from where we are, or what we do, or what we do not do. For some of us life seems a gift.

We learn from the lives of many through the stories and documents that are available. From some of reports from the South Tower during the 16 minutes before Flight 175 a number of things happen.

Some persons see from their windows desperate people in the North Tower jumping to their death, and they then run for their lives.

In the interior conference rooms of the impact zone, people see and hear nothing. Many in the South Tower do not clearly realize what is happening in the North Tower. Many of them do not escape.

A person on the 97th floor sees a jet plane crash into the North Tower. He alerts others and all immediately leave.

Some take elevators, and not the stairs, and die in them.

Some work as financial traders; every transaction is important to them. Some are determined to stay until the firemen come and order them out. They account for nearly half the deaths in the South Towers. Their jobs mean too much to them.

Many are evacuated from the impacted zone in the South Tower, and are told down below that the building is safe. This reduces the level of urgency. The message is made with no knowledge, and no way to know that another jet is heading toward the World Trade Center. The lobby is filled with people heading in both directions. Some leave the building, but many return to work after having made it to safety and then back to their deaths.

One person returns to the 81st floor. While sitting at his desk, he sees a plane coming toward the building, and takes refuge under the desk. After the crash, there were people who were breathing and talking a few seconds earlier. Now they are flat on their back, or torn apart, dead or seriously injured. The person is able to crawl through the devastation to Stairway A, the only passable stairs, and escape. The person is just one of 18 people who are in the impact zone when the second plane hits, and who survives.

Many who remember the 1993 evacuation leave quickly. Others remember that it sometimes took four hours to walk down the steps to safety but everyone made it or was rescued. This is another day. In the end Sept 11th is a new day in all of our lives.

A most troubling issue on my mind after the attack on the North Tower is the fact of people jumping and falling from the upper floors. It is hardly imaginable or conceivable that those individuals would die in such a way. I struggle to accept it. For me they are in as extreme a human situation as possible. I understand that some temperatures reach more than a thousand degrees. I learn that the heat is so unbearable that it is impossible for one to think that he or she might survive. Why continue a moment longer when ones existence is so impossible. It could be that one is in a world where the best way to end the ordeal is to escape through a shattered window or any available opening.

Initially there are 50 people counted who jumped. They jump from both towers but mostly from the North Tower. A later investigation determined the estimate to be at 200. Many of the photos and observations were of the north and east faces of the buildings, which are more accessible to those in Manhattan. However, other witnesses reported numerous persons who jumped from the south and west sides also. Some fall on to a roof next to the center. The jumping starts shortly after Flight 11 crashes at 8:46 and people continue to jump as long as the North Tower stands. Witnesses report that even as the North Tower begins to collapse at 10:28 A.M. that two people jump.

Those who jump fall for ten seconds and encounter instant death on impact, hitting the ground at 150 miles per hour. They jumped from all four sides of the North Tower and are observed jumping in pairs, groups, and alone. Intense smoke and heat create a horror situation making it difficult to breathe and drive people to windows and open spaces 1,000 to 1,300 feet from the ground. More jump from the North Tower than the South Tower as the smoke was more concentrated and twice as many people were trapped. Those in the North Tower are also exposed to the horrific conditions for a longer time. Observers state that a few stumble from an open or broken window hidden by smoke but most die jumping from fire, heat, or smoke.

When Flight 11 hits the North Tower more than 200 fire units go to the center. Nearly all of the 99 elevators are out of service. Without the elevators to carry rescue workers to the upper floors the response will take hours. Though hundreds are killed as the plane crashes at high speed, hundreds more remain alive and some are trapped. There is a strong sense that there is deep trouble and firefighters are going to be lost. They estimate thousands of people may be in danger. They have to try.

It is decided early on that it is not a fire-fighting operation but one of rescue. The plan is to vacate the building, get everyone out, and then for the firefighters to leave. The fire chiefs order the ascending companies to leave half of their gear behind. This is either unheard or ignored. As they head 92 stories above them, many carried hundreds of pounds that no one ever thought they would use. The first firefighters began climbing at 8:57. The 911 telephone operators lack awareness of what is happening and some advise those above and below the impact area to remain where they are for help.

In the higher floors some try to reach the roof living with the reality that they have no way to go but up. All three of the staircases in the North Tower are knocked out in the South Tower only one remains open. Few know about it. There is no notice about roof evacuation. The roof is a place for fresh air and maybe rescue. Though there is never a plan for roof evacuation in the event of an impassable passage down, the security office attempts to open the roof doors but the computer operating them denies access. It is also the case that the thick smoke and intense heat would have likely prevented helicopters from making any rescues. Those inside the towers have little reliable information from the outside, those in the North Tower do not realize the South Tower has fallen and that two commercial planes have hit the buildings is not widely known inside the towers.

There are some individuals in offices who do not assume that in a building with a blazing fire and the elevators not working that they will be rescued by others. Some are still there from 1993 and remember the experience of self-evacuation. Most people do rescue themselves, but that is not a human reality. In actuality some persons are disabled, in poor physical condition, and others are waiting for instructions, and directions. The stronger an organization is committed to a climate of safety, the more effective it is assumed to respond during emergencies. It is also thought to lessen ambiguity and confusion. There are barriers from the 1993 bombing incident that are not dealt with such as communication systems, and rescue agencies coordinating with each other. These things did not happen. A lot of things did not happen. Some do happen such as emergency lights for the stairwells. Only things that are there now matter. There are a lot of things that might have been changed and maybe some things did not have to happen, but they did.

The New York air traffic controllers do not know about the hijacking of Flight 11, or that other planes have been seized, and that another plane is flying toward New York City. No one has all the information. Besides, we are powerless and incapable of reducing life to certainty, and have only our own limited knowledge.

We all need the highest degree of personal responsibility. As strong as each individual is, the reality is that some of us are injured, sick, and disabled. Some of us can do more than others.

In descending the stairs those who survive mainly rescue themselves. Still the sight of the firemen selflessly climbing to rescue those who could not leave, and those who could not cure or save themselves, inspired the survivors. The firemen's presence tempered their fear. The firemen's sense of duty spoke for itself. Some of them struggle hard because to show anxiety and worry is counter-productive to them. Many were overmatched by the climb with the loads they carry. Some are flushed and perspiring, and report chess pain, dehydration, and trouble breathing. At

9:59 the South Tower collapsed in 10 seconds killing all inside. Those in the North Tower have no way to know this. Some think a bomb may have exploded or there is a collapse of the upper floors.

Workers in the North Tower are in awe of the presence of the firefighters. By 10:00 some have reached the 50th floor. Others are ascending and checking floors for survivors, and are helping those down who cannot breathe, injured or unable to walk. Many are killed in the North Tower because when told to leave they do not believe the order is for them. They think it is meant for the persons they are rescuing. Several hundred are estimated to be in the building when it collapsed. The North Tower collapses at 10:28.

No one anticipates the chance of a total building collapse.

On this day, however, nothing is beyond belief.

The September 11 incident is an event of most severe human hardship. In a conversation with a friend, I speak of the remarkable deed and courage of the firemen and persons who lost their lives rescuing others. My friend says it is the job of firemen to save and rescue such persons. For me it is beyond one's routine of work or life. The firemen are there because the life of another is important to them. Saving a life matters to them. No life seems to be taken for granted. For some it is sacrificing oneself through the years for an impersonal goal that frees them from the personal fate and patterns of other human beings.

# 37

## OCTOBER 15TH

October 15, 2002

I travel 150 miles from the Washington DC area, where our daughter lives, to Shanksville, Pennsylvania. I drive through the Pennsylvania countryside, and I see routes to Civil War battlegrounds. Wars and battles do not fascinate me, but the lives lost in them deepen our human reality. The Civil War deaths and those on September 11th are examined to determine the greatest and most severe days of death the country has endured. In the initial estimates the World Trade Center deaths were thought to have exceeded those in the Battle of Antietam of almost 5,000, which is the largest single day's loss of life in America. The total loss of life on September 11, 2001, was later determined to be approximately 3,000. I reach Somerset County and enter Shanksville that I read as being founded in 1803.

It is a quiet drive, just as the map shows it, but getting to the final point of destination is not direct. I drive around in Shanksville looking for a country road there. I see no one around as I drive through the town. Then I see one other person walking along the road with a dog and I ask her how to get to the Flight 93 crash. She gives me the name of the roads, and the turns to get there. She is very helpful, and comforting to talk to as I am a total stranger. I get to the road and I see a sign indicating the direction. I know that I am there when I see a gathering of perhaps 40 people. I see parked cars with licenses from Ohio,

Virginia, Maryland, and Pennsylvania. It is the place where countless persons have come from around the earth to reflect on the significance of the event.

One sees that those who pass through here express deepest feelings. They saturate the area. There are pictures and names of the 40 passengers and crew members. There are poems and messages written as notes, letters, prayers, drawings, flowers and signatures on walls, paper, and rocks from school children. There are statements from motorcycle clubs, family members, friends, and strangers. I am immersed in this world that is dedicated to those of the crash.

There is a constant wind that dominates our presence. I see two bulldozers over a hill and I wonder if this is where the plane crashed. A person from around here later tells me that it is in the opposite direction enclosed by a wire fence and an American flag clearly indicating the site. He tells me that body parts were found forty feet below the earth that is soft here. I learn that this is mining country. We talk about the deaths of those recently murdered by a sniper in the Washington DC area.

The Washington DC sniper is a disruption to the individual and to society. People attempt to carry on their lives doing ordinary things as they go to school, pump gasoline to fill their cars, cut the grass, and visit shopping centers. All of the ten people who are carrying out usual daily activities are in an instant killed; three others are critically wounded. The crime scenes suddenly are extraordinary places. Some swarm with police, federal agents, bloodhounds, and hovering helicopter beams. Those who are close to the scene of the sniper shooting flee and seek shelter. Some have the feeling that the killing is getting closer and closer to them. Nearby traffic comes to a standstill. Those who live on do so with a sharpened sense of peril. The killer seems to stay detached from the victims by firing on them from a distance and viewing them only as targets.

I leave such a life of risk and harm hundreds of miles away to the east. We stand in Western Pennsylvania unprotected from the elements of weather to express respect for the lives lost.

"It's too cold," says a youth, shivering in the howling wind.

Visitors convey what the courage and determination of the passengers means to them. I read some of the things that are expressed and written:

May this land remain forever.
Heroes of our country and our heart.
This was no ordinary life.
This was a life well lived.
Your courage in the siege of the flight cannot be measured in our eyes.
May your deed live forever.
3 Coins—quarter, dime, nickel (symbolizes the forty lives lost).

What is here so deeply are the feelings of respect and humility, in this wind sensing their presence in some mysterious way:

To those who saved our freedom to ride (fly).
From all places near and far, no one will forget your flight.
Peace will reign when all are one.
In our hearts and mind forever.

I leave and drive back through Pennsylvania to Maryland and fly back to California.

The passengers of Flight 93 confronted the attackers and showed they stood for things that mattered to themselves and to us all. They refused to remain silent or invisible to the extreme hatred, violence, and fear they faced, which had already killed thousands of innocent people.

# 38

# SCHOOL EMERGENCY

In seeing the catastrophe and hearing the human dramas, one knows that there is an overload of shock, disbelief, and uncertainty.

There are service and office workers, tourists, and others in battles that they never imagined. We grieve for those we know, and do not know, those who we are. It is an aggression to our common way of life.

Some are taking a train to the World Trade Center and find they are getting off in a war zone.

Some are in schools near the World Trade Center. A high school student thought it was some kid's idea of a joke until the teacher tells them the school is still open and they are to remain in class. Some start listening to the news, and feel like they are hiding in a bomb shelter not knowing what is to happen next. There are stories and crying. Some wonder, "Is my family all right and am I going to be alive tomorrow?" Though they are right next to the disaster it feels like something that just happened somewhere else.

Some persons are going south and across the bridges, others fleeing and escaping the danger get caught up in a migration of masses of people going north, away from the buildings.

An elementary school teacher working in the shadows of the World Trade Center describes their journey. First, she had observed a hole in the North Tower of the World Trade Center, and rushes to call for emergency help, but the rescue vehicles had already arrived at the scene. The students are frightened and parents are distraught. Windows are covered so that the students are not upset by the events outside. The situation worsens, and all classes are moved to the gym and auditorium. Parents tear into the school screaming, roaming the halls, shouting children's names, pulling them out of classes, and running out of the building. Some stand in the stairwell weeping. Nearly one hundred fifty children have been swept from the building during several minutes time. Indescribable loud and rumbling noises are heard, the teacher sees the explosion outside, hears the roar of jet engines, and screaming voices. In a terrifying moment, the entire school shakes, and the lights flicker. It is from the collapse of the South Tower. The first building collapses at 9:45 A.M.

The school is given the order to evacuate just after the collapse of the South Tower. The building is flooded with police as everyone leaves the gym and auditorium to quickly get to the north end of the building. The entire school pours on to the street class by class. They head north. Teachers, and other adults, carry some of the children. In this journey north, they join a sea of refugees coming from further downtown. They are covered in dust and dirt and have dazed looks in their eyes. Moments later a great rumble stops them in their tracks. They look in silence as the North Tower implodes and collapses floor, after floor, after floor. Their world is reduced to ruin and rubble. They turn away from the huge waves of smoke coming toward them, and they keep on walking north. They walk unhurriedly, not troubled by the thousands of troubled and panicking people coming behind them. They are completely cut off from any news, and think that New York, like the entire country, is being bombed.

The teacher says to herself, "I'm probably going to die today, but before that happens I need to get these children to a safe place."

She feels good to have a clear mission in the midst of chaos and destruction. This also kept her from worrying about her own safety. Two miles from the school they turn into a side street, and face getting two hundred fifty children and adults across a six-lane highway with traffic convoys of emergency vehicles hurrying and screaming by at 90 mph. They send the children across in groups of thirty or forty. Fortunately they all make it safely across. They make it safely to a school in Greenwich Village where they all collapse inside the school gym. Some children sit shaking and sobbing. The staff at the Greenwich Village school brings the children snacks and ice cream. Six intense hours pass as the school awaits parents to come to collect their children. In tears they are reunited with their children. Most of the children are united with their parents. Several go home with their teachers, and do not join their parents until the next day. Incredibly they manage to get every child out safely, and pull together as a school to do it. How proud the teacher is of the school.

What followed was the hard struggle of a school community torn apart by the disaster. Most of the families that live near the World Trade Center lose their homes. Many move soon afterwards. Those who remain are devastated, and the entire school staff is traumatized. The school is taken over as an emergency center and they are crowded into another school. Eventually the school is moved to a larger temporary location and continued to strive for normalcy. The teacher writes that the school still existed was an amazing thing in itself.

# 39

# MOVING ON

Flights of Destruction

The youth are impacted by the tragedy in different ways. A fifteen year old left a suicide note. The police reported he had flown a plane into a building in Tampa, Florida, motivated by the September 11 attacks in New York, Washington DC, and Pennsylvania. He lived with his mother, but his father was being investigated about being of Middle East descent just as the attackers were. The student often mentioned that he was. He is believed to have acted alone as he made an unauthorized flight into a forty-two-story building, making no effort to evade it. Others describe him as a loner, and a troubled youth with few friends.

He took flight lessons for two years at the Florida flight school. On January 5, 2002, his flight school instructor left him to perform a pre-flight inspection. The youth has no authority to be in the plane alone, but it is not unusual, or uncommon, for young trainees to be left unsupervised while getting the plane ready to go. Pilots need to be sixteen years old to fly solo, and seventeen years old to carry passengers. He is a ninth grade student who should have an instructor in the plane with him.

While the instructor is performing the pre-flight check of the plane, the youth jumps in the plane without permission. Alone in the plane, he starts the engine, and takes off around 5:00 P.M. When the plane leaves, the instructor contacts the airport control tower. The plane flies over the city for about five minutes in a circled course without any attempt to land, or in any erratic flight. A helicopter making a routine patrol in the vicinity is asked to investigate the flight. It catches up with the plane about fourteen miles from its take-off point. The youth refuses to make radio contact during the approximately ten-minute flight. Minutes before the crash the helicopter pilot and the youth look directly at each other. The pilot gestures for him to land the plane, but soon after the plane crashes into the building's twenty-eighth and twenty-ninth floors. There are no injuries inside the building that is evacuated. The plane leaks fuel but no fire occurs.

As long as there are places in the world that are free and open there are going to be those who stand out as they protest life and society. The youth's school friends and neighbors describe him as a bright and quiet person, and are mystified by his act. We learn we live in a world of uncertainty and sometimes a student's deepest feelings are expressed.

I learn about him and the incident, I understand him as someone in a world where there is power, authority, hatred, and blame. Though he has minimal personal resources, he is able to come upon a situation where he is able to carry out a mission of destruction.

On September 11, the attackers strike with a mission of mass human destruction with trivial resources as compared to those of a nation or a government. They are from some of the poorest and most remote places on earth. They are extremists who are uncompromising about their beliefs as well as highly educated radicals of intense indifference who see the United States as a place of status, wealth, power, envy, and blame. They look for an opportunity to carry out their mission of destruction just as in Kenya, Tanzania, and the 1993 World Trade Center disaster. They are individuals unaccepted in their own countries that seem faraway places to those from the United States. America is closer to them than we realize. They are more informed and understanding of our way of life than we are of theirs, and they seize an opportunity to carry out a seemingly unimaginable act of mass human destruction.

## Going On

After the attack the country is still, alone, and shocked. It is also stirred by uncertainty. What lies ahead for America? Where is the country going? There are things that we suppose and assume will happen. At the time we think that our lives are changed in such an extreme moment, and that we will never be the same again. Even years after the event many persons still make this same comment. However, if one did not lose a close friend or relative, or was not living in Manhattan, or was not involved with the Washington DC military establishment, then it was possible that the September 11th catastrophe did not change one's life very much.

Travel by airplane changes, and attention to national, global, and local security increases, but these changes do not fulfill the thinking that life would end as we knew it. There was the fear that more such attacks were imminent, and threatening to happen, and that there was going to be greater devastation soon afterwards. A second wave of destruction never comes. It is assumed that unprecedented steps would be taken to prevent further attacks of another such national threat. However, four years later the national response to Hurricane Katrina's devastation to the Gulf Coast is a living nightmare, and shows how unprepared for such possible devastation that we still are.

Life goes on and if one outside of our planet observed the current daily life in the world, it is said that there is little evidence showing that something changed forever after September 11 of 2001.

We are unaware of the extraordinary universe we are in. To observe the earth that is so rich and vast and not a planet divided by the pettiness of boundaries and nations is to see it in its actuality. For our seeming security, jobs, and survival we accept this thinking of separate countries, races, and traditions and cease existing as human beings on this planet that belongs to us all.

As to the attack, facts always look clearer from hindsight. There is much talk of missed warning signs, empty threats, and being overwhelmed with endless false leads. There are system breakdowns.

The terrorists were a group that campaigned to recreate an ancient religious empire. They protest against twenty-first century life, then take advantage of it to carry out their attacks. They proclaim the Americans are terrorists as children and other civilians are killed in the Middle East from indiscriminate bombings of their villages. They say they want to be liberated from the presence of America in their countries.

War is an outward expression of who we are. It is a collection of our individual activities and everyday actions. Wars continue as we inwardly seek power, wealth, and domination and do not transform society. We continually contribute to nationalism, religious beliefs, and corruption that cause destruction to society. We cannot rely on another to bring us freedom. Bound by our beliefs and need for self-importance we are willing to die and destroy each other.

Though the attacks bring chaos and uncertainty it is clearly a time for saving persons' lives and protecting the civilians.

The September 11$^{th}$ attack uses human flight for violence and destruction. Those who survive the terror and disaster move on with their lives.

Eight years later not far from the September 11$^{th}$ attack, flight 1549 leaves from New York to Charlotte, North Carolina with 155 people aboard. The airplane strikes a flock of geese; cutting off both engines and the pilot is able to miraculously make an emergency landing on the water of the Hudson River. All passengers and crewmembers survive.

Emergency and extreme situations can happen at anytime to us all. Some of us survive or die for various reasons. All of those in and above the impacted zone of the North Tower, floors 93-floors 98, have no escape. It is more than 1,300 persons and they all die. All of the persons (155) on Flight 1549 in 2009 survived.

Some of us in a severe or extreme crisis may or may not survive. Though lives are beaten down by danger, misfortune, and calamity and those who survive appreciate life deeply, they are like others in that they may be confronted again. All of our lives move on.

# INDIA

# 40

## CALCUTTA

It is late night, and the Calcutta airport is crowded and busy. It is a distant and new world to be in. Though we have been traveling for about twenty hours we are ready to do whatever is needed to get through immigration, find our friend, Shyamoshree, and enter into the city. The process works smoothly as we clear all the formalities and find Shyamoshree, and her niece, Meghna, waiting for us. It is a moving event arriving here and seeing them waiting for us. They are filled with joy to greet us. They are both born here and are so enthusiastic in our having made it.

They bring two cars and drive us away to the city. They are small cars and one is filled with our luggage. The city is quiet and asleep. There is no traffic. It is almost midnight and I am surprised that it seems so shut down. It is a November night and it is cooler than I had imagined. They tell us how human labor builds and transforms the city, not the mechanical and motor-driven mechanisms in America and elsewhere. They saturate us with facts of the places that we move through in the night, from the Cricket stadium to the Chinese section to downtown. It is evident at how much they care about India and living in Calcutta.

At the hotel we encounter a multitude of service workers just as we had when we passed through immigration at the airport. We are uncertain of the day that just passed and all the years that have preceded us. Though they did exist, they have come and

269

gone. The only thing clear to us is that we are here living in an unknown and faraway place.

I awake early the next morning. Just outside the door, I am amazed to be here and observing life. India is a great and interesting place. I often like to run through the streets of cities, but I am not here carrying on any particular routine. I come here as open-minded as I can be to find out things for myself. An Indian friend who drove us to the airport in San Francisco said if there is a way that he would describe India it would be people, people, and people. He said that there will be people everywhere we go in the country. It is not until I am here that I realize that India is about one third the area of the United States, but has three times as many people.

Just outside on the street is a rich and moving life that presents a fascinating view of existence. Just yesterday we went on a road to downtown Singapore on a bus, and I heard only one car horn, and observed but a few cars. Here in Calcutta is the beginning morning traffic the car noise is an endless communication of movement, warning, announcing, emotional expression, impatience, and custom. One sees a teeming street life. It was so quiet when we arrived in the night with no one about. The city was almost dead still. I did see a lone cow, and several persons sleeping on the sidewalks. This morning, outside our living quarters is a man crouched down and sweeping the street with a hand broom, and cars loudly move in both directions in and around the street construction. I make it to the end of the street always cautious and aware of the car traffic from either direction as I walk among others who are as aware of the ever busy street. I reach the corner and I decide to go further. I get to a sidewalk, which frees me from the ever-busy concentration on endless vehicles.

The street and sidewalk life now has my total attention. Immediately I see a barber shaving a customer right on the sidewalk. It seems such a small, impressive, and simple business. There are numerous other such sidewalk businesses and activities that are interesting as I see numerous persons preparing food as they peel potatoes and other fruits and vegetables. At a corner is a vendor selling apples, oranges, and bananas. There is a locksmith sorting and filing keys. Someone is cooking bread in a pot of hot oil. There are gatherings and clusters of conversations, newspaper vendors, children walking to school, cab drivers washing their cars, those washing and hanging clothes, bathing on the street, cooking, and building fires. The pace of life is unhurried.

There are many dogs on the street and trees that are old and battered, which stand on the broken and cracked sidewalk. Some of the places are shacks constructed of tin sheets, scraps of wood and other discarded materials. Sometimes there are streams of water running through the mud alleys. When I see men pulling carts filled with their collected items, I am taken back to San Francisco, where the homeless collect and transport overloaded baskets containing odd and interesting discarded objects. They busily move along, sometimes hardly noticed. In San Francisco such persons have a much more conspicuous and questioning presence.

How common and accepted are poor and homeless individuals to this way of life? There is a much deeper struggle for life here. Recently on a street corner in San Francisco I saw a homeless person start a street fire and cook food. I think to myself that the homeless are as serious about their lives as people in the wilderness who prepare meals with wood and kindling sticks. Some of the San Francisco homeless persons were just as strenuous in their survival as one living in the woods, or one on the streets of Calcutta. On this Indian sidewalk are those immersed in a life that seems to have been refined and perfected using a scarcity of resources, food, and materials to sustain life. To me they are as impressive as those are with sophisticated and expensive tools and modern inventions. The street dwellers seem to live a serious, business minded, and inventive way of life. As one passing through, I do not question the daily routines, but move quietly through the adventure. I am amazed to be in this distant world, with unusual customs and ways that have been existing for hundreds and sometimes thousands of years. I have come from 15,000 miles away and they hardly notice me. I am surprised at how my presence is taken in stride.

A Darker Side

In the midst of those cutting onions and washing clothes and the continuous flow of automobiles, busses, taxicabs, bicycles, and water collectors are the hard and forgotten laborers. There are those who clean the toilets, break stones and cement in the hardest struggle, dig holes and use severe strength and force to move objects, and carry loads in the toughest of conditions. One sees the monotony of their drudgery and the intensity of their subjugation. It seems a hard and struggling life with so little concern and appreciation from others. It seems that those who carry books, and satchels are busy pursuing a life to make a living so as to avoid such travail and physical endurance. They work for what appears to be, and is accepted as a higher quality of life. It said that is why some women prefer sons, as it is often the only way to increase their status in an otherwise subordinate life.

I pass the sidewalk businesses of shoe repairing, food stalls, launderers, and taxi cab drivers. These vendors and craftsmen are engaged in their work. As I travel back I look for a young boy who shines shoes. He is located near the corner. I stand and observe him work; he enthusiastically involves himself in the street activity. I saw him earlier as he busily worked, shining shoes. I am not clear on the price we agree to. It is probably four or five rupees, or about ten cents. It does not take him long and he does a satisfactory job. I appreciate his seriousness and the attention to his work. I was originally going to pay him in rupees, but I surprise him by giving him an American dollar. He puts it to his head and expresses his astonishment and joy. He is shocked at the unexpected amount for his work. I move on with a feeling of having a momentary impact on his conventional custom and a surprise to the street life that he routinely labors in.

We pass through the encounter. Though he is a person on the road whom I am unlikely to meet again, I wonder about his life. I think about him and school. I learn that most street children have never been inside a school.

India, like the African countries I had worked in, has a British system of schools. They were leftover from the colonial rule of the land. I do visit several schools in India. I learn that few of the poor ever attend school. I visit a Catholic secondary school and college in Calcutta. The most impressive thing about the school is the head master and his total attention to our visit.

He welcomes us with enthusiasm and graciousness. He expected us and seemed so glad to have us visit him and the school. He offers us a quiet section of the lobby for conversation and dialogue. Most of the people we meet do not wish to talk about the poor. The headmaster is comfortable with any question about the school that we ask him. The school is St Xavier's. Its motto is Nothing Beyond. It attracts students setting the highest goals in life. There are several places in the school admissions reserved for the poorest students. They come to the school. He did not want to generalize about any class of persons. He discovers that all are capable of learning. Though we may not all be deeply motivated about learning the same things, it is important in finding out what we are good at and are capable of mastering. We find that it is worth dedicating ourselves to such a life. He does find that often the poorest students are fascinated with an opportunity to change their lives, and they may see finding work as a way of transforming themselves from a state of struggling poverty. Some leave the schools for work and to better their lives.

When I lived in Nigeria, I saw students who had excelled in school, and they searched for a place in society. They went to Lagos, Ibadan, and other large cities. Where do they take what they have mastered and contribute to the world? They search for places. Many work hard to go overseas for a more meaningful situation. The Indian students at St Xavier's coming from a poor family, or village probably feel privileged to enter society as an accepted working member. This is real and more important than school. It is a new life.

Moment to moment I appreciate, marvel, and wonder about the pulse of life in Calcutta. I listen to those who say it is a beautiful and unplanned place, as it is an exploding mass of faces and lives that make it almost impossible to travel about. One day we go to lunch with Rajasree, the sister of Shyamoshree. She works in a business section of Calcutta. There is much road construction going on, and the traffic is so slow that it takes more than thirty minutes to drive one block around the corner to the restaurant. The driver is very familiar with the city, but the volume of traffic is overwhelming. We get to the restaurant. It has a quiet atmosphere and the service is excellent. The sister orders many courses, and the quality of the food is very good. The sister is in the travel business. She has been an English teacher, and speaks excellent English. She has visited the United States to attend Shyamoshree's wedding. She had visited our house, and I appreciated her conversation, and her attitude toward life and knowledge of things. We had appreciated having her as a guest. She is now inviting us to this special restaurant and is glad to have us visit her in India.

She tells us about a guru with whom she is studying. She is devoted to his spiritual teachings. This seems to have deepened her life. In reading a journal of an American in nineteenth century India, I learn of an Indian swami who is utterly holy and pure as he had reached a state of perfection. It was said that such a state might be reached once in a thousand years, maybe. This individual is then ready to be released from this world. The writer personally meets the individual and has no personal transformation in this encounter. He has no idea of what to expect with an audience with the swami. He finds it astonishing to be in his presence, but meeting him is not the important and profound thing about this holy man for the writer. That does not move the writer as does the supposed millions of believers who follow him. That makes the individual larger than life to him.

In an adventure to find out the fundamental meaning of the universe I discover an Indian philosopher with deep insight and who contributes to our own existence. I listen to him several times in Ojai, California. From his dialogue and discussion one is asked to set aside all that we know as well as all we have invented to see and to understand life through ones own exploration. He concerns himself with setting all humans free. There is no search for freedom. It is. It exists or it does not. He is not one described by words or any boundary or image created by thought. He stands alone in life and the world.

Life happens now, in the moment. Just this morning I have a conversation with an Indian gentleman from Calcutta who once lived and taught in East Africa. I learn of him through a friend I work with in San Francisco. He is a relative of hers and she tells me how to contact him when I reach Calcutta. I do. We never meet but we engage in a telephone conversation.

We find that nothing rids us of the prejudice of religion, culture, and race. An academic education is closed to the tolerance and compassion of human suffering, tragedy, and injustice. School and education do not rid society of its hatred, greed, and discrimination. The world needs transformation from the inbred systems of knowledge and tradition. We need to live a deeper life not one of images, superstition, and hope for miracles. Technical knowledge and education are necessary to survive, but they do not bring human freedom. We must transcend the knowledge that imprisons us and not accept a world of discrimination, inhumanity, or injustice.

## City Places

Among the cars, buses, trucks, bikes and motorcycles, and rickshaws are people traveling on both sides of the street. One is supposed to drive on the left side, but that often only applies when one wants to avoid an oncoming vehicle, and the car swerves at the last minute. It is always honking your horn while you are driving and keeping your arm and elbows inside the car as there are too many tight and squeezing situations. It is always amazing to get through a narrow space impediment. Drivers force bicyclists and pedestrians off the road. If someone is hit or injured, it is said that only the rich can afford to sue, and that it is impossible to prove anything in court. What can happen if one is hit is that the driver could be beaten up by an angry mob.

Calcutta is a huge urban city and there are no major expressways. It seemingly has too few roads for its enormous traffic problem. People are incessantly walking among trams, trucks, taxicabs, cars, buses, rickshaws, scooters, mopeds, and bicycles. The streets are aflame with noise and sounds of human desperation and resignation among the cows, dogs, pollution, pedestrians, people bathing in the streets, and endless transaction amongst small shops, stalls, and businesses.

Navigating through all of this is Bishu. He is the driver who daily takes us through all the ongoing encounters. Of all the individuals my wife meets or observes, he stands out as the most remarkable. Because of his skills, knowledge of the city, and energy to endure the impossible, we are able to appreciate getting places in the city. We are filled with gratitude to reach every destination that we set out for.

We visit Howrah across the Ganges over the Vidyasagar Bridge, President's College, and College Street bookstores, and meet with one of Meghna's professors. We go to the Bengali Rowing Club for dinner, we see classical Kerala dancers at the Eastern Zonal Cultural Center, we visit Rajasree and her family as well as the brother Abhijit and his wife and daughter, we go to the Metro Railway Station, and to the Calcutta Airport. He takes us everywhere in Calcutta. And then we leave Calcutta for Darjeeling.

# 41

# DARJEELING

Our friend Shyamoshree wants us to travel throughout India. She envisions that we all begin in the east in Calcutta, travel northwest to Darjeeling and the Himalayas. Then we make our way to the plains and then to the west coast on the Arabian Sea. We then travel inland and make our way to Southern India, and the tip of India before again reaching the east coast and returning to Calcutta.

We leave Calcutta first for Bagdogra. At the airport the three of us—my wife, Shyamoshree, and I—meet an Indian friend from San Francisco, and her sister who is from Los Angeles. They are Rupa and Tapasree. We were happy to be traveling together with them to Darjeeling. The plane is late in leaving; we do not depart until 3:00 pm. We arrive in Bagdogra at 5:00 pm. It is evening and as soon as we arrive, we take a taxi as we had planned. The taxi is a jeep, and is larger and a more sturdy vehicle than those seen in Calcutta. At the time I do not realize the small cars and taxis in Calcutta are not strong enough for the mountain road we face. We leave Bagdogra and drive ten miles to Siliguri. We will spend more time here on our return from Darjeeling.

Siliguri lies 398 feet above sea level. We will ascend more than 6,000 feet and travel fifty miles to get to Darjeeling, which is 6,880 feet above sea level. It is getting dark as we ascend. At the time I do not realize the altitude we face and the coming darkness in driving up the mountain road would eventually hide the countryside. Much of the Singalila Range that we climbed I would not discover until we descended days later.

The Singalila Range stretches sixty miles from the plains to the Himalayan plateau, and culminates in the great mountain peaks, which includes Kanchenjunga (28,146 feet above sea level). The driver is familiar with the road and experienced in handling the jeep. It is a winding road that switches back and forth as we climb and climb. Several times the driver reverses and backs down the hill to allow a descending vehicle to pass. The driver keeps a good speed as he untiringly makes it through narrow and sharp turns and negotiates avoiding other vehicles, pedestrians, dogs and cows who occupy the road with us.

In the dark I am not aware that we have reached a much higher elevation but we reach a point when Tapasree and my wife both experience altitude sickness. We stop, and they both get out of the vehicle. They are weakened from vomiting and headaches. After a discussion of going back down to a lower altitude, it is decided that we rest and then continue on. We have come too far. Both are determined to proceed. We get to Darjeeling, and after some confusion and miscommunicated directions, two youth show us where we are going. The cold weather is the unexpected surprise to me as is the different nationality of persons we encounter. The people are the Lepcha, Tibetans, the Sherpa, Nepalese, Bhutanese, and Sikkimese. We are a world away from Calcutta. My wife and Tapasree rest through the night and are slightly better the next day. My wife really never does get over the altitude sickness. She never ventures far and we stay in, while others make trips to the markets, and observation spots to view the mountains.

For my wife it is somewhat like the summer we spend in Italy and France. She is sick in the hotel, and I run and jog through Rome, and come upon such places as the Colosseum, the Vatican, the ruins of the Roman Forum, the Trevi Fountain, the Pantheon or Piazza Navona. Then she, my daughter, and I would visit them together. My wife is overwhelmed with the actuality of being in places of ancient Roman life that she studied in school. It amazes her. In France we stay in a small village called Les Bossons. My wife is seldom well enough to leave the hotel, but wants me to have the opportunity to do some hiking or trekking. I run the roads to Chamonix and back. One day I go there and take the cable car to Aiguille du Midi to the 12,000 ft level, which is where a trail to Mont Blanc begins.

At the time I do not know what is required to get to the summit. I later learn that it is a two-day project. It is advisable to have a guide and one should have crampons, ropes, an ice-axe, a helmet, and a headlamp for the crevasses. One must be ready for uncertain weather, steep ascents, and night climbing. I do hike on the quiet mountain trails and see beautiful wildflowers above the bustling town of Chamonix and small French farms. The air is clean and fresh, and the view is breathtaking. We leave Les Bossons and ride to Geneva, Switzerland, and take a train from there to Paris. My wife's headaches persist throughout our travel just as they are again in Darjeeling.

We are now next to the Himalayan mountain range. Just north of us in Sikkim is Kanchenjunga. We are able to view it from Darjeeling. It is majestic, white with snow, and sacred in nature. Kanchenjunga is the third tallest mountain in the world at 28,169 feet. I have climbed Mt. Kilimanjaro in Tanzania, Mt. Rainier in Washington, Mt. Shasta in California, and mountains in the Sierras in California. They were all awesome sights and great wonders of the earth. The Himalayan mountain range extends 1,500 miles from Tibet to India. It has the grandest and highest mountains in the world. The tallest mountain in the world stands there, Mt. Everest at 29,035 feet. It can be seen from Darjeeling. For my wife and me, its presence is striking, amazing, and unbelievable to us. It is a spectacular world to observe and is a place of great adventure on our planet.

One great Himalayan expedition that I learn about is that of five Nepalese women whose mission it is to summit Everest. Some groups train for years. These Sherpa women of Nepal had two weeks to train before they face the 29,035 feet mountain which is the highest climbing challenge in the world. They have a lifetime of living at high altitude that uniquely prepares them in different ways from many foreign expeditions. They are also unlike the foreign climbers whose faith often lies in physical strength and technology. For these women the mountain, not the climber is in control.

At the 17,500 ft base camp, things start off well for them and their team, but some of them then begin to struggle with altitude sickness and uncertainty, and are unable to continue despite their perseverance and tremendous hope. One by one they discontinue the expedition. The third climber discontinues at 23,000 feet. At the last base camp at 26,300 feet two remain for the final push to the summit. One of the climbers at more than 28,000 feet, who is just a few hundred feet short of the summit, begins to feel ill and says she cannot continue the climb. The last climber beset by howling winds and driving snow reaches the summit. She said that on the mountain she felt no fear. The mission had been accomplished. She had made her family and the team proud. Her adventure impacts us all.

One day my wife felt well enough to travel and the five of us take a back road trip. We go into town into Darjeeling city center, and hire a taxi. Our Indian friends have heard of a religious site to visit, and we accompany them. We set off on the journey. The steep canyon walls make the trip dangerous but we continue on. This mountain road has unsuspected sharp turns and so one is never able to rest. The thick green plant life and vastness of the mountain and the forests give grandeur to the earth. We see places of spectacular beauty and extinction. It is a road where one can just disappear forever, at any point. We ride on. It is a trip of deep wonder, but with a question of getting through it and being alive at each point we descend. The grand view holds one spell bound, but unable to take any moment for granted. It is a breathless descent. We see the earth from a winding road through lofty cliffs that are green with thick vegetation. We move along on the edge of hills and ridges above bottomless chasms. We make it to our destination and later return.

Coming back is not as treacherous. Indeed the taxi is not able to carry the load of all of us, and at one point Rupa and I get out, lightening the load. We walk the hills with a slow and steady pace to reach a hill town. I am amazed at her spirit and energy to make it up the road and reach a plateau and reenter the taxi and continue on to Darjeeling. There we stop at a tea plantation, buy tea and observe the endless rows of tea bushes filling the hills and slopes. We stop at a school. Few students are around, but one member of the staff gives us a tour of the place. The presence of the school shows me how deep education penetrates into every village and in all the places I travel. There are students everywhere. The person who studies subjects to pass examinations is not really a student. A true student is learning everywhere, and from everything. So the school itself is often an illusion in learning.

On another day that my wife feels well enough to leave the hotel, we go back into the city. Darjeeling is a place of walking. We wander through the town and pass shops, stores, hotels, and businesses with garments and wares from around the world. Walking the streets one is aware of a noticeable ethnic presence. There are monks, European visitors, Indian women in saris, people from the plains and the mountains, and an occasional American amongst the Sherpa, Nepalese, Tibetans, and Lepcha.

My wife and I walk up Observatory Hill, pass prayer flags, holy men inviting contributions, some persons praying, others reading sacred scripts, and those in meditation. We observe a Hindu temple, and a Buddhist shrine. It is cloudy, which is not a good day for seeing the Himalayas. The most interesting and intriguing presence in the long peaceful walk is that of the langur monkeys. They have a golden coat and a black face and they roam around the grounds in troops. My wife hardly seems to notice them till they quickly jump around landing right beside us. They scream and flash their teeth as though they are set to attack or demand a confrontation. Before they are able to strike or initiate a seeming attack, I am able to chase them away. We move on beyond them with their gnarling teeth and screams. I leave with a strange feeling about how such creatures disrupt the tranquility of this spiritual world. We descend the hill and I do not think further about them.

It is not until I read about a visitor who was chased down the hill by eight monkeys that I realize their true aggression. They rushed toward him until a guide from the temple came, and the monkeys gave ground and ran away.

An even more surprising incident I learn about is when scores of langur monkeys overrun the nearby women's college in Darjeeling. They are reported to have destroyed thousands of books, disrupted classes, and harassed students. They claw and slap students, take their books and bags, and grab their lunch boxes of food. Such an attack has happened before, several times. The monkeys are the same troops from Observatory Hill where worshipers, and visitors graciously feed them. Some persons think that perfumes and bags used by the students provoked the attack. Wildlife officials captured 30 of the monkeys, and took them to a far away jungle. The town residents protested the encroachment on the temple grounds. It was still not known how and when harmony would come.

We leave Darjeeling early because my wife is still ill. We have an encounter with the desk clerk who is adamant about no refunding a day we already paid for. It seems important to him that he remains firm in carrying out the duties of his position. We are as serious in our determination of not letting him, or the hotel, get away with refusing to return money we have paid. It becomes an intense confrontation and I ask to talk with the manager. She is not there. He tells me there is no need to see her, as this is the practice, and it is our unfortunate situation. I leave and return later to talk to the person in charge. She is already familiar with the case, and says that we are entitled to eighty percent of what we paid to be refunded. She apologizes for the confusion and nothing else is discussed.

Our friends Rupa and Tapasree are traveling on to Sikkim. They are eager to discover new places in India and the Himalayas as we say goodbye to them. We are travelling to stay at the lower altitude in Siliguri.

We again descend from the mountains into the plains and the heat. We ride pass the fields of tea and a meandering road running along the Teesta River, and the rapids and falls. We follow the grand winding river as we pass down deep gorges on either side of the road and the endless green forest. The heat is intense as we reach Siliguri. My wife and Shymoshree rest as I explore the city streets.

Siliguri 2:00 P.M.

It is a contrasting life from the hills. The roads in Darjeeling are winding, hilly, and narrow. Pedestrians compete for space with the vehicles. There is a dominant presence of hill and mountain people from places such as Nepal, Sikkim, Tibet, and Bhutan who bring a lifestyle that thrives in the cold and busy hill streets. In Siliguri there is a steady stream of people along the road but are not immersed in the street traffic. I observe auto rickshaws propelled by drivers carrying people, supplies, and other materials. I see newsstands, men urinating in the grass (as I have seen in the US and elsewhere) a farm with a lone worker, a bricklayer, and even a religious altar along the road.

It is extremely hot and I stop in a small street restaurant to buy a soft drink. It is confusing because I do not drink it there. I tell them I am going to take it with me. The bottle I must also pay for is my understanding. I agree to pay. Then I am told that I cannot pay for it now but that I must bring it back when I am finished. I leave 10 rupees. My thinking is that five is for the drink and five is for the bottle, although I am not allowed to pay for the bottle now. I take the bottle of soft drink back to the room and share it with my wife. I return it to the restaurant and the man seems happy to see me. He acknowledges my return from his workstation where he appears to be cooking.

Another person greets me and is going to invite me to be seated for service. I show him the empty bottle I am returning. He immediately understands and gives me 10 rupees. I am confused because I wonder if I received the drink for free. I then assume that in all of the earlier interaction I may have given them 5 rupees for the drink and left 10 rupees for the bottle (which could not be paid for until I returned) and I receive the 10 rupees for the returned bottle. That possibility of already leaving the deposit makes more sense to me than returning the bottle and getting the entire 10 rupees back again. They seem satisfied that the business had been conducted properly. I acknowledge the transaction but leave uncertain.

Siliguri 7:00 A.M.

I walk by a farmer laboring with a plow pulled by a cow, a welding shop with men working, a multitude of bicycle driven rickshaws carrying people, goods, and food. Some rickshaws are empty. I see a pile of green peppers being sorted, a street barber shaving a customer, black birds searching through litter piles, a pig roaming about, a black cow standing still, car horns blowing, people sweeping the streets, sidewalks and business fronts, and men carrying bananas on their heads. The morning seems busy and things seem to be happening as they normally do. I am unnoticed as I move through the town just as everyone else seems to do. I see an army post as I walk down a side road with a tailoring shop, a chemist and a drug store, a woman carrying firewood on her head, crowded buses, a young boy washing and wiping oranges, those taking baths, those washing dishes. There is a dog barking at a man with a long pole on his shoulder. The dog's owner, with long uncombed hair struggles, to pick up the dog and to quiet him down as the two of them seem to get the issue resolved.

I pass a religious altar, and see closed stores and shops not yet open. There is endless activity with persons walking with their faces covered, scarves around their necks and a continuous multitude of bicyclists moving on the road pass those carrying bricks on their heads and working to build a new place. As in Calcutta, the multitude of people and activity continues and seems endless.

There are school children carrying on conversations, wearing their uniforms, and carrying books that may have engaged their minds. I hope they are serious students who value learning and not the rituals of education.

In the afternoon we hire an auto rickshaw and the three of us travel the main road of the town and visit a market, the railway station, and the stones of the Mahanadi riverbed. Siliguri is situated by this mass of broken stone. In the distance I see persons laboring. There seems to be an endless world of stones and rocks. I later learn that there are children who, because of poverty, illegally work in the stone quarry. Many of the children and their families have no regard for an education. For some it is a cycle of poverty and illiteracy passed down through the generations. For some people in the world poverty is extreme and devastating. They are persons who matter to us and to whom we must give our attention to so that they can climb out of this life on their own.

We leave Siliguri for New Delhi.

# 42

# NEW DELHI

New Delhi 7:00 A.M.

I walk along Subramanian Bharti. Delhi right now is a ghost town compared to the ride through the city the previous night. There were horns blowing, overcrowded buses, and thick pollution. Bicycles and motorized bikes and rickshaws moved in and out of a thick mass of cars, trucks, and carts. The New Delhi area is said to have 16 million people and 4 million vehicles. More than half of the vehicles are a variety of two wheelers that fight for space in the crunch of traffic. So many are coming and going. Many persons walk along the roads. It seems a quiet and sane way of travel, but the persons walking still need to move through the chaos and confusion caused by those in stress to get to their destination. Those who walk through the speeding and pulsating, tangled mass of vehicles are ever cautious, realizing the danger of getting to the locations they pursue. I am aware of the possible hazard every time I cross the street this morning. Though I have seen overwhelming traffic in India, I have rarely seen an accident. I know that they happen.

Today I see several persons on the road that I travel. There are taxi drivers cleaning their cars. I see more luxurious cars here than in other places I have been. As I walk past the Khan Market, I see a security guard standing alone with a rifle around his shoulder. I move cautiously in the event of a human encounter that might awaken any suspicion. I quietly walk by him without notice.

286

I come upon an unexpected sight in which I cross a wide boulevard to reach. Inside its gate I observe a great sanctuary. It is the Lodi Garden. I see walkers, runners, and picnickers. On another day I will return to run through the garden and around this entire area. I see numerous dogs walking the street, and in the garden I am surprised to see two dogs being walked on a lease. Lodi Garden is a royal burial ground for Sayyid and Lodi rulers of Delhi. I was not certain of where I was when I first reached the place so I asked a guard at a gate. "Is this Lodi Garden?" His response, "Yes," is the only interaction I have as I walk along the street. The Lodi Garden seemed a place where one exists in some other time. I wear a jacket as it is colder than I had anticipated.

I leave the garden and I turn a corner. I am almost lost until I am able to retrace my path, and get back to the Khan Market. It seems to be a wealthy shopping center. Just outside the market area I see a woman sweeping the street. I then notice on the street three handmade tent-like-structures. I immediately realize that this is where the woman lives. It is a place where the poor reside. It is somewhat like a San Francisco homeless street shelter but this is much larger and seems to be allowed to remain where it stands. Those who reside there seem to be getting ready for the day. The woman who is sweeping the street is wearing a beautiful and colorful sari, and seems unaware of me or anyone else who is walking about. She seems totally alone in her work. Her world on the street is distinct from affluent Delhi life, and is a universe away. As close as she seems to this wealthy world she never enters its realm.

I cross the wide street, and look at both the street light and the quiet traffic. Where I am in Delhi is a place of grandeur and opulence, and seems another India in some ways.

In the afternoon we visit Dastkar, which is a society for crafts and craftspeople. We know about coming to this place from Shyamoshree's brother who is an artist. We visited him and his wife and daughter in Calcutta. My wife had been interested in an Indian scroll painting at his house, and he told us about the artist whose work it was, and where we could find her. It took us a while to get there, but we did locate the center and the artist. The Dastkar organization was founded to help craftspeople, especially women, to use their crafts to produce work and employment and to generate economic self-sufficiency. The goal of the center is to allow the craftspeople to be self-reliant in developing modern markets that are sustainable. The products they produce include garments and accessories, home furnishings, toys, stationary, and objects of art. There is a group that creates work depicting traditional folktales. My wife was elated to have found the woman who produced the exact work she sought. It was a scroll painting to propitiate the spirits. The artist was from the Midnapore District of West Bengal.

It is said that income generation is not enough for the women and they must have a place of their own. Women in the traditional rural social system own nothing and they need such an organization most of all.

I learn that the women were once asked for what would they use the earnings they hoped to make. They responded to purchase silver jewelry, to buy better seeds and a buffalo, or to buy a well. They would send their children to a fee paying private school, receive hospital medical treatment, or get a proper latrine were also some of the hopes expressed.

Agra, Uttar Pradesh

We leave New Delhi for Agra at 6:00 A.M. in the morning. It is 128 miles away. We leave in a large van. It is a four hour drive. I ask our driver about the population of the two Indian cities. He says that New Delhi is 15 million and Agra is 3 million. In leaving New Delhi we pass expensive homes and the Apollo Hospital which provides an international standard of healthcare, and is at the forefront of medical technology and expertise. Persons from all over the world come here for treatment. It is a tribute to the level of competence and excellence that exists in India.

The highway surprisingly is not very busy at times. We do encounter the accustomed traffic tie ups as we pass through towns along the way. It is what we were accustomed to in Calcutta and New Delhi. There are seven of us who paid 1500 rupees each for this bus trip: 2 Americans, 2 British, 2 Indians, and 1 Israeli. One of the British, married to an Indian passenger, was from Nottingham. He was asked if he was friends with Robin Hood. The British woman replied that Robin Hood was from Sherwood. In a conversation I had with the British woman she told me that she had started her Indian stay by being in Mumbai (Bombay) for four days. She says that her husband, who is not with her, was born in Bombay and they are returning to India for a visit. She tells me that Bombay has 17 million people and that 12 million live on the street. I have no idea as to the accuracy of this figure. I know by being on the street in Calcutta and Saliguri how amazed I am at the capability and inventiveness of masses of people in poverty to live off minimal material and sustain such vitality and to stay alive.

We encounter new scenes all along the way, and at the toll stops are a variety of animals, and along the road are rice and wheat fields, mud huts, granaries, water buffalo, plows, and tractors.

Many people live along the road. Towns are alive with people conducting business as they buy and sell vegetables and other goods in open markets. Some are collecting and carrying water as townspeople go from place to place in cars trucks, bicycles, and motor scooters. When cows cross the road the traffic stops. The driver is experienced, but there is always concern about the conditions of the road, horns blowing, the traveling speed, and what is coming the other way. There is a constant presence of life and people clinging to the side of the van whenever we stop or slow down. There is a continuing interest in selling us things. The journey has a sometimes circus atmosphere as ones sees muzzled bears, camels, a snake charmer, pigs, cows, and horses. It takes us four hours to get to Agra.

Seth is our guide. He was born in Agra and has been talking about the Taj Mahal for more than thirty years to visitors. He is tall, thin, elderly, knowledgeable, and answers all questions. As we get close to the Taj Mahal I feel overwhelmed by the thousands of people and the heat. Though it is a most anticipated view, I am exhausted. Seth seems to understand the mass movement of people, and why each one of us is here. I learn that as many as 200,000 people in a day sometimes visit the Taj Mahal. Before we enter the main gate, he shows me a view through an opening in the gate all the way though the entrance of the Taj. It is straight as a laser and it becomes such a mathematical, geometrical, flat, and symmetrical world that surrounds me. The precision seems astonishing. We enter the gate and see the grand architecture.

Why is it there and how it is so exceptional? The Mughal Empire, like the British, ruled over India. As conquerors they were powerful and rich. The Mughal emperor, Shah Jahan, had taken over the throne on the death of his father. He had the Taj Mahal built in memory of his wife, Mumtaz Mahal, who died, and whom he deeply loved. In the 17th century the Taj Mahal was built at tremendous cost for its day. It was millions of rupees to finish. It took 22 years to complete and 20,000 workers. The emperor was later deposed by his son, and imprisoned in Agra Fort until his death and then buried besides his wife in the Taj Mahal. Seth says that the workers were not ordinary, and worked and labored beyond normal work days and weeks for very long hours for the emperor in memory of his wife. He said that they had a mission and a dedication to produce this work. I find it is a world beyond the artificial measure of time and wealth.

One understands the Taj Mahal is a sacred resting place inspired by great love, using architecture to express glory and greatness. It is timeless and unique in the world.

We visited the Agra Fort to see where the son imprisoned the emperor and where the emperor was able to view the Yamuna River and the Taj Mahal. We return on the Delhi-Agra road and we reached New Delhi at 11:00 PM.

Death is hard. I know this when I learn about four young American women who were killed some years ago on the Delhi-Agra road. It was late at night. The bus swerved off the road killing seven people and others were critically injured. The families were devastated. I read an account submitted by a family member that investigated driving on the road. It was described as a road that narrowed and widened constantly without warning with extensive potholes. It was called the busiest highway in India and was predominantly stampeded by trucks with no dividing barriers on the road. The chaos of the trucks sometimes three or four abreast, vying for position, crossed lanes regardless of the traveling direction. Speed limits were completely ignored and entirely self imposed. There is a strong tradition of not using headlamps at night. They may be switched on and off rapidly at the last moment. As we returned on the same road we did not know that the risk was always so monumental and was particularly hazardous at night.

Jaipur, Rajasthan

Rajasthan is a flat desert country that is brown and barren. It is a land of grand forts and palaces that have survived the desert life.

In Jaipur, I see new travelers on the road. There are the three wheel autos, buses, cabs, motorcycles, bicycles, rickshaws, and pedestrians crowding the road. I see camels carrying people and I see more cows, pigs, horses, and dogs than before. Elephants are used to carry passengers up roads to Amber Fort. Heavy structured walls were built to defend its residents. Inside the gate of the fort is a courtyard and structures that deteriorated, disappeared or stood in ruins, but some do remarkably remain. There are passageways, a hall of mirrors, gardens, pavilions, royal apartments, palaces, and temples. Its construction began in the late 17th century and took more than a century to complete. From the top of a hill it has an expansive view over the valley and plains beyond.

It is a surprise to see contemporary and medieval ways of life resonate and survive among the multitude of people, vehicles, and animals. All fit in and form an ever-moving wave of life that is divergent and striking but not conflicting as life goes on. A cow standing alone on the road as life directs itself around it is an interesting phenomenon to me, as are the folk musicians with their instruments. Also interesting to me is the holy man appearing on the road and walking into town. The most unusual individual that I observe is an Italian man walking along the road. I am told that he came to town, became penniless, and was unable to leave. Now those in the town say that he is a crazy and insane person. I had thought of trying to talk to him. Though I had wanted to meet him it never worked out. It seemed as though many people knew about him. I hope that he is able to free himself from his mental and economic prison.

When we walk in the town a beggar follows me. She singles me out and is determined that I give her money. She has a baby on her back. As I walk and walk she never gives up. There are a lot of beggars here, and this is their way of life. I am unable to contribute to all who approach me, so I give to no one. In the end I give the woman with the baby five rupees. I genuinely want her to have the money. She communicates that it is not enough. Once she understands the situation is final she stops asking and moves on. The amount of money one gives in such situations is indeterminate. One day I was running in Golden Gate Park in San Francisco and I found a quarter. I gave it to a homeless person who was sitting down under a bridge in the dirt. My presence had surprised him. I told him that I had found the quarter on the road and it might change his day. He broke down in tears because he had been so astonished and surprised.

There are so many people in India and elsewhere who depend on help and donations from others on the streets, at the restaurants, in hotels, and in taxicabs. And as one moves through life some individuals view the world differently. In our hotel in Jaipur an employee at the hotel, who works in the office, graciously assists us in our stay in many ways. He does it without reward other than our gratitude for his quality of work. He adamantly refuses any money for the assistance he provides. He is content doing his job as well as he is able to do it. The staff who manages the hotel is exemplary, and unique in India.

Another time I am in such a situation is in Geneva. My wife is ill and we take the taxi from Les Bossons, France to Geneva,

Switzerland. The cab driver has been exorbitant in his charges, but it is an emergency. We later take a taxicab from our hotel to the train station in Geneva. The driver charged exactly what is registered. He refuses a cent more. He is very clear that this is fair. He thanks us for our riding with him, and says that he deserves nothing more. He stands out as such a unique person, because when we go to Paris, again the taxi service is exorbitant. The individuals in Jaipur and Geneva are persons who to me search for truth in life through the work they do.

Jantar Mantar is an observatory that we visit in Jaipur. It is one of five such places for viewing the heavens. They were built in the early 18th century. The observatory in Jaipur is the largest and best preserved. It contains thirteen different instruments for calculating the movement of celestial bodies. Each piece of equipment is used for specific purposes. I hear elaborate detail on how they work. It is interesting and arduous for my mind to follow these tortuous and twisting exercises. These methods are supposedly used to find such measurements as the position of the stars and planets, the calculation of eclipses, the determination of celestial longitude and latitude, and the altitude of the sun. It is a medieval tradition of viewing the universe that is continued and maintained. This Jaipur geocentric model of the earth as the center of the universe was never questioned or challenged until a sun-centered solar system replaced this view. It is irrelevant in today's world of understanding the universe.

"Are we alone in space?" is a question we ask.

I observe the deep energy of the human adventure, and I know children and other minds that are here as unprejudiced explorers probing our world and trying to make sense of life and our place in space.

"Have we been visited, will we be, or are we being visited now?"

We who are alive now may never know. It is not knowledge that we need, but to find our own way.

From the very beginning of life we probe, and understand things. We find ourselves on this planet alone, and we are on our own. We use inquiry and discovery to move further into this existence and world, realizing the earth is no more significant than we are. We must be self-taught and not assume others have the answers as we exist in this universe and its adventure.

Bandra

Bombay (Mumbai) has a very modern airport, but there are tents of the poor at the edge of the land. We decide to take a taxi to Bandra as we are just passing through the city on the way to Goa. To me Bandra exemplifies an affluent life. I find it somewhat like life in a wealthy neighborhood of Manhattan in New York. There is a fashion world of fabric and clothes. There are health food stores as well as stores of wedding garments, and men's and women's wear. There is a baby's shop and shoe store. I see a doctor's office that describes prenatal diagnosis and ultra sonogram services. We see the fashionable area of the film stars, the joggers' park, the promenades, and the shopping malls. We visit a girl's college campus, where it seems as though its graduates may be assimilated into the wealth and world around them. What happens with affluence is that one wants to sustain prosperity and not question it. The poor and others are excluded from participation.

I read that Bandra was once a place where people came to breathe fresh air and enjoy open space, and the sea, and to rest and reflect. Before that, the Portuguese and the British had come to dominate its life. These days I notice a more British influence than Portuguese.

I see no poverty in Bandra. I am reminded of San Francisco where poor people are unable to live there and quietly vanish. Some persons envision San Francisco as becoming a special place. It is like those who pursue the best school, the greatest city, the richest people, the most powerful nation, or the truest religion. These become images that are significant to us. It is a way for us to impress, dominate, and make things important in the world. It is a form of self-worship that diminishes, and lessens the lives of others, and the world we live in. Some people have called San Francisco a world class city. However, the conditions of the homeless, and the education of the poor, show that in many ways it is an artificial and meaningless city. We leave Bandra for Bangalore.

# 43

## BANGALORE

Bangalore

On the ride from the airport, the taxicab driver goes to the wrong hotel. It seems as though the name of the hotel has not been clearly understood. So we go to another place. Still I am not certain if this is the right hotel or not. There is room and we do register. There is a misunderstanding between Shymoshree and the driver. He asks to be paid for the entire ride from the airport. She tells him that he has not taken us to the right hotel as directed. They both are adamant in their positions. The driver is so annoyed that he refuses any pay unless it is all he is owed or nothing at all. In the end he refuses any pay and leaves unpaid. He is very annoyed, but unyielding. He is not paid and we never see him again. Shymoshree seems unbothered as we all check in.

The hotel itself has the latest computer equipment at the desk, and throughout the facility. Bangalore as a technology center in India is compared to Silicon Valley near San Francisco. The city is known as a productive place in computer and informational technology, and I learn does research in aerospace and biotechnology and has excellent educational institutions.

Once we settle into our rooms, we venture into the city. Our goal is to get Shymoshree's video camera repaired. Though it is night, we have looked forward to getting to this place of technology to finally get it functioning. We are in the center of town and there is a multitude of people as there is in all of

India. We hire an auto rickshaw. It begins with a quiet entry into the existing swarm of vehicles moving in this world of traffic. The driver seems able to take the vehicle anywhere in and out of impossible entanglements and traffic jams and maneuvers through the oncoming buses, trucks, motorcycles, and other autos. The vehicle we are in seems unstoppable and all such auto rickshaw drivers seem fearless as they encounter no problem that cannot be overcome in getting them to their destination. They are on a mission that drives them. Some have no passengers and are always drifting in and out of the madness looking for riders. These drivers and vehicles are all over the country tying up traffic, moving through it, and keeping cities vibrant, active, and alive.

The driver knows several shops to take us to. We state the problem and they look at the camera, but in each case, no technician is on duty so we are to return tomorrow during the day. In three such shops we were told the same information. However, on the next day Shymoshree takes a government bus to visit Mysore. She comes back moved by the vibrancy of the city and the magnificence of the palaces, gardens, and temples. She leaves at 7:00 A.M. and returns at 10:30 P.M.

My wife and I visit the botanical gardens, and several other places. The most interesting place is the Bull Temple. We leave the Sri Dodda Ganapathi Temple and walk up Bugle Hill to reach the Bull Temple. It is a Dravidian style temple that houses a grand black granite stone statue of a bull that stands 15 feet tall and over 20 feet long and is carved out of a single stone block. There is a yearly groundnut festival near the temple to honor the sacred bull. As we travel around Bangalore, it seems of immense size and it takes a long time to travel across town. The traffic, the distance, and the number of people are much more than we have expected. The task of crossing a large city of more than five million people is more intense than we imagine.

Bangalore is an interesting city with masses of people as well as expensive stores and a presence of wealthy merchants. In the hotel are persons moving through daily from the United States, Europe, and other parts of Asia. It is evident that the technology world is present here. As we travel through the city, this world is not evident. Technology has no impact on the ordinary citizen. Though the technology world is hidden to many, I learn that half of the engineering graduates in India have studied in Bangalore's eighty engineering colleges. About 1,000 technology firms have set up businesses in Bangalore. Like every place in India, it is unique. It is a spiritual city that is vibrant and with great technological capability. To what extent will its wonder further impact the ordinary citizen, the country, and the world? From Bangalore we go to Kerala.

# 44

# KERALA AND MADRAS

One morning in Southern India I walk along the shore of the Arabian Sea in the sunshine, appreciating the ocean breeze. I watch children playing Cricket in the sand, joggers running by food vendors who are starting the day. In the near vicinity are men working in unison hauling a net from the sea. Tomorrow we are traveling from here in Kovalum in Kerala to Cape Comorin at the southern tip of India in Tamil Nadu.

Before coming to Kerala we were further up the coast in Goa. We see its waterways, hills, coconut palm trees, green rice fields, villages surrounded by the sylvan countryside, and the great coastline of beaches. We journey to Calanguti and to Panjim, the capital, and then travel through the colonial past and see thousands of people who were on a religious pilgrimage.

Portuguese ships came centuries ago and reached Goa and Kerala. Sometimes it is interesting to see firsthand where others have come and have left from.

We once passed through England where ships had sailed from there to the Jamestown settlement in America. The colonists had gone there for new-world riches. They encountered famine, disease, malnutrition, insanity, and death. Some abandoned the settlement, and some survived. For the American Indians, the colonists brought dominance, and near extinction. For the Africans shipped to the new world plantations the colonists brought inhumane slavery. Our venture into Jamestown gives us a more profound view of the world when we observe where the ship originates from that reaches the Jamestown shores.

Two eye surgeons live in Kerala. They are friends of Shyamoshree. They invite us to have dinner with them at a restaurant in Trivandrum, the capital of Kerala. The husband and wife are both physicians. They are quiet, respectful, and serious. They have also brought his mother to join us. She has lived in Chicago with her other son, and seems comfortable and excited about discussing her time there. I had visited Chicago several times, but I knew very little about the city. Still we talk. She sat next to me. I understand about one half of her English. She does not talk a great deal but our conversation kept both of us focused on getting meaning from our sometimes-questionable communication situation. The husband quietly orders and suggests food we can share. His wife is unusually quiet and attentive and he also is calm and clear in his actions. He and his wife have a quiet, reflective, and understanding nature. They seem aware of our journey and what it means to travel in India.

I ask them about the literacy of the people of Kerala. I had heard that it was the most literate state in India. The wife who is from Kerala feels that this no longer is the case as it was based on an ability such as writing ones name and that these skills and capabilities are now diminishing. It was very interesting to hear this from her, because others in India still looked to those past days of acclaim. I learn that twelve years ago there was such jubilation in Kerala because of the unique accomplishment of achieving complete literacy. Now a 68-year-old grandmother who was the leading celebrity has forgotten how to write her name. It is said that hundreds of thousands have lapsed back to illiteracy, and have forgotten their ability to read and write. Those who had been so driven by the mission to find a campaign to change the mass and poverty population at a grass root-level of participation find the movement has collapsed after inactivity and the time lapse in beginning the second phase of work. The second phase of the project, which was to further literacy awareness, and to teach those left out of the first phase, meanders into nothingness. This is the view expressed.

I ask them about socialism and communism here. The doctor says that it is sometimes an obstacle, and an impediment to others who do not support their views. He had wanted to move furniture into his house, but the local government and its workers insisted on a rate that was not acceptable to him. He challenged them and, in the end, was able to move on his own terms. I learn that communism flourished in the earlier days of Kerala but then was unable to bring about social and economic change, and could not transform the downtrodden people who joined the movement. Its decline it is said resulted when an unchecked government was given complete control of the economy and the personal freedom of its citizens.

The next day the doctors have paid for a driver, a car, and a guide to accompany us to Cape Comorin, the Southern tip of India. It was a great evening for us in Trivandrum. The doctors had two children who were unable to join us, because they were studying for school. They seem satisfied with the school and they have the highest expectation for their children to perform at their best. We looked forward to their visiting us in the States. When we returned, they came and we all had a wonderful San Francisco visit.

In coming to India I realize we are going to a distant place far from home. When I travel to Africa the towns, the food, the language, and the people are all new to me. The heat, the rainforest, the Savannah, and the wildlife are all fascinating. It is a new world that I am in. To those who live there it is the only place they know. I am an outsider and once they realize this fact I am a fascinating subject to them. In Africa my language, nationality, clothes, and the food I eat become curious and interesting things for them to think about and discuss. As we drive through the towns of Madras and Tamil Nadu we are hardly noticed, if at all. We may be thought to be strangers at times, but for the most part not thought about at all.

The places we pass through seem new and foreign to me. And though the villages we travel through along the road from New Delhi to Agra—to encounter unexpected crowds, vendors, objects, and the unlikeliest variations of livelihoods like snake charmers, owners of camels, elephants, and monkeys, book vendors and others—it is vastly different from Southern India. As we travel to the tip of India, the road follows coastal villages along the Arabian Sea. The towns are filled with women, men, and children walking along the road. What is most noticeable to me is the lungi garment worn by the men. It is a long garment worn as a wrap around the lower half of the body. For me, it contributes to making these places interesting and unique in India.

I also learn about the lives of those who live in these places from our guide who the doctors have hired to accompany us. He is an expert on the life we see and he answers all the questions he can. I wonder about the workers who live here. I learn from him and also in reading about the places that some of the people work in the coir industry. Coir is coconut fiber that is made into doormats and accounts for almost twenty percent of Kerala's export. The coir industry is unionized. The doctor had talked about how the unions can become demanding and hard to work with. I talk to the guide and I also read articles about the business.

I find a report of a person who visited a company. He writes about his conversation with the director of the company and some of the workers. The situation of the unions here was described as having overpaid and militant workers, too many strikes, and as driving away investors. The director of the company says that Northern India has trouble doing business here. He says that in the North they are used to getting workers for fifteen or sixteen rupees a day. (At this time there are 45 rupees to the US dollar.) He also says that those who live on the streets in the North don't know their rights. In Kerala he states that labor is more expensive, and one can do business, but must pay higher wages to avoid strikes. It is said that at some companies the workers make 60 to 70 rupees a day, with equal pay for men and women.

In the account that I read about the company director allows a person to talk to several of the workers. These workers are not hired by the company, but to a subcontractor who employees them. The first person is a loom weaver who says that he makes 35 rupees a day. He is asked if he can live on that amount of money. He says that he is barely able to manage. A woman working nearby preparing fiber for a loom earns 12 rupees a day. The person says to the director that this is less than the street dwellers earn in the North. He admits that it is very little. The woman is asked if she belongs to a union. She says that she does not and doesn't want to. She says that she knows her employer so that it is not necessary for her.

Another business is visited. A subcontractor also runs it. One woman is a fast worker and earns 18 rupees a day. She is doing the hardest work and worst paying job that is beating the husks of the coconuts for fibers. Many women suffer from a prolapsed uterus because of the squatting position in which they work. A coconut tree climber who has great agility retrieves and brings down a coconut. He says that he makes 90 rupees a day. He does belong to a union. He says that it is because he does not want to be exploited. His hope is that his children get government jobs. The company director says that this is possible because the Indian government does reserve jobs for people from the low castes.

It seems that so few people are able to transform their lives. Our human struggles are everywhere.

We leave Kerala and unknowingly are in Tamil Nadu. I wonder about the citizens in these coastal towns and the village life here. It is a slow pace and places are quiet with the townspeople walking through the town and along the road. I ask the guide what the villagers do for a living. He tells me they are mainly fishermen. That is how they make a living. When I observed the fishermen pulling in nets from the sea yesterday, it seemed as though there was not a lot of work. As I sat on the shore, I wonder how much they are paid for their work. I learn on a good day a boatload of four fishermen can make as much as a thousand rupees or twenty-three US dollars. On a bad day they could come back in an empty boat, making nothing. Ten years ago the fishing was better, but these days though they work hard they still take a loss. I ask the guide how much the boats cost. He says that they cost 100,000 rupees (2,300 US dollars). The catamarans are worth 70,000 rupees (1,600 US dollars) he says.

It is about fifty miles from Trivandrum in Kerala to Kanyakumari in Tamil Nadu at the tip of India. We left at 8:00 am and arrive at 11:00 am. We walk through Kanyakumari, and observe the festivities with many visitors and local townspeople. We are aware of the three mighty oceans the Bay of Bengal, the Indian Ocean, and the Arabian Sea. A ferry takes us a quarter of a mile to Valluvar Rock. It has a 133 foot statue of Thiruvalluvar, a great Tamil saint and poet who lived more than 2000 years ago. It is next to Vivekananda Rock which is a short ferry ride away. Vivekananda Rock is the larger of the two and provides more sheltered space for the visitors. Vivekananda Rock is a memorial and a sacred monument that comemorates the visit of Swami Vivekananda over 100 years ago. There is a bookstore where we stop. I buy a book and read about his life just as I had done on Valluvar Rock with Thiruvallar. We do not know if Valluvar Rock and Vivekananda Rock will ever have any special importance to us again, but the next year they become places of life and death. We leave the rocks and eat food in a local restaurant. We then travel the road back to Kerala, and then on to Madras (Chennai).

The Next Year

Sometimes there are hard school stories such as those about a teacher and children who encounter destruction and disaster from the sea. Before the 2004 tsunami struck south Asia off the coast of Indonesia and spread to India, Sri Lanka, and Africa, I had read about destructive ocean waves in the Pacific Ocean. An incident happened sixty years ago. School children were the first on the island to see the ocean recede and disappear from the shore. They were amazed and awestruck as they watched the sand emerge and sparkle in the sunshine for hundreds of feet. Some of those curious and daring ventured into the exposed sand. The water came roaring back. There was not the realization of the distance between the oncoming waves. The children were swept away along with the entire waterfront of the town. A teacher in her twenties hung to a piece of driftwood for nine hours until she was rescued by boat. The teacher saw a number of children floating around her, clinging to the debris and wreckage. They just kept floating out to sea. Some of the children disappeared. An underwater earthquake had erupted hours before off the coast of Alaska that had caused the destructive waves.

On Sunday, December 24, 2004, one year after we left India, a chain reaction that started more than six miles below the ocean surface, off the coast of Indonesia sent enormous and destructive tidal waves crashing into the coasts of Asia and Africa. Billions of tons of seawater were causing an enormous disturbance. Waves moving at 500 miles per hour took more than two hours to reach Sri Lanka. It took less than two hours to cross the Bay of Bengal to India. The waves moved across the sea early that Sunday morning. Children along the coast went to collect stranded fish in the sand after the first wave receded; a second wave sweeps them out to sea. That Sunday the water also had receded dramatically from Kanyakumari almost an hour before the waves arrived. The destructive waves caused from the earthquake off the Sumatra, Indonesia coast, lashed the Tamil Nadu coast, killing thousands. Some were helpless and were swept out to sea.

Hundreds of people were injured as the raging sea entered houses in fishing villages along the coast. A large number of fishing boats and equipment were washed away as the tsunami hit. Villagers walked dazed along the roads unable to comprehend what was taking place. Those lucky enough to survive were left in total confusion. The sea had no mercy and no help seemed forthcoming. Almost a thousand people were killed in the Kanyakumari district. Those on the two rocks had been rescued and no one was killed. I learn from reports that the tsunami hit on Sunday at 9:45 am. Over three thousand tickets for the ferries were sold from 8:00-9:30 A.M. Ferry service to the Valluvar Rock was stopped at 9:00 A.M. because of rough seas. This probably prevented another 500 people from being on the rocks. When the tsunami hit Kanyakumari, 1,200 people on the memorial rocks were stranded. The rescue operations were started after the enormous waves stopped at about 3:00 P.M. The ferry boats were not operating so fishermen from the area rescued those stranded which took to 8:30 P.M.

Following the catastrophe along the southeastern coast where the tsunami struck, I also learn about the plight of the untouchables. It is said that they have been forced to live in inland villages, while upper-caste fishermen lived in the most favorable seafront property. The fishermen would bring in the catch, and the untouchables would sell it. During the tsunami disaster the untouchables suffered less loss of life and home, but their loss of income and livelihood were just as severe. In the relief camps there were reports of their being deprived of food, water, and shelter and were often forced out of the camps. Some officials acknowledge that there were some problems with supplies reaching the untouchables, and others said there was no deliberate caste discrimination. The complaints about discrimination against lower-caste groups in the distribution of aid is said to be a problem due to local officials who are reluctant to go against local customs which include caste distinctions.

It is also very interesting to me that the Indian government refused to accept international or outside aid after the tsunami, even though 10,000 of its citizens were killed. They demonstrate their self-reliance as a nation. They have shown the capability of dealing with nature's disasters it faces such as drought, floods, earthquakes, and tidal waves.

Madras

We reach Madras (Chennai) Airport and Shymoshree's brother, Indrajit and his wife Aloka, are there to greet us. We ride into town to a hotel and later in the evening we visit the restaurant run by Aloka. Indrajit helps her out with the business. He is a retired military officer and says that running errands for his wife and helping her out with the business are things he loves to do. It is an impressive place with fine food and great waiters. Aloka diligently looks at each detail of the food served and has excellent service. I, my wife, Shymoshree, Indrajit, the daughter Seruti, and son Samudra all sit at the same table. Aloka is busy running the restaurant as well as tending to our table. Many delightful dishes are served. During the meal I talk to Indrajit about his career in the Indian army and the various places he was stationed. He is a quiet and reserved person. On the other side of me is the son Samudra. He is full of life and energy. He loves talking about science, math, and sports.

I have a math puzzle that I brought for him and his sister. He is fascinated by it and cannot stop asking questions about possible approaches to solving it. This puzzle like others did not have an obvious or trivial solution. He never tires of it and will have much time to study it after I am gone. I do discuss some facts about how the puzzle is assembled and about the position and orientation of its elements and the rotation of the faces. He seemed so fascinated by it all. He is also very interested in his uncle Steve, Shymoshree's husband, and what he is doing. We also talk about space travel and American basketball players. He seems interested in everything. His sister Seruti talks mainly to my wife. She has a school examination she had been studying hard for. Coming to the dinner had been an opportunity for her to take a needed break. Both parents are very interested in the education of their children. Nothing is probably more important to them right now.

The next day, while the children are in school, the five of us drive around Madras. Both Aloka and Indrajit are easy to converse with. Aloka tells us about the guru with whom she is studying. Aloka says that everyone should just do the best they can in life and give up ones self-importance. One must internalize and live this life. She is very excited and spirited about living such a life.

In my travel through India I read statements by several swamis. They talk of unity among the Hindus, a ban on cow slaughter, and eradication of the untouchable-caste. They say that untouchability is still prevalent in Indian rural areas, and is a blemish on Hindu society, and should be ended. They say the scriptures teach to look for God even in the house of the poorest person.

While the three women shop, Indrajit and I walk through the streets. As I am walking a woman beggar with a child in her arms approaches me. Sometimes I fit into the crowd, and sometimes I seem like the most visible person on the road. She is the only person I see begging amongst a crowd of moving people. She is patient and persistent. She carries on a conversation with me that I do not understand the words, but her appeal to be helped is clear. I quietly give her several coins. She takes the money, but continues to ask for further assistance. She points to her baby and calls for more help. I give her another coin. It is interesting how she stands out as the neediest person on the street. She is living a clearly visible life of poverty at the deepest level. We both stand out on the street. I appreciate her presence. She is genuine in her mission and determined to communicate her need. Her presence brings energy to our lives and connects us to the same human journey. What is the journey for? It is for human freedom.

There are also poor people in Madras who are not begging on the streets. I read about a woman who tells about her life in a slum area of Madras. She says that she sells bananas because no one will employ her since she is illiterate and from a low caste family. Some days she is lucky and gets a good selling spot, but on other days evil men take the spot and make her sit somewhere else. She is a poor woman and nobody cares what she says. She is always in debt because she has to pay back more than she borrows. She has to care for herself, her husband, her son's wife and their children with the income she makes. It is not enough money and sometimes the grandchildren go to bed without any food. Her son works a few days a week and the money he makes he spends on drinks. He beats his wife when he is drunk. Her husband's health is weak and he cannot do any kind of work.

The slum area they live in has no electricity, or running water, and no real roads.

Throughout my travel in India seldom has any person ever talked to me about the human condition, the poor, poverty, or freedom. I ask Indrajit what he thinks about the poor and the cast system. He says that some changes have been made. He also knows that Indian civilization is five thousand years old and that has some significance. In the end he feels that it is inexcusable and should be stopped. He said India owes a great debt to those who have labored as they have and much more needs to be done.

Freedom as a mission transcends class, race, education, and all other barriers. Recently I read about the lives of those who were once wealthy in high caste land owning families, subsisting on what they can beg each day. Sometimes when women in such a family husband's die, their land and possessions are taken over by strong men. They are left nothing. One woman had been begging and taking care of herself for fifty years, and taking care of her mother for forty-eight years. There are hundreds more like them in the ashram where they live. When they are young they never imagine their lives would end as they have. None of us know right now what we will make of our lives or of this world.

We leave Chennai and return to Kolkota (Calcutta).

# 45

## RETURN TO CALCUTTA

The Sadhu

India is a spiritual and religious place. Religion seems present everywhere and happening all the time. One observes this clear and deep religious presence and wonders in what way it impacts our world.

As we continue to move through India, our return to Calcutta sustains the life of the journey. I wait outside on a Calcutta street as my wife and Shyamoshree are buying cloth. As I do so a sadhu appears and sits nearby.

Sadhus are persons who stand out from the vast multitudes everywhere I go in India. A sadhu is a holy man travelling the country looking for enlightenment. They are interesting to observe as they are poor, unpretentious, and unconventional. He is unaware of my presence. They standout, but probably seldom know of the attention they receive as they pass through places. What makes his presence different from others? Most of us in society seek to acquire money, power, property, authority and other such conventional objects. We are dependent on society and imprisoned by it. If one does not desire any of these things and lives with great humility, then one is not of this societal life. The sadhu revolts against it, and breaks away from the society. All old practices are abandoned and past patterns are eliminated and thrown into the air as one acts in new ways. I observe the sadhu from a distance to see he has no possessions, and seems without impediment and worry.

I read about one sadhu, who says, "When you end your desire, everything is possible."

One hears of such men who come from wealthy families and who never intended in living such a life. Some find it is hard at first. It is because one is no longer a businessman, attorney, or civic leader. That life has ended. Vanished. Those who dedicate themselves to a selfless life can deepen society and the world.

I also wonder about one who is a sadhu who is in a spiritual search, using meditation, sacred texts, and self journey. He surrenders family, and social custom, his obligations, and material possessions. Some even abandon clothing. I also read about religious incidents between themselves, and sometimes where violence, and anarchy can erupt. I realize that any religion is a destructive force when extreme practices are followed. A religious direction with extreme believers and followers can pursue a fixed and unyielding path to carry out their view of the world. Revolution and change happen, but transforming the planet does not come from a religious philosophy or a political practice but comes from an inner discovery outside of thought, belief, time or knowledge.

The black Hole of Calcutta

The black Hole of Calcutta is a disputed incident in which 146 captured British prisoners were held captive in a small chamber, 18 ft by 18 ft, in 1756. Of the 145 men and one woman placed in the small room only 23 survived. To the British they considered the Indian captors who had imprisoned them as evidence of cruelty. The account was based on a story by a survivor, Joseph Holwell. His story described how he, perishing with thirst, kept himself alive. It seems a stirring account of survival. The Indians to whom I talk to accept the fact of this incident happening but are not clear on the details. To some, this event provoked the British to mark the beginning of its empire in India. The British domination and subjugation of India for almost 200 years showed a need to rule and to express its power. Any oppression over another human being destroys and diminishes us.

When human freedom exists there is an end to those who oppress other people or their own people.

Poverty and overcrowding explodes in Calcutta. Its millions of people and endless energy make it a place forever alive. Though there is pollution, unemployment, homelessness, and overpopulation. There is also a vitality of life. There are the ill and the dying but there are also those who are dedicated to treating the sick and neglected.

Dr. Banerji

In a modest size red brick building, in an always crowded section of Calcutta, the poor and the sick assemble. This morning, like any other day, almost 800 people come for treatment. It is mostly the poor who bring their sick and dying relatives with a hope that the doctor in the house will be able to help them. They quietly wait for the opportunity to be helped and healed. They are unlike the chaotic and confused masses that are elsewhere. This is a quiet sanctuary with those who discipline themselves and are very serious as they wait to be seen. They realize that like thousands of others who have come through here seeking medical help that they are fortunate to have this medical visit. Many are poor and are unable to afford medical treatment. Here they do not have to pay any money at all.

They patiently wait for the legendary homeopath by the name of Dr Prasanta Banerji. He has been practicing medicine for more than fifty years. His grandfather and father had learned homeopathy and treated the very poor of their villages for free. They also treated aristocrats, presidents, and prime ministers. Dr Prasanta Banerji gained international prominence with his homeopathic treatment of cancer. Our friend, Shyamoshree, introduces my wife and me to him in his Calcutta office. He had cured her of a spinal disc injury as a youth. It is interesting sitting with him as he discusses his observations and remedies for my wife and her migraine headaches. She has visited another prominent physician in San Francisco. They are probing and curious as they explore the situation first-handed. After his thorough and diligent examination he discusses the problem with us. He listens intently and gives her a prescription to be filled. Homeopathy uses remedies prepared from natural substances and work by stimulating the body's own healing power. I am impressed with the vast number of patients that he sees and his concern for alleviating illness and suffering among the poor.

City Youth

The youth and their energy help to sustain the life of our cities and our world. In Calcutta, I read about two boys who push a battered metal cart through the streets looking for a place to have a show in the evening after the workday. They have a hundred-year-old machine. They turn its crank and the children come to watch. Inside the cart is a small movie screen that is about eighteen inches by twelve inches in size. It is a nineteenth century projector, marked 1898, flashing an unordered collection of clips from Indian musicals. The first such machine arrived in Calcutta in 1896. The scenes are blurred and the sound is poor. In the neighborhoods of poverty the family's portable machine, called a bioscope, but referred to as, "the machine," brings excitement for ten minutes for a penny. The father of the two adolescent boys said that his father began showing movies on Calcutta's streets years ago, and now his sons work the machine most nights. Once the music is on, the children gather, and it does not really seem to matter what is on. The audience could see much of the same on television, but that does not move them like the biosphere. It is novel. They can watch its gears rattle.

Once, I took an old computer into a special education classroom of Steve Diamond, Shomoshree Gupta-Diamond's husband. The students were not interested in playing chess against the computer as they were in taking the keyboard loose and fooling around with the mouse. It was the parts to the machine that fascinated them.

The Calcutta youth were able to spend a small amount of money and participate in an engaging activity. "I love this thing," some would say. Some spend as much as an hour a night with it. Up to twelve children can crowd along its sides, watching through a slot with a blanket hanging over their heads, keeping out the light. The movies are pieced together from those that have been shown for the last ten years. Sifting through the recycled film, dance scenes are spliced into one film. The children don't care about the quality just as long as people are moving on the screen.

The film is an illusion of life through the movement of still pictures.

Indian Impact

Traveling in India and observing the profound life that dwells here makes it as interesting place as I have visited. Though there is vast poverty, illiteracy, environmental destruction, and an ancient religious caste system it is a unique place on earth. It is transforming the world in information technology, altering a society to middle class life, and independently manages great natural catastrophes. It is also producing great talent that is exported to other countries. It launches its own satellites into space. India is as capable as any place there is in bringing human freedom to the planet.

In India, like the United States, I find there are voices that are deeply motivated toward a world where the poor and downtrodden can transform their lives. They realize the rich through their greed fail to end the poverty of the world and turn themselves into gods. India is a place of great hope and staggering problems. For some it is a country where education matters. Students stream into colleges and institutes. It is said that the students in India study mathematics and science with a passion that may be unrivaled in the world. Some feel that it is through education that the poor will be empowered to express their individuality and creativity. In our lives can we educate ourselves and human society to the fullest extent? Humankind changes continuously. We move through conquest, slavery, war, famine, and other destruction. In our existence in this world as humankind we struggle, prosper, survive, and explore this planet in an adventure where we find ourselves discovering and learning all the time.

# THE WILDERNESS

# 46

# WILDERNESS PROLOGUE

Life is a struggle and a gift.

The wilderness immerses us in this existence.

There life pulsates through us.

One works to revitalize the human spirit in learning elements to sustain one's self.

On the city street corners those who are in rigorous struggle, those studying the toughest courses in schools, live in artificial and invented places, and do not encounter the adventure of the mountain world.

In nature I find myself empowered to go on.

Life in the wilderness can be beyond the mind and the imagination.

On a mountain road I pass through the natural world, understanding we educate the planet by educating ourselves.

Immersed in nature one encounters the possibility of
death and the presence of adventure.

The earth is our origin and where we begin.

As a youth I learn that the universe is billions of years old. A
billion years after the earth was formed life appeared, dinosaurs
inhabited the earth several hundred million years ago, and the
first flowering plants on the planet started blooming more than
one hundred million years ago.

My first trip through East Africa was into Northern Tanzania.
I travel an African road to Olduvai Gorge and I learn that it is the
place where humankind may have emerged. The fossil remains
provided evidence that revolutionized the thinking of the origin
of humankind. I was wandering through the same area more
than a million years later.

The early human inhabitants began their journey on a
mountain road to an outside world and discovered the elements
of survival on their planet. It was a world without nations,
borders, or other human division. Where did the road lead them?
They settled in a new place and from there a new population left
to form other new places until the entire world is settled. There
were multiple migrations across generations, all travelling across
the earth.

After tens of thousands of years, the roads out of Africa now
traverse the planet. Today the paths of the earliest human journey
are tracked and the migration is defined by genetic differences
from one population group to another now living along all these
roads. The original road is gone as are those who traveled along
it. It is as impermanent as all else that exists.

The early human journey moved from its beginning and
probed further into the world we now live in. We discovered
an escape velocity and are able to break free from the earth's
pull that moves the original road into the vast darkness of
space. One day as a teacher in Africa, I examine with my class
a photograph of the earth taken from space. I feel that it is

such an extraordinary world we see. It seems a miraculous place where we exist. This is the world where we all begin our own human journey.

The deprovincialization of our obscure world in a vast universe encourages and empowers us to explore what exists on our planet and what lies unknown in our journey of the human adventure.

# 47

# THE SEA AND THE HILLS

San Francisco is surrounded by a wilderness, which is the sea. It touches all of our lives. The universe and the sea are vast and seemingly endless worlds. They challenge and compel us to inquire further into our own existence.

Entering the sea from the San Francisco shore is an expedition into wilderness and adventure. The wind from the sea sometimes rushes swiftly across the city and the bay, as it has for probably millions of years, bringing with it endless waves against the shore, rocks, and cliffs. Along the shore are walkers, runners, and schoolchildren as well as objects from encounters and misfortunes within the sea that have been deposited in the sand. The San Francisco coast is a sanctuary for birds that fly for thousands of miles, as well as for the shore birds and tides that come and go. As humans we are able to marvel at nature as we maintain a fascination to understand how some creatures are able to fly in space, sometimes traveling the earth for thousands of miles.

Twenty-seven miles off the San Francisco coast are the Farallon Islands where there are observations on the effect of ocean climate conditions on seabirds and other ocean life. Sometimes I run along the sea, and leave it to begin a school day. The sea means different things to us all. Through the countless years of existence it still surges, drifts, rests, and alters the planet, and changes us sometimes quietly and sometimes profoundly.

Those who work on the sea and who live with its danger and destruction observe how it sometimes discounts fishermen, youth, and others who come and go. Those who bravely sail and test the sea must live with its indifference to them. There are written signs along the shore in San Francisco, which communicate to all of us the lives of those who struggle and who die here. The calm and serene sea runs deep. The cool and restful water is not as dead quiet and peaceful as we think and imagine it to be, but a world that can be more than we can handle or endure. Some signs warn of the dangerous and hazardous currents and surf, others signs tell of those who swam and waded in the sea who died here. Suddenly, in a brief moment, rip currents take the lives of the unsuspecting.

A riptide is a strong surface current flowing outward from the shore. Along the coastal water it is the hidden killer that the signs warn us of. The riptide currents are strong enough to sweep the most experienced swimmers far out to sea. Those who panic can tire and drown. The currents can be strong enough to knock someone off his or her feet, especially a child. Most drown who struggle against the current and become exhausted, as they try to swim back to the shore rather than riding it out until it dissipates.

Some years there are more deaths than others. One year searchers gave up hope of finding a 13-year-old San Francisco school student who was swept away into heavy surf at the beach. Several students were taking photographs and the youth was dragged into the water. His friends leaped into the 50-degree water to save him, but were unable to make the rescue. They all managed to get out of the water on their own, and were given medical treatment and hospital care. The Coast Guard stated that the maximum survival time was about three hours. They gave up the search after twenty hours.

Another time I think of life after death as I hear sirens filling the air as rescue vehicles rush through the city. My wife says that some person has drowned in the sea. She is certain when she sees an emergency rescue vehicle racing to the sea. It is really our own death we witness, as it is the same response that is being followed as though we ourselves had died. The world continues in its course with us or without us. We observe how life ends and the world goes on.

The ambulance is rushing past us, because moments ago in the waves at Ocean Beach, a man raced into the sea to save two drowning children. The children eventually make it to the shore with the help of others, but the man, after reaching them gets caught in a strong current. The waves get stronger, and take him further into the ocean. When the Ocean Beach patrol lifeguards pull him from the sea, their efforts to revive him fails and he later dies at a local hospital.

We all learn from the sea.
The sea is everything.
We live beside it, die beside it.

Hills
About thirty years ago I am running a hill in San Francisco for the first time. It is a mile and a half long and I manage to get to the top. It seems hardly surmountable to me when I start, but it is good to get to the top and realize that I can make it. That is a new discovery for me. It becomes just another passing thought, because when I do reach the top another person runs by me and continues running up to Twin Peaks. It does not enter my mind to run to an even higher elevation. This person seems to run effortlessly into the distance, not stopping at the top of the hill, where I stand, but taking on an even steeper ascent. Not long after that day I also run to the top of Twin Peaks. I find it in me to do so and to also go further in my running. It is a great and strenuous run, along trails, through grassland, and on red rock dirt. There are many small birds but no sign of the nocturnal raccoon or skunk that I sometimes see in running through Golden Gate Park. The twin peaks stand 900 feet above sea level,

and from them one is able to see other hills and mountains in the area such as Mt. Diablo across the bay.

Running the hills makes living in San Francisco a more serious adventure for me. A life of running takes one to interesting places in the city and places beyond. I also discover that it can be a way where one is fit for wilderness adventure.

There is a foot race in San Francisco that has 80,000 runners. It has been run here for a hundred years. I have been running this race for about the last twenty-five years. It is 12 km, or 7.5 miles, long as it goes across the city starting downtown at the bay and ending at the ocean. Though there are those who dress in costumes and those who take to the street to party, most are serious runners. They work hard and are aware of the distance as well as the hills. There are things to be observed and learned as one runs. With tens of thousands of runners I seldom encounter the same runner more than once as I run in the crowd. It is a multitude of different faces that drift in and out of my field of attention.

The last race I was in a fellow runner tells me that we have phased in and out together for the entire race. I would never have known this if he had not told me that the two of us had seldom separated. It was interesting to know that an unknown person was running the same pace, stride for stride, as I was throughout the length of the race. In one race the runner next to me received a call on his cell phone. It was a time where there were not a lot of such phones around. It was the first time I had seen such communication, which had distinguished this race from all others. We had just entered Golden Gate Park, and the runner had told the caller his location. The person to whom he is speaking is just coming up Hayes Street Hill. Technology, communication, and the monitoring of our activities seems to me a capability that can exist everywhere and all of the time.

Usually by the time I am entering Golden Gate Park, about three miles from the end, the fastest runners have crossed the finish line. It is invariably a Kenyan who has come from half a world away, and who lives at an altitude of 8,000 feet at the edge of the Rift Valley. My wife, daughter, and I had once lived in the same Kenyan highlands where these runners existed with the earth. Their lives there and their attention to running the hills could take them from a subsistence farm to become one of a dominant group of world distance runners.

From a window in our house as I write and study I can see Mount Diablo in the East Bay. For thirty years I have seen it on clear days, and days of haze, fog, and rain. It is always there to behold. In all of the days that have passed before me I have not been moved to hike to the top. I have known several people who have climbed it. The summit is 3,849 feet and many drive their cars there. These days I am intent on learning and traveling paths that are close to our home.

One day I drive across the San Francisco Bay Bridge through Oakland, Berkeley, Walnut Creek, and Clayton to get there. It is a thirty five mile drive that takes me forty five minutes to reach the mountain. I start the hike from the Mitchell Canyon Road that is about 600 feet above sea level. It is fourteen miles round trip to the summit and back. I estimate eight hours for the hike. I start the climb in Mitchell Canyon along Mitchell Creek, and I take the first several miles at any easy pace. It is a grassland of wildflowers, sagebrush, chaparral, poison oak, pine and oak trees, and other wildlife. After the first several miles, the climb is steeper and a more strenuous pace is needed. There are switchbacks for the next thousand feet up to Deer Flat. It is a long and sustained climb. I have only seen one other hiker. It is a lone and quiet world. One wonders about the animal wildlife that lives in these hills. I continue up Deer Flat Road to Juniper Campground.

To get to the summit I go through the lower parking lot and follow the trail to the Summit Museum in the old sandstone building at the top of the mountain. There I talk to the ranger about the hike down. There are photographs, exhibits, and Native American history displays. As I wonder about the fossils, native plants, and the earliest inhabitants, there is an interesting journey through these mountain trails that I learn about. It was by a horseman who left Germany from a town on the Rhine River on an expedition to travel around the world on horseback. It was a trip that had not been done before. In six months he traveled 2,700 miles across Germany, Poland and Southern Russia, then 4,000 miles across Russia and Mongolia. He then went through China and Korea and along the way he encountered border problems, questions from governmental authorities, thieves, and robbers. His vision of an around the world journey, his love of horses, and meeting people with energy and understanding sustained him. When he arrived in the United States he followed trails through Walnut Creek and over Mount Diablo. So the mountain trail has been a place of great journeys.

On the way down the mountain I encountered animal wildlife for the only time. I come upon deer whose eyes continuously follow my trail as we coexist in the moment. It is a quiet standoff till they quietly disappear into the wild and I continue the hike down through the switchbacks. I follow the trail down through Mitchell Canyon. It took me four hours to descend and four hours to reach the top. I leave from Mitchell Canyon Road to go through Clayton and return to San Francisco.

In my travel back I see the Golden Gate Bridge in the distance.

The Golden Gate Bridge is a symbol of urban wonder, surrounded by the Marin Hills, Alcatraz, Angel Island, and the shoreline of San Francisco. This is the same view for the great majority of suicide jumpers from the bridge who face east toward San Francisco instead of west toward the Pacific Ocean. More suicides take place on the bridge than any other structure in the world.

# 48

# THE BRIDGE

The Golden Gate Strait is about four miles long and a mile wide. It is the entrance to the San Francisco Bay and links it to the Pacific Ocean. There still is a ferry that crosses the strait and travels between San Francisco and Sausalito in Marin County. In visits I make to schools around the bay I learn of a Latin teacher who, before the bridge, rides the ferry from San Francisco to Sausalito twice a day and continues this commute for 43 years. In 1937 the Golden Gate Bridge is completed. It takes four years for its construction. It is a place of immense interest. On its fiftieth anniversary an estimated 300,000 people surged on it in celebration. Now more than one hundred thousand cars a day cross it and a person dies from jumping off the bridge every fifteen days.

In the San Francisco Public Library are newspapers and magazine articles about Golden Gate Bridge suicides. I read many of them. The bridge stands as a technological achievement, but at times is a socially tragic destination. The suicidal behavior of those attracted there is of a crisis driven state and acute nature. Some people are more likely to develop mental illness than others, but the capacity for suicide is in all of us. Some deaths from the bridge are from an absence of connection of the human mind to the outside world. One person who died left a note behind saying, "I'm going to walk to the bridge. If one person smiles at me on the way, I will not jump."

One story I read in the library is about a survivor who tells of his jump on Monday, September 25, 2000. I call him survivor 1. On this day he thinks that if only one person would show he or she cares, he wouldn't jump. While he is thinking this, an attractive woman wearing sunglasses approaches him. Everything seems okay he thinks. She cares. The woman holds out a camera and asks him to take her picture. She ignores his tears. When she walks away, he turns, takes several running steps and plunges into the water below.

It is said that the 220 foot fall takes four seconds as the jumper's body hits the water at 75 miles per hour. The force of impact and the inertia of the internal organs to maintain their motion cause jumpers to endure broken ribs and lacerated organs. There are also broken bones to such places as the sternum, clavicle, pelvis, and neck. Skull fractures are also common. Some jumpers die from the impact and some are knocked unconscious. Some survive the impact and for a time while they struggle to stay afloat and then yield to extensive internal bleeding. Others are asphyxiated as they breathe in saltwater and die by drowning.

The rare survivors hit feet first, and at a slight angle. Some are able to stay alert as they fall. One survivor reports that in realizing the impact, he is able to adjust to a vertical feet-first position and almost achieves a perfect entry. Though he is dazed he is able to reach the shore and admit himself into a hospital. His worst injury turns out to be several cracked vertebrae. A more typical outcome is that reported of a stuntman who jumps off the bridge trying to set a free-fall record. He lands flat on his back and is dead when pulled from the water with massive internal injuries.

Sometimes there are second thoughts about taking one's life. After one takes poison or drugs one may question going through with ones death. When one is jumping from the bridge, second thoughts are rarely significant. Survivors often regret their action in midair. One person in flight to the water recalls saying to himself, "I instantly realize that everything in my life I thought was unfixable is totally fixable—except for having just jumped."

Survivor 1 jumps headfirst. He changes his mind and doesn't want to die. What is he going to do? In mid-fall he is strong enough to turn his body into a sitting position and hits the water feet first. The deeper he sank in the water, the darker it became. The pain is extreme as the impact broke his back and shattered vertebrae. Like any animal with an instinct for survival he swims up to the light and air. When he breaks through the surface of the water he is stunned to be alive, and wonders if it is all real. He is unable to swim for the shore as the pain overwhelms him and he sinks back in the water again, fighting against dying. He manages to bring his head above the water, and feels something alive, a sea creature, brush his legs. He later thinks this to be a seal but a person taking a photograph from the bridge says it is a sea lion. At first he thinks he may have survived to be eaten by a shark, but the creature keeps nudging him and preventing his sinking again into the dreaded darkness.

A man in a uniform from the Coast Guard who rescues him asks,

What did he do?

He tells him he jumped off the Golden Gate Bridge

He asks why

He tells him to kill himself.

He is nineteen years old.

(The man did not know that he jumped to step out of reality.)

Sometimes suicides are carried out with uncertainty and ambivalence and have not been thought out; other times there are those who only want to die.

The bridge like the sea itself is alive. Eleven men died during its construction. The first suicide happens weeks after the bridge opening in 1937. Millions of sightseers visit it each year. Daily many pedestrians, motorists, and bicyclists move through its world. Some die. The bridge is said to demonstrate humankind's control over nature. It does.

Sometimes, however, we are not able to discover ways to understand and deal with the wilderness aspect of the bridge and its significance. There have been over a thousand known deaths of those jumping off the bridge. Less than a mile away, off the Oakland Bay Bridge, there are no suicides or jumps occurring as no persons are able to walk on or across the bridge. Those who have known to jump from the Golden Gate Bridge provide a human measurement. The actual count in nature is unknown and is possibly thousands more have jumped who have not been found or counted. They are now buried in the land or a part of the sea.

The interest and fascination with the human stories and the bridge seem to ever live on. Recently a high school student on a field trip jumped from the bridge and survived with no major injuries. He was helped ashore by surfers. He says that he has made jumps like this before. There is talk about what action should be taken for what he did. I find it amazing that he is able to carry out such a daring venture. Someone commented that he wanted to succeed where others did not and could not.

# 49

# MOUNT WHITNEY

The first time I come to Lone Pine, California my wife accompanies me. I am almost sixty years old when I decide to climb Mount Whitney. It is the first mountain I am climbing alone, without special equipment, and without a climbing team. The only concern I have about climbing the mountain is hiking up rocky terrain. It slows me down. I would have attempted the climb when I was younger, but I was more interested in climbing other mountains in other places. I have known several people who have climbed Whitney, and I feel that I am in condition to make it to the top. I read that one in three climbers make it to the summit. The first day we get to Lone Pine I want to get familiar with the mountain, so I hike past Lone Pine Creek to the first of the switchbacks and I return.

The next day I am enthusiastic about the climb. I begin at 5:30 A.M.; it is cool as I set out. I get to the first series of switchbacks and continue on at an even pace to Lone Pine Lake that is at 2.5 miles and an elevation of 9,000 feet. The trail works around the lake to another set of switchbacks and through Outpost Camp, at 3.5 miles and 10,365 feet, and then to Mirror Lake. An older man with a trekking pole passes me several times in our climb. We acknowledge each other as we advance up the mountain. It is too tiring for much talk. He seems a confident and capable climber. I continue through Trailside Meadows to Trail Camp, at 6 miles and 12,000 feet. The rock steps seem to never stop.

This part of the hike is the most wearing on me as it is laboring on the large rocks to get up the mountain. It takes the most time of the climb and the sun is pouring down which wears, exhausts, and weakens my stamina. I am just over half way there. There are many campers at Trail Camp. They stay the night, and summit the next morning, or they may have just returned from the top of the mountain. It is a resting point for many, but my permit is for a one-day climb so I never consider rest or sleeping overnight. I carry no overnight gear with me. This is also where the two-mile trail of 97 switchbacks begins. They lead to Trail Crest.

Once one gets to Trail Crest the major part of the climb is said to be over. I want to push on. I do not want to turn back. I feel strong enough to continue. I am concerned about how rocky the switchbacks are. It is trouble if they are as hard to traverse as the last two miles were. If so it may be that I am unable to get to the summit. Just as I am approaching the switchbacks to Trail Crest, the older man with the trekking poles has turned back and is descending. I ask him why he is going back. We both have been climbing for six hours. It is noon.

He says that we are at the halfway point and it will take just as long to reach the top. That would mean that one would not reach the summit until 6:00 P.M. He is going back. It does not make sense to be on the summit that late in the day under uncertain weather conditions. He is clear in his action and is on his way back down the mountain. I do consider exploring the trail to see how rocky the switchbacks are, but I do not get very far. I know I have to turn back. It had taken six hours to get to this elevation and I feel I can descend the same trail in four hours. I might be able to have the energy to get to the summit, but to get through the weather, the darkness, and the unknown trail is too overwhelming a world to confront. I do get back down the mountain in four hours. It troubles my mind to have made it halfway there and then to return on the same path one had struggled so hard to climb. I had underestimated the impact of climbing the rocky terrain. My wife is glad to see me. She is pleased that I have made it back safely. We drive back to San

Francisco, and I do not know if I will ever ascend Whitney or even see it again. Though I had climbed other mountains, this is the one that I have not climbed.

The next summer I come again. This time I obtain an overnight permit so I can sleep on the mountain. I bring a sleeping bag and other gear. I am now familiar with the route through the rocky terrain and the hike to Trail Camp. There are many people camped out when I get there. I am exhausted. It is a harder climb because of the added weight I have packed with me. I find a big rock to sleep beside. My body is so drained and exhausted that I have leg cramps. It is a miserable night. I lay thinking that I should have climbed Whitney when I was younger. Climbing the mountain, however, is not about ones age but having the energy to make it. I am unable to sleep. The next morning I know that I have to descend the mountain. I am not in any condition to go on. The walk back down the mountain is more devastating than before. It had meant so much that I made it this time.

On the journey down Whitney I encounter a man and his son on the mountain. I learn that the son is in the fifth grade. It is a great day to be on the mountain. I ask the youth if he likes school. He seemingly tolerates it. I ask him what is his best subject in school and without hesitation he tells me that it is physical education. His father states he does well in all of his subjects. It is a friendly conversation as we continue on our way. I am impressed with them both in their enthusiasm to work their way up the mountain. How excited they are. I know for the youth that this mountain road is deepening his life and enhancing his education. I met a teacher in Africa whose class climbed Kilimanjaro as a field trip. I do wonder about youth and the adventures and worlds they enter.

It is not until some years later that I learn about a youth who climbs Everest at age thirteen and Kilimanjaro at nine years old. I also learn about youth who sail around the earth alone. What does such energy tell about humankind? There are those who can seemingly accomplish any task or adventure. I read that the youth's passion for climbing mountains began in his school hallway where a painting of the highest peaks in the seven continents inspired him to conquer them all.

On the way back to San Francisco from Lone Pine, I drive through Death Valley. It is 120 degrees at Furnace Creek. My wife, daughter and I have traveled here before. The names such as Starvation Canyon and Dead Man Pass reflect the troubled adventure endured by those who once traveled here. The abandoned towns and the remains of mineral and metal ore mines still stand. One observes a unique land where the Panamint Mountains rise above the salt flats and painted canyons. The stark landscape marks one of the most inhospitable places on earth. It is a distinct, extraordinary, and stunning place on the planet that is brutal and harsh to stand and exist in. The temperature sometimes surges to 130 degrees cracking and drying the earth's surface. From the wind one tastes dust and salt.

I am so profoundly disappointed with the second attempt that I am driven to try a third time. I am determined that I make it this time. In reality there is no way of being sure I can reach the summit. In both previous attempts I have only gone halfway. I am still unfamiliar with the upper switchbacks and terrain and the 2.5 mile hike from Trail Crest to the summit. For me there is no significance given to any previous time of climbing the mountain, but only to my seriousness in getting to the summit now. I come with that vision. It is my only goal.

I am enthusiastic when I arrive in Lone Pine. I want to rest well and to start very early in the morning. I feel grateful in being here. The wilderness awakens me. It does not present the usual patterns of city life. For me it provides a new world to explore, discover and investigate. I climb, struggle, and survive as I am engaged in its wonder as well as its formidable and demanding challenges. Since I would start in the darkness I bring my headlamp. The only time I had used it was in the climb of Mount Rainier in Washington. We started from Muir base camp at 2:15 A.M. and we reached the summit at 9:30 A.M.; the headlamp had worked well. I have new batteries in it and it seems to be all right. That evening though I decide to drive to a store in Lone Pine and buy a flashlight. It is new and works perfectly. I also buy extra batteries.

When I leave early in the morning to begin the ascent, it is pitch black outside. I do see another light in the distance but away from the mountain. I see no lights from climbers on the trail as I begin the climb. It is not yet 4:00 A.M., and it is total darkness. I am alone on the mountain, I feel fortunate to be here and have the chance to climb the mountain. It is a great adventure I am on. It is cool but good weather to begin a climb. It is totally quiet and still everywhere. I am enthusiastic about the world I am entering. Forty-five minutes into the climb there is trouble. The new flashlight goes out. It devastates me; I struggle in the dark to fix it. At first I think that it is a minor problem as it is new and was bought from a store selling mountain climbing gear. I change the batteries and it still does not work. It may be a defective bulb or faulty connection I think to myself. I never get it to work. This is the first event of a journey that only gets worse.

I try to walk in the dark. It is impossible to know where one is headed and what objects are on the trail. It is a long way to fall in the blackness of night. It is disappointing and frustrating, but all I can do is wait. I may wait until daylight, or until other hikers ascend the mountain along the road. I probably wait for thirty to forty five minutes until a group of three climbers come along. I hear them in the distance and I observe their light moving in and out of the twisting trail.

I tell them about my situation with the light. I join them as we move on from my location. They maintain a fast pace. They are intent on sustaining this climbing rate. I climb at a slower pace. One of them has an extra light. He loans it to me and says that I can return it to him in our next encounter on the trail. I am grateful as they continue on and I proceed at a slower but a steady pace. I make it past Mirror Lake with still at an even pace. The second light I had was getting ever weaker until it went out. I know I am unlucky, and I wonder about the chance of two lights going out in such a situation. In frustration I wait in the dark along the road until it is light enough to continue. I think to myself that I may have had as much as two hours of total dead time. I have no watch and do not know for certain. I do get to Trail Camp around 10:30 A.M. I am totally exhausted.

I meet a group of women campers who have an extra flashlight bulb. It does not seem to work but I take it along anyway and thank them for their assistance. I move through the tents and campers, and on to the two-mile trail of 97 switchbacks. They are rocky in places and the boulders are hard on the knees. They slow my pace considerably. There are many climbers ascending and descending the mountain. I have several conversations. A couple from the San Francisco area gives me a small packet of an energy food. It is miracle nourishment that adds strength to travel on.

When I am almost at the top of the switchbacks, I see the fellow who gave me the flashlight. The three of them are descending. I tell him how it had gone out at Mirror Lake but I did appreciate his assistance. He is glad that we see each other again. I reach Trail Crest and surprisingly I come to the John Muir Trail and am able to see the route leading to Whitney from Sequoia National Park. Many of the persons ascending the mountain from this trail take six to ten days to complete their journey. It is not a day hike. The final two miles to Whitney are not easy. There are rocks as far as one can see. I walk toward the stone hut but I do not get all the way there and I do not sign the register. The sky turns black. It starts to rain and is getting cold. The rain turns to hail. Flashes of lightning bring electrical activity. I see a person rush away with his hair standing straight up. I move on. As I work my way back through the rocks to descend the mountain the few people who were once there are now gone. They know the danger of such an open exposure to this electrical storm.

The sky is ominous and threatening and the dark clouds gather quickly when the hail begins to fall and everyone leaves the summit. I work at leaving the mountain and on keeping to the trail through the rocks. It is tedious and difficult following the trail back. Once there were others on the trail moving around the mountain. I was not on my own then as I am now. I look for the John Muir Trail where I can connect back to Trail Crest and the switchbacks to Lone Pine. It is probably about four or five o'clock in the evening. I was exhausted when I was struggling to ascend the mountain, but I was aware of those ascending and descending around me and I took the mountain for granted, unknowingly. Overcome with fatigue I abandon trying to find the Trail Crest road back down the mountain. I am too overwhelmed and exhausted to continue in the search.

# 50

# THE DESCENT

Before the climb I tell my wife, who is in San Francisco, that I am going be late in getting back down the mountain. I am now alone as I look for a trail down the east side of the mountain. Just as I started in the morning the mountain is dead still and there are no other individuals around. The lightning flashes seem so close and capable of striking anything and anywhere. It is time to leave, but the path back is just not there. I cannot find it. I am lost. I do not know if this is a life and death situation. Again, I am exhausted and lack the energy to continue to look for the trail that got me here.

Suddenly there is this disruption in my life. My imagined descent has ended. I know that getting down the mountain for me is an adventure that is going wildly wrong. Though I am getting confused I know not to panic. It is a shocking situation, but I am not desperate. I must stay with the situation and get through it. I came alone, and this is what I now face. Whatever is to happen is beyond me at the moment. The lightly falling snow melts quickly. I am faced with finding another way down the mountain. I am glad to have made the summit. I am not elated or exhilarated about it, but I am glad that it is now behind me and I did get there. I had been determined and certain in my mind that I would reach there, but nothing is ever guaranteed.

After reaching the summit I now think about other paths I may have tried and explored in coming down the mountain. In

this world I am in, in this present tense, it is now too late to undo
the expedition in which I find myself. The summit and other
possible paths down the mountain are only my dead thoughts. It
is too late to dive back into the past. I just have to face whatever
obstacles or misfortunes that I encounter in the journey. It is
evening and I have no interest in the food and water that are in
my backpack. I look for the John Muir Trail that I had crossed
in coming. It is another way down, but I am unable to connect
with it. It is not there.

I had been very surprised to see the trail on the way up the
mountain as it seemed as though it was a much less strenuous
expedition than what I had faced in the eleven hard miles of rock,
sun, and elevation that one forces oneself to overcome. I knew
there were also more technical routes to the summit. And though
my stamina is weakened and diminished, I know the body and
mind are capable of renewal and recovery, but I also realize this
is theory and possibility, and nothing more. I do know that it
is going to take strength and energy to descend the mountain
and reach the valley below. Surprisingly I observe life at a vast
distance below me, but it is there and is a place that my mind can
process, and can clearly see. As desperate, exhausted, lost, and
confused as I am, I suddenly am able to see how fortunate I am
that others are carrying on beneath me. It seems miraculous that
I can see life and activity that gives me something to struggle to
reach. I am aware that I am immersed and plunged into an ordeal
that puts me in a vast, ancient, and timeless place.

Seeing hikers far below me makes an interesting situation
as my mind deals with solving the challenge of finding ways to
wind through the endless labyrinth of rock formations and piles.
One cannot give up or wander around like a prisoner of hope.
I know that routes through and around the rocks and boulders
must be found. These ancient monolithic giant bodies must be
traversed and descended to a place where I am free again. It is an
unknown world I must penetrate, move through and get beyond.
For me it is damnably real because it is life as it is. I must find
my own way out. At first I struggle, but I am grateful that it

is not the magnitude of endurance that it takes to ascend the mountain. I am in a more restful state as I try to work my way down. I find it at times seemingly insurmountable to descend and to negotiate the immense rocks and boulders that cover and dominate this world. I am able to recognize life in the valley below as others hike through the plain and wilderness there. I deeply engage myself in seeking out possibilities, in connecting to them and their world.

I bruise my body continuously as I slide and fall and damage my arms and legs, trying to get down. I wonder how wrecked and damaged my body really is. In my mind I try to envision places that seem strategic islands to land on that will be bridges to other sanctuaries. It is a vast and uncertain world to move in. In my mind I do see other people who are living here, and I think that I can possibly work my way to them. They seem to live on a road that connects them to a place outside the mountain. I am driven to reach them and to get out of this mountain rock world. They are as real as the rocks to me and I work hard to find paths among the stones that lead to them. I shout out to them from afar but they never hear me. I never reach them or their houses. Eventually I never think about them again.

I am in this stone settlement in the sky with no trails to be seen. The rocky slopes and their deep drops seem to lie unaltered over many ages. There have not ever been road crews through here with their levers and muscle. It seems if I do not find a way out no one will ever find me. It is as though no one has ever been here and no one will ever be here again. It is such a strong feeling of human absence. I am alone. I never imagined there being such a lonely place. It is so cut off that no soul would ever seem to have wandered here. The fact is I am here now and it is like being in a new and hidden world on earth. I look for skeletons or remains from animals that may have roamed here. Nothing. There is total absence of existence or any prior life.

I am cut off from my wife as there is no way to communicate. I told her to expect my return to Lone Pine in the late night or early morning. I must endure a world I find myself in and be able to exist in its narrow limits of heat and cold. I do not come dressed in warm gear for the night as my goal is to make the summit and back within the day. So now I accept this new road I am on and the journey into this night. I do not know exactly when darkness comes. I am not that aware of it, probably from the tiredness and futility of getting nowhere in my effort to make a significant descent as my goal. I see the sky, the moon, and the stars. I see seas of stars that are bright and luminous in the night sky. The light of the universe is bright, clear, and unobscured.

Planetary Cities

I struggle down this steep path to reach those who continually travel the mountain road below me. They come from the outside.

Lying here I realize that humankind began in the wilderness in its journey. From the wilderness we form villages, towns, and cities. The cities are engines that step up our advancement on earth. The explosion of city life changes our planetary society and transforms our way of life.

The cities also contribute to our planet as an island in space that we are destroying to live on.

The growth and development of our cities and planet must be viewed in terms of the resources necessary to sustain their population. Our actions must be based on understanding the causes of environmental degradation as well as the uncertainties that go along with it.

Dinosaurs lived for more than 100 million years and humankind has lived for one million years. If we do not destroy the natural world and ourselves, our planet can be where we began our continual journey across space. We are making small increments yet significant steps in our travel. How deep do we reach into space?

We are one planet traversing space and we can do the things and travel to places we find we are capable of reaching. We have begun and must sustain our energy to discover new places in the universe.

We realize that we do not dominate or conquer the natural world but exist with it as we continue in the journey. Why do we climb mountains or journey into space? We are motivated from within and live with a sense of discovery.

We explore the universe because of the adventure to find out if life is out there in our search for ourselves and how far we can reach.

The Frontier of Space

On the mountain in the night are stars thousands of light years away. We observe them by the light they emit or reflect or by the energy we detect transmitted through space.

The journey to the moon and the planets of the solar system are recent worlds where we are able to reach. Those on earth are now seeking to travel deeper into space.

As humans we are able to transcend the planet.

In our own way we search for new worlds in space by sending robots, rovers, and orbiters to deeply examine and understand the universe from our landing and exploration.

Those traveling in space may encounter dangers we do not find on earth. Space is not as empty as it is imagined. What about shipwrecks and the destruction of the spacecraft? Coasting in space where there is no time and where landings are uncertain, even if we are robots. How do we transform ourselves?

We search the universe because of the awesome journey to find out if there is life elsewhere besides us, how far we can go, and what other matter and energy exist in it.

———◦◦◦◦◦———

The earth is seen as a dot from four billion miles in space taken from the spacecraft Voyager that views it as a mere point in the cosmos. Our imagined self-importance lies on this dot in cosmic darkness. There is no one to save us from ourselves. We are alone.

Voyager journeys through space as we may have once left Africa to move across the earth to the moon, planets, and beyond. With the earth as our origin, we leave it and establish shuttles and space stations, and again we set out as humans or we construct probes to explore unknown worlds, using what resources these new places have to allow us to establish ourselves there, then moving on into the universe. The frontier of space seems unbound and everywhere. Our new journey is in the open universe. How many worlds do we traverse before we find our way?

Here I lie like other creatures on a cold night mimicking death and clinging to a fragile life, waiting for sunlight. The stars are clear and visible, but my mind is entangled in seeing and imaging the presence of other beings and forms that never materialize. My whole life and this night is dominated by the tremendous cold that so imprisons my world in which I cannot escape. I never remember falling asleep.

I find myself immersed in a state of cold and darkness. The beings who fill my mind and dominate my thought talk about temperature and how it is a fundamental element in the life that must be dealt with. They seem to want to manage their activities to exist with the cold. I am an outsider who hears their conversation but I do not interact with them. I see them as creatures that are living in the cold, whose dark rooms and cells and places seldom seem clear. They are strange beings who have their own order and way of doing things but are of a nature that is fragile, amorphous, and uncertain. I become accustomed to being amongst them as I carry on in their world. They are busy moving about in their activities that are unclear and vague. I find myself inside a complex housing compound that I am unable to leave. I am locked into this place in a similar way that I am locked into the mountain. The creatures who surround me never speak to me. I am a curious outsider who is frustrated and confused with my situation. I am exhausted in my continued confinement as I am unable to escape, leave or breakout. I realize it is probably both an imagined and an actual state that I am in. It is very disappointing and discouraging not to be able to liberate myself from this life and this circumstance. I am struggling to move from here. How far am I from anywhere? I live through the night not knowing when it was the coldest and the darkest. It was damnably cold throughout the night. Unknowingly sleep came and quieted my mind.

I do not know when the next day comes. The sun brings me to life as I awaken with the mountain. I feel like a cold-blooded creature whose temperature changes with the surroundings. I am warmed by the sun just as the rocks and air. I find myself standing on the mountain in the sunlight. I feel great joy and energy.

I seem to be in the center of activity as though the mountain setting itself is now a marketplace. I see various activities and persons conducting business. My wife is amongst those who are selling things to those who come and go. There are merchants who are located at various levels of the rocks in which people move about as the vendors arrange and assemble their items and goods for sell. They operate in a patient and unhurried manner. Briefly I seem to talk to my wife about driving the car back from Whitney to San Francisco. She tells me about closing things up before I leave. I look around at the things being sold. I see strange rocks with engravings on them among the items. They seem unusual. I am comfortable standing in the sun. I seem to fall asleep on my feet standing in the mountain market. I awake and no one is there. Everyone is gone. I look for the rocks that had the engravings and they are no longer there.

I find myself locked into the mountain again with no way out. I am deeply disappointed because I had not left the place soon enough it seems. Why had I fallen asleep?

In my mind I had thought that I had already descended the mountain and had driven back to San Francisco, and somehow I had found myself locked into the mountain, again. I was very frustrated with my action. In actuality I had never left the mountain and am still trying to descend it to the valley below. In my thinking I do not want to have my wife worrying about me, but I have no way to communicate to her because I am still surrounded by the immense mountain. I look at the world beyond the mountain. The valley and lakes are far below, and hikers continuously move along the trails in organized groups. My goal is very clear; it is to get down the mountain to the valley and to contact my wife. I need to speak to her about returning to San Francisco. I will ask her to send me money because in my mind I had driven the car back to San Francisco. But I know I still have a difficult job getting down the mountain. Descending amongst the deep drops and boulders, I know with a fall that one could die, become unconscious, or encounter body injury. I had slipped before and knew the danger.

I stand on steep slopes and massive rocks and carefully work my way from place to place. I only slip and fall twice. Each time I slowly get back up and continue down. It is interesting the further down the mountain I reach I am able to find paths that lead to the foot of the mountain. It seems that I am fortunate that these paths are there and that I can actually descend the mountain. I do take paths that lead to dead ends. I retrace my steps back to the branching point and try another road down. It is a long way down and it has probably taken me four hours to finally descend to the valley I had seen from above. I feel it is a miracle to be where I have worked so hard to reach. I marvel at being here, at the fact that I am not locked in the rocks and the cold. I rejoice in the warmth of the sun. I do see hikers in the distance. I am too weak to catch up to them. My world is so slow and weary as they trek through on their journeys.

One group sits and rests and I am able to talk to the leader. It is evident that he is not able to help me. He says that there is a park ranger that is coming along the road and that I should talk to him. He is not interested in any hardship I endured. It is a life of survival for everyone in the mountains. I had counted so much on reaching the valley and finding help, and getting back to the road to San Francisco. The person had helped because I did see a ranger in the distance. There also seems a slow moving car in the distance. It gives me hope of getting out of here. I am exhausted and can hardly move. Two people pass me as I sat on the ground. They notice how weak I am, but are unable to help, but they too point out the ranger who is coming this way and that I should make sure that I stop him and tell him about my situation. The ranger walks by me across the road from where I am sitting. It is exhausting for me to walk. I get his attention. He comes and talks to me. I tell him about how I was unable to locate Trail Crest and connect to the switchback trail from the summit and had taken another path down and pointed to the rocks above where I had struggled to sleep in the night. He seemed amazed at the story and that I had gotten through the night, but what he is able to do is limited. I ask him about the car or truck I had seen in the distance. I am not clear on what his response was.

I must have never even seen any vehicle, or else I would have probably been able to be assisted more. We never talked at all about it, so I knew there was not that possibility of getting out of the mountains. I am probably so out of my mind that the conversation had gone as meaningless and not worth further energy. He did observe my severe exhaustion and dehydration. I drank the water in my backpack. He had only one bottle of water he was carrying. There was a pool of stagnant water nearby that he filled my bottle with. We agreed that it was not safe but there was no other alternative due to my total exhaustive state. I drank the water. My situation was that I was on the west side of the mountain and that I had to climb back up and connect to the trial I originally ascended to get back to Whitney Portal. I now understood exactly what had happened.

My problem is making it back up the mountain and down again. My main problem is my weak state and lack of strength. He tells me that he is going in that direction and that I should follow him. He would get me on the trail there. I fought hard to keep up with him. Soon I drifted further and further behind. It seemed as though he felt that I could match his stride. In the far distance I did see him point to the trail up the mountain that I was to take. I do have a new surge of energy just from the small source of energy food I still have with me. I surprise myself that I am able to again ascend the mountain at a steady climbing pace. Different things pass through my mind. My hope is to make it to the top of the trail so that I can connect to Trail Crest. The top of the trail is not as direct as it seems, and I know it is going to be hard work to get there. As I am climbing I am met by another park ranger. He tells me that he has been looking for me, because my wife had called the park service when she had not heard from me. I told him that I had slept on the mountain because I had been unable to find the Whitney trail down the other side of the mountain.

I later learned that my daughter in Maryland had awakened at three o'clock in the morning and called my wife in San Francisco because she felt that I was in danger. Once, my wife, daughter, and I went to Mexico. Our daughter, with several friends, was to take a bus from Cuernavaca to Taxco, a city with a natural wealth of silver and craftsmen of jewelry and works of art. The night before the trip my daughter was awakened with disturbing news that the bus would be robbed and so she refused to take the trip. On the road there bandits did force the bus to stop and robbed the foreign passengers on the bus. They took mainly money and jewelry. No one was injured, but several were troubled and frightened.

The situation does happen though, just as it had come to my daughter. So the ranger talks to me about my physical condition. He had followed me for some time and knew that I had endured a hard, and troubling climb to the summit as well as sleeping on the mountain. He had also talked to other climbers who had come across me. He said that he wanted me to undergo some medical tests to determine my condition. He said that a helicopter was going to take me to a nearby hospital to assess my physical state. I tell him that I am physically fit to make my way back and that I do not need a helicopter to take me for any medical assistance. I tell him to use it for someone in greater need. The ranger is very diligent, but he does not discuss things about my altered mental status that he is aware has some significance.

I do know that my mind is not as clear as I think it is. I realize this when I tell the ranger that I need to talk to my wife so that she can send me money to get back to San Francisco. I told him that I had driven the car back there and needed a way to get home. He then tells me that the car is still where I left it at the Whitney campsite. This was puzzling and confusing to me and he was very clear in his knowledge of the matter. I say that I am physically and mentally capable of getting back to San Francisco, but some things are not clear to me. The ranger did not want to have any confrontations and told me to keep an open mind until I talked to the paramedic who was flying in. The ranger and I get to a lake, and I take as much water as I can consume from him and a nearby camper. The helicopter lands very near us and I am adamant with the paramedic about my condition and that I do not need any medical attention. The paramedic says that the blood tests he is taking will determine my condition. He is focused and deliberate in doing the job he flew in for. My blood sugar was so low he said that I needed immediate attention. No way was he going to leave me, so I was flown out.

Both the ranger and the paramedic were very concerned about my well being and serious in their work. They were both competent and enthusiastic in doing their jobs and were an effective team in getting me out. I was grateful to both of them. We flew over land that would have been strange and unworldly to me if I had not just traveled through it. It is Death Valley and I recognize much of its detail. We landed at the hospital in Lone Pine where the medical team took charge and kept me for two days hydrating me, administering electrolytes, and getting my blood sugar in balance. The doctor and nurses are an interesting team. They closely monitor my activities.

The head nurse had climbed Whitney along several technical routes. The doctor has lived in West Africa and we share experiences of living there. It is evident that the African road he traveled has deepened his journey in life. He has also climbed Mount Kilimanjaro and we also share that climb. To encounter him as I do from our similar African experience makes me appreciate the world as it is and our place in it.

After two days when I am fit to leave, the doctor drives me to my car at the Whitney campsite. The car is still there. Before leaving Lone Pine I stop at the ranger station. One of the rangers is from San Francisco, and he has helped me with permits and followed all of my climbs up Whitney. His only question is did I make the summit. I tell him I did but that I had some problems coming down. I made it and that is all that matters to him. He celebrates the news. It is significant to both of us and is something that counted, at least for a brief moment. I had come to climb to the mountain summit and drive back to San Francisco. It was something I had never done before and I had lived to climb another day. I get back to San Francisco and my wife is happy to see me.

My daughter is also glad that I made it back. She asks me to write our grandson so he has an account of the adventure when he is able to read. I write him this note:

"I climb to the summit of Mt Whitney. I get lost coming down and have to find a new way. I sleep on the mountain. On the way down a park ranger locates me and calls for a helicopter that flies me to medical help. I then drive home to San Francisco."

Later on I further my thinking on the journey.

Traveling in nature and the wilderness or to new and unknown places, we do not know the world that we may come upon, or the intensity of the journey. One may enter into a profound encounter in a vast and extraordinary world. I am fortunate to survive the day. On a mountain road I am in a world where I observe the monotony as well as the freshness of life. It is the hard, remarkable, and demanding times on our planet that we deepen our adventure.

# Author Biography

Hoover Liddell has been a mathematics teacher in Africa and San Francisco. In forty-two years in San Francisco schools he has been a parent, head of high schools, a member of a federal court desegregation team, and a district consultant to city schools.

Printed in the United States
By Bookmasters